Finding Om

44 Ways to Increase Joy, Happiness, and Inner peace

by
Kristy M. Ayala, M.A.

Copyright © 2016 Kristy M. Ayala, M.A.

Published By: Kristy M. Ayala Press

Cover Layout: Rudy Cortez
Photo Credits: Jen Arntzen

All Rights Reserved. No part of this book may be reproduced by any mechanical, photographic, or electronic process, or in the form of a phonographic recording; nor may it be stored in a retrieval system, transmitted, or otherwise be copied for public or private use-other than for "fair use" as brief quotations embodied in articles and reviews-without prior written permission of the publisher.

The author of this book does not dispense medical advice or prescribe the use of any technique as a form of treatment for physical, emotional, or medical problems without the advice of a physician, either directly or indirectly. The intent of the author is only to offer information of a general nature to help you in your quest for emotional and spiritual well-being. In the event you use any of the information in this book for yourself, which is your constitutional right, the author and publisher assume no responsibility for your actions.

ISBN: 978-0-578-18442-5

1st Edition: 2016

Printed in the United States of America

Table of Contents

Prologue	5
How To Use This Book	9
Physical Support	12
1. Time. Time. Time.	13
2. Clearing the Noise	17
3. Clearing the clutter	20
4. Streamlining and Making room for the new	26
5. The Heart of the Home	30
6. Shake that Body	46
7. Breathe/Breath work	52
8. H2O Power-Drinking, Dunking, Soaking	63
9. Sound Therapy	71
10. Visual Therapy	77
11. Home Sweet Om	90
12. Space Clearing	99
13. Workplace Wonderland vs. Workplace Woes	106
14. Who Am I? Where Am I? How Did I Get Here?	114
15. The New You	120
16. Writing	126
17. Creativity	136
18. Learn something new	146

19. Move Out Of Your Comfort Zone	162
20. Go Outside	169
21. Get grounded	176
22. Nap	186
Emotional/Mental Support	192
23. Balance	193
24. Burn out	200
25. Decompress and Detox from Machines	208
26. Create Time for Fun	214
27. Clean Up Your Friend and Family Circle	221
28. Create Time for the People in Your World	230
29. Clean Up Your Inner Junk Drawer	236
30. Financial Literacy	242
31. Framily	249
32. 10 Minute Quickies	254
33. Affirmations and Mantras	260
Spiritual Support	268
34. Prayer	269
35. Meditation	277
36. Spiritual Connection	284
37. Energy work	292
38. Aromatherapy/Essential oils	297

39. Guided Action Clears Tension	306
40. Choose You	320
41. Life Long Learning	328
42. Set Up Your Day	336
43. Refilling Your Well	342
44. Honoring Number 1	346
Epilogue	351
Acknowledgements	352
References	353
Notes	354

Prologue

After the second edition of my first book came out, I started to get the idea for this book. Since 2008 I've been running my own business offering a wide range of counseling, healing, and support services. I found that there was a specific cross section of people that were guided to come in for sessions with me. I found that I tended to give some similar activities, homework, and follow up work to each of my clients. I found that there were many common themes which ran throughout my clients' lives. I found that it didn't matter if my client was the head of a department at the university where she taught, a business owner, a graduate student, a full time parent, or anywhere in between, the same themes were prevalent. Many of my clients would come back and tell me that the follow up work really supported them in grounding in the work we had done in our private sessions. They told me story after story about how the work supported them in taking what they knew needed to be done within their lives and apply it by taking guided action. They told me about how their lives had been shifted for the better and how they had gained confidence, clarity, and momentum along the way.

Of course this kind of feedback and the shifts for my clients made me really happy. As someone who has been in the support service and counseling field since 2000, I really know that supporting people on their path is what I am here to do. When I see and hear about people being able to maximize their own best potential with support from me, well I am over the moon about being able to have been a part of their support system.

Some of my clients asked me if I had a book or a collection of PDf's they could purchase which would have support systems, tools, or activities that they could use for other areas of their lives; things we didn't cover in our private sessions. I would always say the same thing, "No, I don't have anything like that put together, but what a great idea. I'll think about doing that when I get around to it." So, I am finally getting around to it. This is by no means a be all end all list or anything like that. Rather it is a small collection of things that I have found to really work for me and for my clients. These are things that I use in my own life and things that my clients have folded into the fabric of their lives as well. My intention here is to offer you a support system as you continue to move forward upon your personal path of peace. I hope that you will find some things that really speak to you within the pages of this book and find ways to fold them into the fabric of your life. Please feel free to adjust, tweak, and shift things as you see fit. This is meant to be a genuine support system and I hope will serve as an inspiration to you and anyone in your world who picks up this book to take a peek inside.

As I always tell my clients, you are your very own best guide for what is right for you. The ideas and activities tucked away inside of this book are just some things to help you reconnect with your own inner knowing, inner truth, and your higher self. You know, that beautiful voice that has always been with you; reminding you how much you have to offer the world just by being you. Yes, that one. I hope you will enjoy this collection of support tools. Thank you so much for allowing me to share this book with you and yours.

For those of you who may be wondering why I have included 44 ways rather than 40 or 50; yes, that was a conscious choice. Rather, I should say, clear guidance.

Many of you know that I work very closely with the angelic realm and the number 44 in angel numbers means that the angels are with you. So in addition to the things inside, when you hold or use this book, know that you are also connecting to the pure and loving energy of the angels. Yes, you (and everyone) have angels with you right now, right this second. You can connect with your angels at any time you choose, you simply need to ask for their support and allow them to be a part of your life.

I am wishing you a wonderful rest of your journey.
Yes, you can take steps toward the life of your dreams.
It is possible. You do have what you need. You do have what it takes. You can make changes beginning today.
Happy Travels.

With deepest love and respect,

Kristy~

For all who are guided to make changes
that resonate with their inner wisdom; this book is for you.

How to Use This Book

My intention for this book is to offer you support and guidance as you take guided action steps to get back to the place within you that feels like home. Now I know that some of you may be feeling a teeny bit of trepidation as you read this. You are what I affectionately refer to as "the list" people. (I love you list folks, hang in there with me, I promise you can do this.) This is by no means a book which will add more "things to do" to your seemingly never ending lists. Rather, this book is meant to be a guide and a support system to help you release some of the things, situations, and dynamics which can keep you feeling disconnected and out of your natural rhythm. (This is also the experience of never having any time for yourself because you are always chasing the end of your lists.) This book is meant to help you increase things, situations, and dynamics which are supportive, uplifting, nurturing, and conducive to true balance. This book is intended to support you in honoring your true self.

I've worked with a lot of people from different cross sections of life experience and I have found that implementing the tools within this book can create deep and lasting positive change. There is no one way to use this book. The book has been divided into 3 parts: Physical, Mental/Emotional, and Spiritual Support. Some of you will feel guided to work through this book from the beginning right through to the very last page. That is a wonderful way to move through each of the areas within the book. However, some of you may feel that there is a particular life area which needs your attention first. If that is the case, I recommend honoring that inner knowing and start there and then work your way out to the next area and then the next. Some of you may feel guided to read the entire book and then go back to the areas which resonate with you right now. This is also a great way to implement the tools that are needed within your life right now. Some of you will be guided to use this book as a way to receive a message and divine guidance. This book is wonderful at providing insight into what you need to know right now and what you are being guided to work through.

For those of you who feel guided to receive a message from this book:

Hold the book in your hands

Then, you can either ask a question, such as,
What do I need to know today? or *What am I being guided to work on right now?*

- ❖ Then, allow the book to open to your page. You will always be guided to the right page for you.
- ❖ Some people will feel guided to pass their thumb over the pages until they are guided to stop. When you are guided to stop, you will see your message.
- ❖ Some people will hear a number from 1-44. This number represents the method within the book you are being guided to work on at this time. Simply turn to the corresponding method to read your message.

Any of these methods for receiving a message are supportive, useful, and accurate ways to use this book.

I recommend having a notebook and something to write with as you work through this book. You can purchase a special journal or a spiral bound notebook, whichever is right for you. If you prefer to use your tablet or your computer as a way to work through this book, great. I have found that there is something very cathartic and healing for people when they physically write down their thoughts during this process. The writing process also allows you to better hear you inner voice and connect to the feelings which will come up for you as you write.

* For those of you who are not able to write: I recommend using a voice recorder or free ware like Audacity or Garage Band which will allow you to record and listen to your thoughts, insights, and feelings as you move through this process. You can listen back to them as many times as you are guided, offering you additional support throughout your process.

I am wishing you all a gentle, healing, and revealing journey throughout this book.

Part One

Physical Support

1.

Time. Time. Time.

Getting a clear and concise understanding of your schedule and a true break down of time is paramount. Once you have a clear understanding of where your time is going, you will have a much easier time making room for the things that are important to you.

This tends to be one of the biggest issues for my clients when they first begin their sessions with me. Perhaps you know this is a big issue for you too. You may notice that you say or think, "I don't have enough time for that." or "I would be able to do so much more if I only had the time." or "No matter what I do I never have time for myself."

This experience of not having enough time is a real challenge for people when they are trying to make changes within their lives. This can feel like a road block for people which can lead them to believe that they aren't able to make real and lasting changes within their world. However, I have found that by taking an honest and sometimes uncomfortable inventory of where the time is going, there is always room for movement. Always.

This important inventory is the catalyst for all of the other change that you will be able to implement within your life. It is really important to be completely honest as you create your inventory. If you feel guided to stretch the truth while filling it out; definitely take a look at why. The truth is that the more honest you are about this, the better you will be able to experience a more meaningful life. You won't have to show this to anyone if you don't want to. So please tell the truth and allow this to be a snap shot of where you are right now. Allow this inventory to serve as a blue print of where you are and where you want to be.

Breathe Through It:

If you are noticing any emotional or physical push back to reading this, take a breath. If you feel that your scenario is the one exception to this exercise, then allow this to be a support system to you. You can benefit from this in a really big way. Any push back or anxiety you may be feeling is a red flag letting you know that this is an area that really needs your attention.

I promise you that you can do this. I have worked with many people who are scheduled to the max and also felt they were the exception to the exercise. Guess what? They gained a lot of deep personal insight from the exercise and we found room for movement within their schedules. You will too.

Activity:

You will need to use a tablet, computer, or graph paper for this exercise. If you are using a computer, you will need to open a brand new *Excel* file or some other kind of graphing program. If you prefer to write, then get out some graph paper and some pens and or colored pencils.

Across the top of your file or page write in the days of the week. Along the side of your file or page begin with 12:00 am and using 30 minute intervals create blocks of time ending with 11:30 pm to Midnight as your final box. (Please do not make one hour blocks of time.)

Here comes the important part. You need to fill in every single box of time with the activity that you are doing at each time frame. This will take you an entire week. Yes.

You need to commit to filling it out as you go for an entire week. This is why it is so important to be honest when you are filling it out. You need to go about your week in the way you normally would to create a baseline. (You may want to print out your document so you can easily carry it around with you.)

Every time you "quickly" check your Facebook page, Pin a few things to Pinterist, Answer Emails, Return Phone calls, Watch TV, or a few YouTube videos; you need to document it. In addition to these quick activities, you will also need to document everything else you do throughout your day for an entire week. If you spend time "doing nothing" write that in too. If you commute, document it. You get the idea, write everything down. At the end of the week you will have a very clear understanding of where your time is being spent. (If you are honest and I know you will be.)

Now, you will need to take a good look at the areas within your schedule where you have flex time. Yes, you do have flex time. These are the times within your schedule that are being eaten up by things and activities that can be reduced or even in some cases eliminated.

Take some time to really reflect on the schedule and the life that you have created for yourself. What areas of this schedule feel great to you? Which areas feel not so great and why? Does anything within your schedule surprise you? How do you feel as you look at your schedule?

Now you are going to create another document exactly like the first one. Then, with both of your documents side by side; you are going to fill out the second one in its entirety. Schedule in all of the things that feel great to you. Now, go back to the places from your first schedule and look for the places where you feel there was some misuse of time or too much time going by the wayside. Schedule something else into part of that place. For example. If you tend to lose time when you come home from work because you are _____. Look at where that time is going in your schedule. Schedule in something that you want to do for yourself and honor it. That may mean reducing TV time, or whatever is eating up those hours and make a change.

This is a really powerful way to get a clear understanding of where your time is going and how you can regain control over your schedule and your life. This may sound simple and in truth it is, however its simplicity does not reduce its efficacy in creating big change.

Clients who committed to this exercise were able to make huge changes within their lives immediately which led to lasting change and positive outcomes in many life areas. You will too.

2
Shhhhh, It's Quiet Time

Clearing the noise from your daily life creates a huge positive shift in the way you think, feel, and move through your world. Often times we are not even aware of how much noise we are exposed to as we go about our day to day lives. Like anything, over time we get used to something and in some ways we are able to shut it out. However, even though we may not realize that we are being impacted by noise within our world, we are.

Too much excessive or abrasive noise can increase tension and stress within the body, and even distractions within our thinking process. Many times when clients have experienced issues or problems with sleeping, low grade frustration, anger, and feeling "off" they are being impacted by too much outside stimulation.

When clients tell me that they feel like they can't hear themselves think, or they feel a restlessness within them or that they are having a hard time finding a quiet place within; they are usually being impacted by too much outside stimulation.

Whether you can relate to any of the above examples or not, carving out quiet time is very healing and supportive. Creating quiet zones within your home for a few hours or a few days can lead to a reconnection to yourself, your inner guidance, clarity, and a feeling of inner peace. Many people who carve out regular quiet time find that they are able to increase their connection to their spirituality, receive divine guidance, increase their sensitivity, feel more like themselves, and actually hear more.

Breathe Through It:

If you are feeling any nervousness about carving out quiet time for yourself, take a breath. If you are feeling like this would not be possible for you due to the number of people in your household or the level of clients and colleagues who are constantly contacting you, take a breath. If you tend to lead a loud lifestyle and have a lot of things happening around you all the time, this can feel a bit unnerving at first. However, if you have a lot of noise and commotion around you regularly, you can benefit from this quiet time in big ways. Creating quiet time won't keep you from following through with your responsibilities to your family, friends, organizations, or career. It can however support you in being better focused when you return to these life areas after carving out this much needed quiet time. The more you practice this support system, the easier it will become and the more benefits you will experience within your life.

Activity:

Create Your Quiet Zone. You will need to decide where you are going to create this quiet space. You may want to make your entire home a quiet zone, or perhaps one single room. (You can also do this at your work place.) Once you have decided where you are going to hold your space, next you will need to choose the amount of time. You can create a 20 minute time frame to several hours to several days. This is completely up to you. Then, turn off all the background noise within that space. Televisions, radios, appliances, cell phones computers, etc. and allow yourself to be in your quiet space.

In the beginning you may feel like you need to be doing something or that it is too quiet. This is normal and just an adjustment period for you as you decompress from the amount of noise that you have grown accustomed to. As you continue with this practice you will notice that you can relax more quickly each time. You will also find that you can connect to your inner voice and personal peace more quickly as well.

In addition to creating a quiet zone for yourself; you can also reduce the amount of background noise within your world. For example if you tend to keep the television on for background noise, make a concerted effort to turn it off when you aren't sitting down watching it. This will also support you in decompressing from additional tension and stress from too much noise overload.

If you have children at home, you can support them in fostering quiet time too. We all need down time and this is a great way to support self-soothing and self-care for everyone within your home.

If you need to create a quiet zone in your home while other people are doing other things; you can hang a Shhhhh sign on your door and let everyone know that you are going into your quiet zone.

While you are in your quiet zone, you can journal to connect with your thoughts, you can do some breath work, you can meditate, or simply enjoy the stillness. Enjoy a cup of tea, color in a coloring book, stitch, paint or close your eyes and relax.

3

Clearing The Clutter

I know, I know this is the one you tend to put off until _____ is all done. However, this is a really big one. In fact, what many people don't realize is how interconnected clutter is with lots of areas within our life. Not only is it interconnected but it is also the catalyst for clearing up issues, problems, and challenges.

So, if when you walk into your home, office, room, garage, etc. and you feel overwhelmed with the clutter, piles, stacks, and stuff all over the place; this one is for you. (This also applies to your car, trunk, storage unit, and any other spaces including closets that need attention in this area.)

For some people, the clutter can feel like it appears overnight. This group doesn't really remember the clutter building up. One day they just look around and finally see it.

For others the clutter is an issue that the person is aware of; but they keep telling themselves that they are going to deal with it when they "have more time."

For another group, the clutter doesn't look like clutter to them, but rather piles of things that are about to be organized, recycled, filed, and put into a great new functional system. However when you ask this group when they started this process, they might tell you it's been months and even years that they have been living among the stacks.

As you read through the above examples, you could probably tell which one resonated with you most. You may even be a combination of the groups. But, no matter where you lie within the list; clutter is an issue that makes a big impact in life.

When clients tell me that they feel overwhelmed with the way their home/office looks or feels; that they can't finish projects while they are at home; that they don't feel good about people coming over to their house; that they are experiencing some financial challenges; that they are experiencing some self-worth/self-love issues; I ask them to talk to me about their clutter.

At first, clients can feel a little uncomfortable talking about this issue. It tends to bring up some of the feedback/excuses that come with each of the examples above. Many times clients don't believe these areas are connected to the experiences they are having. Plus, cleaning out our clutter forces us to take an honest inventory of the way we have been living and the things that we have been procrastinating and why. However, once we get down to the bigger issues, clients find they are able to see the bigger picture and make some changes.

Doing the clean out in all the areas that are impacted leads to huge shifts, clarity, and big change. Clients tend to find that the clutter not only creates emotional and body stress but it also leads to procrastination and represents some kind of area within their lives that they have been shelving. Whether that issue is about getting on track with their life purpose, ending a challenging relationship, going back to school, eating better, standing up for themselves or creating healthy boundaries. Once the de-cluttering process begins, the other "shelved" areas show up too.

I have found that once we are able to move through the mess, we could begin to really clean up any old fears that had been holding space about moving forward. As each cluttered area is addressed and cleared up in its entirety, other life areas are also cleared up as well. Reduced stress and anxiety, increased self-worth, life satisfaction, and happiness are all examples of areas that become positively impacted during this process.

Breathe Through It:

If the thought of clearing out the clutter makes you nervous and or anxious; stop, sit, and breathe. Take a breath in through your nose, and out through your mouth. Good. Repeat.

If you are thinking of all the reasons this doesn't apply to you. Stop, Sit, and Breathe. If you are feeling like you turned to this page on accident. Stop, Sit, and Breathe. It is going to be okay; you can do this. In fact, if you are having a challenging time reading through this area of support it just means this is something that really wants your attention. You will find that as you begin to clear the clutter away from your world, you will experience more calm, clarity, and the ability to enjoy your life even more than before. You are absolutely ready to begin this exciting and healing path which begins with clearing away the clutter.

Activity:

With a pen, notebook, and camera; walk through the spaces and places that are holding clutter. No matter how much there may be, if there are things piled, stacked, or out of place, it counts as clutter. Take a picture of the space. (A camera phone is great, any camera will be fine.)

- ❖ Write down the way you *Feel* as you walk into these rooms and storage buildings.

- ❖ What kinds of clutter do you see?
- ❖ Where is it being stacked?
- ❖ How long has it been there?
- ❖ Now do the same thing in any other places you store clutter; for example: your vehicle, closets, attics, basements etc.

Take some time to look over the things that you have written down in your notebook.

- ❖ Do you see any common themes? If so, what are they?
- ❖ Is there a specific time that this started for you?
- ❖ If so, what was happening within your life when the clutter began to build?
- ❖ Have you always had clutter around you?
- ❖ Did your childhood home or place where you were raised also have clutter?

Commit to a schedule which will have you cleaning out one room or area each week. You may need to ask a trusted friend or an organizational professional to support you through this part of the activity. Some people will need support to get started. You will need to determine what things will need to be recycled, donated, and kept. This is usually an area where a second opinion is important. I promise you, not everything needs to be kept. You will release some things that are no longer being used or needed.

While you begin working through the places and spaces, pay attention to the things that you are releasing as they will be significant for you. Many times people don't even realize what they have been holding onto and for how long. You may find this process to be emotional. Allow yourself to move through any thoughts, feelings, memories, and emotions that may come up for you.

Once you have the things that are leaving your home/office remove them immediately. This can be the challenge for some people. If they don't take them to be donated or recycled right away, they may bring them back into the space. (Get support if this is a challenge for you.)

Place the things that are staying back into the closet, room, office, or out building. You may need to invest in some organizational materials to help you get your things put away in a functional way. It is important to finish one space in its entirety before beginning another space or place.

Once you are done get out your camera and take another picture. Get out your notebook and write down some words that describe the way the room looks and feels now. Tune into your body and notice if you feel lighter.

- ❖ Do you find it easier to breathe in this space now?
- ❖ Do you feel happier in this room?
- ❖ How do you feel about yourself after completing this project?
- ❖ What was the biggest surprise you found as you moved through this activity?
- ❖ What did you learn about yourself during this process?
- ❖ What is the biggest thing that stands out to you as you look at both pictures?

Continue this process throughout all the areas that need attention. In addition to the physical changes that happen as a result of this activity; pay attention to the changes that happen within yourself. You may notice a renewed relationship with yourself, others, and an increased self-esteem and self-worth. You may also notice that you have more confidence, clarity, and the desire to move forward with things that are important to you that have been shelved for some time. Be gentle with yourself during this process but stay on task and committed to your time table and schedule. Finishing what you start is a very important component of this activity.

4.
Making Room for the New

This support tool is a great follow up to number 3, Clearing the Clutter. For those of you who just did a huge clear out of your homes and offices, way to go! Sometimes clients get confused about this technique that I refer to as Streamlining. Clients often think clearing the clutter and streamlining are one in the same. These two techniques work together beautifully, much like a key in a lock. However, they are not the same thing.

Streamlining is a powerful way to take your newly cleared space and power it up to the next level. So many clients tell me that they want to bring in new people, experiences, opportunities, and ways of living into their lives. They tell me that they feel stuck or that things seem to remain the same no matter what they are doing. What I find when working with people who are having these feelings or experiences is a need for streamlining.

When you are trying to make room for the new in your life, in no matter what capacity that may be, you first need to create the space for it to enter. If your home, office, social schedule, work schedule etc. is already jam packed then there is no room for the new to come in. We look to nature in this case, and we can see that nature abhors a vacuum. This applies in all areas of our lives as well. We need to consciously create physical space (a vacuum) so that the new can be ushered into our lives.

So, even though your have a clear and de-cluttered space which is wonderful, we need to go further. This technique asks you to look at the areas that need to be streamlined within your space/lifestyle and to make changes accordingly.

For example: If you are working on bringing new things into your home, you will need to streamline what you already have. Perhaps you have created a vision board with beautiful design components you want to incorporate into your home. The next thing you would need to do is take an inventory of the things which don't match your vision, and release them. (You can donate, gift, and recycle these items.) If you want to bring in big bold colors and geometric shaped fabrics, you will first need to release the things that don't match your vision.

You would move through one space at a time and streamline the areas you can focus on and make changes. In this example, if you had lots of floral throw pillows everywhere; you could streamline some of those down; thus creating space for something new to come in to replace those old pillows. This does not mean you are being asked to remove everything that doesn't work, but rather streamline down to less and less stuff that doesn't match your vision.

As you do this, you will automatically create space for the new to move into your world. This is something that I have seen work over and over again as if by magic. For many this technique can seem counterintuitive at first. Some people feel uncomfortable releasing their items or situations until they have the "new" thing or situation first. In truth, this is backwards, you must first release the old so that the new can come in. For many clients who feel stuck and like things are always the same, this in lies the paradox for them. They know what they want to change, yet they feel like it is always evading them. So, by creating a vacuum, you can then allow the shift to happen.

This is true for every area of our lives, not just for physical items or design components of a home or office. If you desire more down time, high quality friends, or new opportunities within your world; this is the key to opening up that door.

Breathe Through It:

If you find yourself thinking or saying, "Yes, but..." as you read through this; it's okay. You may be experiencing some of the tension and stress that so many people experience as they realize they have been placing the cart before the horse.

If you have been waiting to have all the things you need before making changes within your life and it hasn't worked out as planned; try streamlining. I recommend reaching out for some support as you go through this process. Contact a life coach or a professional who understands this technique.

Often, clients who feel nervous about this technique have been pushing against the natural flow of allowing things to come in by trying to force things to happen. It may take some outside support and hand holding to guide you through this new way of approaching your desired changes. As you work with a trusted professional throughout this process, you will find big shifts happening within and around you. Many clients find that they can release a lot of old controlling tendencies in addition to better understanding the natural law of allowing while utilizing streamlining.

Activity:

This requires you to take an honest inventory of the things or situations that you would like to shift. Once you have an understanding of what you would like to bring in; it is time to look at what has been standing in the way.

Sometimes the realization of the overflow of stuff, out of balance relationships, and unnecessary demands on our time can bring up some deep emotions. This is natural because it forces us to look at the stand in's we have been investing in which keep us from actualizing what we really want. Be gentle with yourself when any emotions come up and allow yourself to move through them in ways that work for you.

Now that you have a clear understanding of what you want to bring in and what has been in the way; it's time to streamline. This is where the rubber meets the road in this support technique. This is where the changes must be implemented. This is where the releasing of the old and creating healthy boundaries comes into play. As you actualize these important shifts and changes, the desired result must come in to your world. This is that magical quality that I referred to earlier. This in lies the action which creates a vacuum which ultimately brings in your desired changes.

As you continue to move through your personal list by implementing this streamlining technique, you will experience huge change.

5.

The Heart of the Home

This is such a fitting name for this sacred space which is housed in all of our homes; otherwise known as the Kitchen. This room and space creates, supports, and nourishes all who dwell and visit your home. This is the true heart of the home indeed as it is constantly pumping out love and life force to all who cross your threshold.

For many of us we can pull up happy memories of loved ones who have prepared favorite dishes for us on holidays and other special occasions. We may hold fond memories of laughter and conversation with loved ones within our kitchen or the kitchen of someone near and dear to us, perhaps a Grandmother or another loved one. Maybe it is us who creates, nourishes, and creates community within the kitchen for our friends, family, and neighbors. No matter how you personally use your kitchen, it holds a sacred energy within its space which impacts your entire home; including you.

As I have worked with clients over the last 15 years I have found that there is a very strong connection between the relationship with the kitchen and one's connection to self. For example I have found that people can fit into different groups when we look at this connection between the kitchen and ourselves. Based on these groups there are different themes that seem to impact each group. No matter which group feels more like us at this time, making small shifts to the way we move through this area of our lives yields big benefits; physically, mentally, emotionally, and spiritually.

Yes, I Walk Through that Room Every Day:

When clients tell me that they are run down, exhausted, and can't seem to keep up with the demands of their daily lives; I ask them about their daily food preparation and eating experience. The answers that I get tend to be about the same. Perhaps you can relate to these feelings as well. Most people within this group respond by saying that they barely have enough time to shove some packaged food into their mouths as they rush from one thing to the next.

These clients tend to find that no matter what they do they can't seem to find the magic elixir which will allow them to do all of the things that they need to get done within their day. This group tends to find themselves experiencing burn out, stress, and even sleep disturbances on a pretty regular basis. These clients tend to be the quintessential "burning the candle at both ends" group. This group also tends to use lists to help them remember all of the things that they need to get done. They come home from a long day and don't know how they weren't able to accomplish more; thus setting up their next day already "behind."

Overtime this group can feel like each day is the same as the day before. This kind of monotony takes a toll on people especially when there is not enough time to nourish the body and soul with real food. This kind of experience can create feelings of being disconnected, and that the magic or wonderment of life has dissipated completely. This group overtime can feel that they no longer enjoy their lives but just keep putting one foot in front of the other to make it through the day. Often people within this group report that they can't believe how quickly 1, 5, 10, or more years has passed by. This group can often feel that no matter what they do they can't catch up. This group tends to report that they don't understand why everyone else is able to have fun and live exciting and successful lives. This group can feel lost and like they are constantly treading water.

Many times the kitchens within this group can look one of two ways. Beautiful and Untouched or a Catch All.

Beautiful and Untouched
Many within this group have lovely kitchens and wish they had more time to utilize this beautiful space. They just can't seem to find the time. Many may even fantasize about a time when they will be able to host and prepare lovely meals for their friends and families. This group tends to feel a longing or a sadness as they connect to their kitchen. They feel that sadness and longing within their own lives as well. This group is out of balance and can never seem to find enough time for themselves or to nourish the parts of their lives that aren't about work and responsibility. They tell themselves that once everything is finished, then they will have more time. However, this is the opposite of the truth. This disconnect and misunderstanding in thinking compounds the sadness, hardship, and perpetual hamster wheel of trying to play catch up.

Catch All
The other extreme looks exactly the opposite. In these homes you may tend to see items that do not belong within the kitchen at all. The space becomes a catch all for things that haven't been put away. Because the room is not being used, it can begin to collect piles, clutter, and other stuff. Many times this collection is a reflection of the sadness or overwhelming feelings that many experience from being unnourished within their lives on many levels. This group often reports feeling lethargic and that they have given up

on trying to change the situation. This group unlike the other group doesn't fantasize about the time when they can use their kitchen. This group doesn't believe anything will ever change. This group has decided to believe that this is the way it is; so why fight it. This group has accepted this way of living and in some ways tries to settle into it. Even though there is a level of acceptance here; you can physically see the discord within the space which also shows up within their bodies and emotions as well. This group is living out of balance and it is evident in the physical space and within their lives.

Yes, I Cook. I Defrost, Zap, and Heat up My Meals Every Day:

People who fall into this group tend to lead very busy lives as well. However, they tend to carve out time to eat meals on a pretty regular basis whether they live alone or with other people; family or roommates. These are the folks who have lots of food in the freezer, pantry, and many times an overflow of food in some kind of out building; maybe a garage or even a basement.

This kind of food and kitchen experience creates a sense of understanding that eating meals is important. This group really does understand the importance of making time to eat even though they are really busy; however the energy around this kind of food experience is also hurried and contains an energy of "get 'er done." Its wham bam, thank you ma'am and onto the next thing that needs to get done today.

People who find themselves in this situation also tend to be really overloaded in their day to day responsibilities and see the key to nourishment as another thing to quickly and effectively take off of their to do lists. This is why this group gravitates toward items that are prepackaged and can be heated up and eaten in a fast manner. This group loves microwaves, toaster ovens, and the ability to defrost food.

Even though this group understands the importance of eating meals regularly and makes a commitment to do so; there is still a sense of urgency which can contribute to a low grade anxiety over time. That low grade anxiety or feeling of needing to hurry all the time can create stress within the body. This hurried feeling can also train the body and brain to remain in this state for long periods of time which can teach the person that this feeling is normal. This can lead to a belief or experience of the body's natural state: Rest and Restore, as feeling foreign or "non-productive."

People in this group can carry a bit of nervous energy and it can be overwhelming for other people to be around them as they are constantly moving and doing things. This group often reports that it is challenging for them to sit still. This group often has a challenging time slowing down or doing things for themselves. This group tends to have challenges with receiving. People in this group tend to be the doers, givers, and helpers within their inner circle yet, they show outward signs of needing a great deal of self-care. This group tends to put everything and everyone else before themselves. This group also tends to lean into out of balance relationships. People in this group can tend to attract natural takers; which can leave them feeling taken advantage of and sad.

Professional Students tend to fall into this group as well. Due to the overwhelming academic and often work schedules students are managing while in school; they can experience this kind of relationship with food during college. The slippery slope for professional students is in finding a way not to transfer this style into their professional lives as they move into the working world. It can become so easy for students to become accustomed to this way of life that it naturally transitions with them as they leave their university.

Some students can tend to push so hard that they can end up in the first group, "Beautiful and Untouched" or "Catch All" as they move into the professional world. Mastering balance is important for everyone and especially critical for professional students.

Oh Yes, I cook all the time. To Me, Food Is Life.

So, you know these people right? They are the all time food foodies. They love food and food seems to love them too. They tend to have subscriptions to food magazines; they talk about food on a regular basis, they plan their lives around food, and trips to the farmers market are moments of complete bliss and enjoyment for them. Many of these people tend to live the majority of their lives within their kitchens. The Kitchen truly is the heart of their homes and when they are in that space you can feel their deep spiritual connection to the food they are preparing. These are the kitchens that you love to hang out in because they feel so comforting. These are the people who you love to watch work with food because you can see their art come to life with the slicing, sautéing, and mixing of foods.

These people tend to nurture, love, and heal their friends and family with their food. These tend to be the comforters within their group. These folks will listen to you and offer you support as they make you something to eat to nourish you from the inside out. They will brew a pot of tea that is especially healing for you on that cold balmy day. They feed the souls of the people within their world.

Life Purpose:
Many people who fall into this group tend to have a life purpose that involves food. They may dream of owning a restaurant, have already owned one, or currently work with food professionally. Food bloggers, cook book authors, food to table advocates etc, anything to do with the world of food is right on target for these folks. As this group honors this natural talent, gift, and connection with food they will be able to maintain the balance within their lives. It is really important for this group to really accept that their love of food is a part of their life purpose and not trivialize this deep soul connection. When people in this group find themselves out of balance; often it can be because they are not allowing themselves to fully invest in their food calling. No that doesn't mean you must quit your non food related job to honor this calling; but it is important for these people to integrate and respect this part of their life purpose on a regular basis. People within this group will feel more fulfilled on an overall level if they can find ways to be connected to food while also making money. This feels like a huge win win to this group and they feel so blessed to be able to be paid for doing the things that they love. Working with food and connecting said food with others is their true love and passion.

Putting Food Over Responsibilities:
Okay so there can be a slippery slope for folks who absolutely love food but get out of balance with that

relationship. Unlike the above group; this group can use food and food preparation as a delay tactic. Let's face it creating 7 course meals everyday takes a great deal of time and planning.

Sometimes people in this group find that they use this time to delay them from working on what it is that they know they are meant to do. These delay tactics come from fear; fear of success and fear of failure. Using up all of their spare time to create elaborate meals can serve as a buffer for this group.

This group tells themselves that working with food nourishes them and they are passionate about it; so they are on track. However, like anyone who is not working on their life purpose, feelings of anxiety, stress, and a pressure to be doing something else is a constant experience. This does not feel good and can compound the fear which can feel paralyzing for people. This create a vicious cycle which can make people feel like they are caught on a hamster wheel and not sure how to stop.

This group does great with outside support in taking small but effective steps forward. Breaking goals up into small steps allows people from this group to experience success which helps to lift the heavy feelings of pressure, stress, and anxiety. This allows forward motion to become easier and easier. This group does wonderful working with counselors and coaches to support them in moving into a career they are passionate about. This group does great with consistent support sessions so they can begin to make real progress while replacing old fears with confidence, actions steps, and positive results.

Using Food To Numb Pain:
Some people in this group who find themselves out of balance can at times use food to push down their feelings. Old painful memories, stress, sadness, fears, etc, can become overwhelming; and sometimes people within this group can turn to food to self medicate. There is a large body of published research on the correlation between food, emotions, and brain chemistry. (1) We know that foods hold the same chemical compounds as some pharmaceutical medications used to reduce feelings of stress, depression, and anxiety. (2) Many within this group can slip into a state of using food to soothe any challenging feelings they may be experiencing.

Overtime this self medicating style can create even more sadness, upset, disappointment, etc. for the person because they feel out of control in relationship to food. It is really important for this group to reach out for professional support to gain insight, information, and tools to work through their feelings without using food as numbing technique. By reaching out for support this group can find that they feel more confident and self assured in moving forward once they find they have more tools to work through their emotions or memories from the past.

Somewhere in the Middle:
Maybe you have found that you resonate with a little bit or maybe more in each of the groups. This means that you tend to connect to your food and the heart of your home in different ways depending upon the things that are happening within your world.

This chapter will help you to better identify how you can make subtle shifts when you notice your life and food connection becoming unbalanced. By making these seemingly small yet effective changes you will be able to maintain balance more easily and over longer periods of time. You will also find ways to enjoy your food and kitchen experience on an even deeper level.

Breathe Through It:

So as you read through each of these groups, you probably found your main group really easily. You may have found little tidbits of yourself in other groups as well. If you found some of the things within your group/s challenging to read; that okay. If you found yourself experiencing deep emotions; that is absolutely okay and natural.

The truth is that when we look at food and the kitchen; we realize that this area impacts us on every level. The kitchen is not a place which only represents a physical component of our lives. This sacred space impacts us physically, emotionally, mentally, and spiritually. This place connects us to all times within our lives no matter how old we are today. The kitchen connects us to our ancestors who have passed before us and to those we love who are still with us today. The kitchen is a very powerful place and just by reading through this chapter, you can really feel the depth to this truth.

Honor your spirit by allowing yourself to feel all the emotions, memories, insights, and aha moments that are coming forward or you. Don't push them down or try to deny their presence. These feelings and memories are support systems for you; helping you to move forward.

Activity:

Yes, I walk Through that Room Every Day:

Beautiful and Untouched:

Okay, you need to go back and work through Chapter 1 again so you can gain a better understanding of how to honor your time. I know you don't believe you have any more time; and I promise you that as you really work through this area you will create more space within your schedule.

As you choose to release the people, things, and situations which no longer match your desire and dreams for your life; you will be able to open up that much needed space. Your feelings of missing out on your life will be lifted from you as you take back control over your schedule and your life. This is your life, right now, right this very second. It is important for you to be able to enjoy and live the life that you dream of within your soul. It is possible for you.

You may need to work with a counselor or a coach to support you in effectively making changes to your schedule. It is important to make the changes rather than talking about your "understanding" of why it is important. The key here for you is to take action and implement these important changes now. Waiting will only compound the experience of your life passing you by.

Catch All

The clutter and stuff that is building up in your kitchen represents a deeper issue that is happening within you. Reaching out for professional support from someone who specializes in the connection between clutter and emotions will be a huge help for you. It is important for you to really understand the bigger picture that is happening for you inside of your home and inside of your heart, body, and spirit. As you begin to move through the stuff and to consciously change your day to day patterns; you will find a simultaneous shift happening within you and within all areas of your life.

Yes, I Cook. I Defrost, Zap, and Heat up My Meals Every Day:

The big underlying issue here is a combination of reprioritizing your time table and self worth issues. Because you are so used to doing everything all by yourself; it can be challenging for you to ask for and then to receive help. However, this is key for you to move into a more balanced space.

Working with a professional who can support you in understanding the importance of reprioritizing and making yourself a number one priority is very important. In addition to learning to honor yourself first; creating healthy boundaries with others, learning to say no without guilt, and slowing down are key issues to support you in releasing the anxiety and hurried lifestyle that you experience.

This is a practice that takes time to shift as you have probably been investing in out of balance relationships and lifestyles for a significant amount of time. The big issue here is learning that loving yourself, receiving, and weeding out your schedule doesn't mean you don't love the people within your world. You will learn that this change will allow you to love your friends, family, and passion projects even more.

Students:
The issue here is that you are scheduled to the max nearly every day. Taking tiny slices of time to slow down even if only for 5 minutes will support you in reducing the anxiety and intensity that you feel on a regular basis.

Taking some meditation courses, whether through free online videos or through your university will be invaluable for you. Learning to do simple but effective clearing and breath work will allow you to increase your memory and ability to work longer while also releasing the build-up of stress that can be holding space within you.

Learning to master this skill while you are a full time professional student will allow you to yield dividends forever. This life skill is applicable to every area of your life. This simple but effective way of shifting the way you move through your day can be the difference between maximizing your best potential or feeling like you can never catch up.

Oh Yes, I cook all the time. To Me, Food Is Life.

Life Purpose:
If as you read this part of the chapter you could feel your heart and soul longing to work with food in a professional way; this is your life purpose. So, take some time to get clear about your dreams in relationship to working with food in a professional way; and then begin taking action.

You may want to contact a professional life coach to support you in getting clear about your goals and to help you move forward. You may also be guided to reach out to professionals who are already working in the food area of your interest so you can ask them questions about what a typical day looks like for them and how they got started.

You may even be guided to participate in an internship or training program.

The important issue here is to take action in the direction of your calling without delay. Avoiding action steps will not make your life purpose go away; the call will only become louder until you take action.

Putting Food Over Responsibilities:

If you resonate with using food as a delay tactic; take a breath and release any tension or guilt. Acknowledging this truth is the first step in moving through this pattern. It will be very important for you to reach out for support from someone who has a background in helping people better understand the root cause of the fears you are experiencing and support you in working through them. You may want to find a counselor who you feel comfortable working with so you can begin the healing process which will allow you to experience forward motion.

As you begin to work through this pattern, you will find that the heaviness and the recurring stress and anxiety begins to organically lift from you. Even seemingly small steps lead to huge relief while simultaneously creating a pathway toward your life purpose. As you work on your life purpose you will find that you feel better, have more focus, and feel more confident in all areas of your life. You will also find that you no longer need to use delay tactics.

Using Food To Numb Pain:
If this category resonated with you while reading this chapter; you may have also connected to the many times throughout your life that you used food to numb your pain. You may have connected to the cycles or issues that have triggered this pattern for you in the past.

Finding a trained professional counselor who specializes in eating disorders and food related issues will be a huge support system for you. This is an issue that connects to other areas of your life that involve strong emotions, pain, and even past trauma in some cases. It is important to reach out for and accept support so you can begin to work through this issue with a professional you trust.

Joining a 12 step program such as *Overeaters Anonymous* can offer you an additional support system. These groups allow you to create a support system of people who are working through the same kinds of issues that you are experiencing. There are groups located all over the planet including groups which meet online.

It is important to work with someone in this situation so you can learn ways to move through your emotions and food triggers. It is important for you to create a community of support rather than suffering alone. It is safe for you to reach out and ask for help and then to receive it once it is offered to you.

Somewhere in the Middle:

When you find that you are experiencing any of the areas covered within this chapter; re-read the sections that apply to you. Then, work through the activities and make a conscious effort to take action daily to shift the experience that you are having. If you make the shifts consistently you will find that you can move back into a balanced state really quickly. For you it is about acknowledging what kinds of things are happening or are about to happen so you can prepare accordingly.

Since you find that your heart of the home experience fluctuates with the events of your life; you can plan ahead.

If you know that you tend to have a great deal of pressure around the holidays for example. Plan ahead and work through your schedule and build in support systems to help you so that you can enjoy a more balanced holiday season.

Or if you have a huge work project deadline coming up and you are going to be working nearly around the clock; prepare ahead of time. Make a whole bunch of something, soup or stew is great. Separate the bathes and freeze some and refrigerate some so you can heat up a nourishing meal while you are working without the pressure of needing to stop and prepare an entire meal. (This will also help you avoid fast food or snacks eaten as meal substitutes.) Bring a new bag down from the freezer to the refrigerator as needed. You can have some salad ready to go too. Anything like this will be a great fit for you. You tend to move through the ebbs and flows of your life pretty well already. This planning ahead method will allow you to shift into a space that feels better to you more quickly.

You can also use the techniques in this chapter to help you maximize your Kitchen and food experience. If you want to increase your connection to food and try new things for example; re read the foodie section. Maybe you can spend some time at your local farmers market. Begin growing a garden, try new ways to prepare food etc.

You can use this chapter as a way to power up the things that you want to experience and add more balance and ease to the areas that you want to as well.

6.

Shake That Body

Ah, yes the exercise message. So for most people this message tends to resonate in one of two ways:
1. I love exercise and I make it a regular part of my life.
or
2. Yeah, I know I know; I need to do more but I just haven't gotten around to it.

No matter where you fall within this range or maybe somewhere in between; this message is one that supports all of us. Exercise has many physical benefits along with emotional and spiritual support as well.

The truth is that our bodies, like any physical structure tend to hold onto energy. As you move through your world doing the day to day things that you are used to doing; your body is impacted. No matter what it is that you are doing. Even if you feel that your day doesn't tend to put a great deal of physical stress or strain onto your body; the truth is that your body is still being impacted.

Oftentimes when working with clients who find that they feel a bit off or have been experiencing low energy; we come around to talking about exercise. For most who don't have a regular exercise schedule; they can tend to experience a lot of ups and downs with their energy and even with their overall health. Often times these clients also tend to be highly sensitive people who are very impacted by the moods of others, their work environments, and stressful life events.

Let's go back to the body and its natural ability to absorb energy for a moment. Let's use the analogy of the body as a sponge. Our bodies are constantly being impacted by everything that we do; and everything that we don't do.

Imagine using the same sponge to clean your home day in and day out for weeks but never washing it or wringing it out after you finish using it. What kinds of things do you imagine you would see and even smell when you picked up that sponge to use it the following day? Right, not a pretty sight.

When working with clients who are highly sensitive and who are experiencing low energy; I tend to find the same kind of "full sponge" experience happening within their bodies. Because the body is constantly absorbing the day to day impact that we put it through, it continues to store that energy until we move it out.

For example, if you sit at a desk working at your computer for 8 hours a day; by the end of the day your lower back, shoulders, arms, and wrists will be tired. Your body will send you messages during that time letting you know that it needs to be supported. Some people may take regular breaks to move and walk to help their body get back into alignment. Some will choose to keep working until they are done for the day. Some people will do some kind of restorative stretching at the end of the day to bring their body back into balance. Some people will not do anything until they begin to experience pain or some other physical issue.

Once the body begins to experience pain it can lead to other issues like sleep disturbances and other kinds of stress. This collective stress within the body can then begin to impact other areas of life including energy levels, focus, and happiness to name only a few.

One of the most effective ways to clear this experience and build up from the body is though movement. Exercise that resonates with your body's needs, ability level, and your personal interest will help you to not only wring out the stuff that you have been collecting; but it will increase strength at the same time.

When the body has increased strength, flexibility, and clarity from regular movement; all other areas of your life are positively impacted at the same time. Increased energy, consistent energy, (less highs and lows) clearer thinking, better sleep, increased happiness etc. These are all bonuses that come from regular exercise.

Over the years I've worked with clients who had limited mobility due to a variety of reasons. We found that integrating seemingly small amounts of movement on a regular basis added up to big results. It's also important to remember that there are a variety of ways to integrate and introduce movement into your life.

One of the common things that I found for people who were putting exercise at the bottom of their list for long periods of time was due to timidity. Clients would tell me that they weren't really sure where to start in finding something that they liked to do. Clients would also tell me that they didn't feel confident signing up for a class series or a program because they felt everyone else would be really far ahead of them; and they felt insecure about being a new student or group member.

These are all understandable and natural feelings when beginning anything new. The great news is that there are lots of ways to try new styles of exercise without having to join a group if that doesn't resonate with you.

Across the board exercise and movement are essential for overall health and wellbeing. For those of you who fall into the first group; you understand that plethora of benefits that come from regular exercise. For those of you in the second group or somewhere in between; know that you do have what it takes to integrate and experience the benefits that come from moving your body.

Breathe Through It:
If you find yourself thinking or saying yeah, but…..then this is an area that can really use your attention at this time. If you feel uncomfortable thinking about exercise or you feel like you don't have enough time or you aren't athletic enough; rest assured all is well. No matter what level or ability you believe your body to be in at this time; you can always start from where you are.

Just think about anything that you have done which has taken some commitment on your part. In the beginning you may have felt unsure of how you were going to get there, but in the end you realized it was just about taking one step at a time and continuing to move forward. This is the same thing. Even if you've experienced challenges in the past with your exercise plan; that's okay. Like all practices in life; this is about progress and not perfection.

So, take a breath with me and release any tension, stress, or low grade anxiety that you could be holding within your body and release it on the exhale.
Ready, inhale ….1…2….3…..and release…….good.
Now, let's look at the Activity section so you can find some areas that feel like a great place for you to begin.

Activity:
If you make exercise a priority in your daily life already, continue on in a way that supports you and your lifestyle.

First things first, consult your primary healthcare professional before beginning any new exercise routine. Afterward it will be important to begin some research to find the program that is right for you.

If you feel that you don't have the ability to incorporate exercise within your life due to your schedule; re-read chapter one. You may want to work with a professional coach who can support you in making some life style changes so you can create the space for your physical health and well-being. When you make your health a priority; the other areas of your life will automatically receive a positive boost.

If you used to do a certain kind of exercise and you can still do it and you miss it; you may want to begin integrating that style of movement back into your life. For example, if you used to love running, swimming, or cycling and you are physically able to continue those sports; begin bringing them back into your world. For example, maybe you will need to find out if there is a running club in your area you can connect with. Or maybe it's time to get your bike down from the rafters and tuned up for a ride. Any steps that you take to reconnect to the activities that you loved will help to reignite that spark and connection you had in the past.

Connecting with other people who enjoy the same kind of exercise as you can be a great support system. You can make new friends, exercise together, and support each other. Anytime you participate in any kind of community atmosphere; you automatically receive the added benefits of connecting with like-minded people.

If you tend to shy away from exercise because you don't feel comfortable joining teams or groups, that's okay. There are so many ways that you can find the right movement practice for you. Thanks to the internet you can dabble in lots of different styles of movement right from the comfort of your own home.

There are endless free videos online via YouTube and other places where you can try out different instructors, styles of exercise and decide for yourself what feels like the best fit. There are fantastic DVD programs that you can purchase at big box stores like Target if you prefer to have physical discs that you can pop into your player for your workouts.

Once you find some things that you enjoy, you can then decide how you want to move forward. You may decide that you want to work with a professional instructor or trainer in person or you may love the freedom of working with your favorite Online or DVD instructors. It doesn't really matter how you choose to embrace and practice your regular body movement. The important part here is that you find something or a combination of things that you enjoy and implement them regularly.

As you continue your exercise practice you will find that in addition to physical strength and mental clarity; you will also gain confidence, balance and a sense of inner peace.

7.

Breathe | Breath Work

Okay, so you may be wondering why there would be an entire chapter devoted to breathing. You may even be thinking, "Why would I need to focus on something that I do automatically?" That question in and of itself is in many ways an answer to why this chapter is here.

Breathing is something that as humans we do "automatically" yes, that is true. However after working with clients from all different walks of life for many years; I have found that breathing is a big issue for many people. In truth breathing is a big issue for all of us.

Most people are not breathing in ways that are best for their bodies. This pattern of not breathing "correctly" or not breathing deeply on a regular basis can lead to several issues for the body: physically, mentally, emotionally, and spiritually. When working with clients to help them recognize and rectify this issue big shifts happened for people across the board. Learning to reframe and retrain your mind and body to move back into a natural body rhythm is absolutely possible. The benefits that you will yield will pay out dividends, daily.

Often times when people are experiencing a great deal of tension or stress; they tend to move into a pattern of mouth breathing. Most people don't even realize that they are doing this. Our bodies are incredibly amazing on so many levels and are set up to support us even when we don't recognize it. Think for a moment about a time when a child (maybe a memory of yourself, maybe a child of your own) fell off of their bike or hurt themselves in some way. When you were trying to ask them what happened and how they got hurt; you may have realized they couldn't really talk because they were crying so hard and they were taking oxygen in through their mouths. So you get the experience of trying to feed the information to them and then have the child nod their head in response to your questions. "Did you fall off of your bike?" "Can you move your leg?" "Did someone push you?"

This experience of mouth breathing sets in automatically when we are under a great deal of stress. We begin breathing through our mouths so that oxygen goes directly into our lungs, keeping us alive. As our stressful situation begins to dissipate and our body begins to normalize; we automatically begin to breathe through our nose again. This allows oxygen to go into the brain and then to be distributed throughout the entire body. As we increase oxygen we increase calm throughout the whole body. (This is also the reason that during an accident where you take a ride in an ambulance, you receive oxygen. This helps to bring a calm and homeostasis to your body quickly.)

I have found some variations within the clients that I have worked with. Each group experienced some level of challenge in respect to their breathing; however there were noticeable differences. I have included some of the key points for those groups below.

Over booked | Over Scheduled | Over Stressed:
When I work with clients who have been under a great deal of stress for long periods of time; I tend to find that they have breathing issues. Many of these clients tend to have really busy day to day lives. They tend to be scheduled to the max and always have something going on. On many levels they feel like no matter what they do, they can't

seem to catch up. Many of these clients tell me that they physically have a hard time "catching their breath" throughout the day. These clients tend to breathe through their mouths for a majority if not all of their day.

When we spend long periods of time mouth breathing, we aren't able to get the deep quality breathing that is needed for overall health and wellness. This can take a toll on the body. Because the body and brain are so malleable we can actually train ourselves to maintain this style of breathing throughout the day. For many who experience this near constant style of breathing, it has become really normal for them. Many of these clients don't even realize that they are doing it.

The 3:00 Witching Hour:
Some clients find that their breathing changes and tightness in their chest, neck, and shoulders shows up around 3:00 pm. These clients tend to have a great deal going on within their lives as well. However, the difference here is that these people tend to feel great up until that 3:00 time frame. These clients report that they feel good in the morning and throughout lunch time and then all of a sudden they seem to hit a wall. Many of these people tend to be really hard workers, natural overachievers, and self-starters. They are the people who tend to continue working until they have completed what they are working on. These people will often skip breaks and just "power" through. This group finds that it may take a while for them to unwind or decompress after work. Once they are able to make the shift from their work day they can feel the tension and tightness dissipate.

Yawners:
Another group tends to find that even when they get a full

night of quality sleep; they are yawning throughout the day. Sometimes these folks are shift workers and other times they aren't. Shift work can be really hard on the body for some people. The full spectrum light is important for all of us as it creates serotonin and melatonin; which we need every day. So if people are asleep during the full spectrum lighting and working during the dark; it can create challenges.

When we yawn, we are take air in through our mouths and it is goes directly into our lungs. (aka mouth breathing) For some people in this group learning to increase deep breathing will help to alleviate the yawning experience.

Shallow Breathers:
The last group tends to report that they experience shallow breathing. Many of these clients reported that they had experienced shallow breathing for many years for a variety of reasons. Some of these clients had minimal mobility and didn't participate in regular exercise to increase their heart rate and clean out their lungs. Others reported that they tended to stay indoors throughout the day for a variety of reasons; and weren't exposed to fresh air very often. Some reported that they had a very sedentary lifestyle. Some reported that they had physical health issues within their lungs which contributed to their shallow breathing.

The great news is that no matter where you might recognize your own breathing patterns; you can always increase the quality of your breathing. I've found that everyone can reap benefits from breath work. Even if you almost never mouth breath, you can still deepen your breathing.

Breathe Through It:

No pun intended here. If reading this has brought your attention to your breathing, great. If this has made you nervous about something you don't tend to think about; please just let that go. This is by no means meant to increase stress in any way. This is only meant to be a support system for you so you can increase all the benefits that breathing offers.

Take a nice deep breath with me in through your nose……hold it…….and exhale out your mouth, good. Release any tension, tightness, or stress that could be holding space within your neck, shoulders, or chest…good. Repeat if necessary.

Activity:

Over booked | Over Scheduled | Over Stressed:
It is really important for those of you who resonate with this group to reach out to a professional who can support you in re-learning how to breathe. This is not something to put on the bottom of your to do list. Working with a breathing professional will support you in reducing stress, increasing oxygen to your brain and body which will allow you to have more energy and ability to focus. This will also allow you to more easily shut out distractions and get centered as needed. The ability to reduce your day to day stress will support you in all life areas.

Those of you who resonate with this group have an issue with being out of balance. In many ways you have become accustomed to this out of balance way of living. By taking the time to bring your physical breathing back to homeostasis, you will find that you are able to bring other areas of your life into balance as well.

There are a lot of professionals available who can help you with this issue. Many Yoga Instructors or Pranayama teachers can guide you in shifting your breathing patterns. Meditation Instructors and many Wellness Coaches can also support you in reframing and retraining your breathing patterns. This is something that a few sessions can correct for most people. The big take away here is about integrating the information that you learn into your daily life. Like anything, the more you do something, the easier it becomes.

Re-reading chapter one and working with a professional to create some much needed space within your schedule will also support you in big ways.

The 3:00 Witching Hour:
For those of you within this group; balance is an issue for you too. However, your shift back to balance looks different from the first group. You tend to commit to things 100% in all areas of your life. So, no matter what you are doing, you tend to go all in; whether at work or at play. That is a great commitment, however, it is important for you to balance that commitment with breaks.

The reason the 3:00 time frame is so hard for you is because you forget to take time to regroup and move your body throughout the day. By the time 3:00 creeps up on you; your body has already been pushed to the limit. So your body begins to give you signs that it wants to decompress. You may notice that your shoulders end up around your ears, your back becomes hunched over, your breathing becomes tight, and your neck and shoulders begin to hurt. These are all stress responses from your body begging you to stop, drop, and breathe.

You are great at shaking off the stress after work is over. However, you need to find ways to integrate this shaking off and resetting throughout your day.

Small shifts make a huge impact for you; try integrating some of the things below to create a support system for you.

- ❖ Set an alarm to go off on your phone every hour (or two hours) during your work day. When this alarm goes off: simply push away from your desk and Stop Drop and Breathe. Take a moment to inhale a long breath in through your nose, hold, it, and exhale out of your mouth. Then, physically move your arms and legs. Stand up if you can and move your body. Stretch and repeat your breathing 3 times. Then go back to your work. (This only takes one or two minutes.)
- ❖ Listen to relaxing music or nature sounds at your desk if possible. Relaxing music physically supports your body in decompressing stress and tension.
- ❖ Go outside to eat your lunch if possible. Getting away from your desk or project allows you to get into a new environment which allows you reset your body and breathing naturally.
- ❖ Listen to a guided meditation to help you slow down, reset your breathing, and reduce stress. You can listen to free meditations online or purchase a low cost MP3 and listen to it with head phones when you feel you are under a great deal of stress.
- ❖ You can also take a yoga or pranayama class to learn how to integrate breath work into your day.

- ❖ Watch a free video online about how to do pranayama and integrate this into your week.

Yawners:
If you are a shift worker and you find that you are yawning throughout most of your day; you may want to make an appointment with your health care professional. You may be experiencing some challenges due to the time of day you are working.

If you tend to find that you are getting enough sleep, you don't feel tired, but yet can't seem to stop yawning try some of the things listed below. Often times, if you fall into this group, you are not getting enough deep breaths in through your nose. Like the group above, you can make huge shifts by incorporating seeming small changes.

- ❖ Set aside 5 minutes in the morning before you begin your morning routine. Do one to two minutes of deep breathing in through your nose and out through your mouth. If you can go into a quiet place in your home to do this, even better. This will allow you to bring some fresh clean air into your brain and body first thing in the morning. This will also help to set you up for a better breathing pattern throughout your day. After you are finished with the one to two minutes of breathing; stretch your body a little bit. If you notice the yawning beginning to show up again later in the day, just do a few cycles of deep breathing to reset. (This may only take one minute.)
- ❖ Sign up for a yoga class or purchase a yoga DVD and begin a practice at home. Yoga is a great way to learn how to breathe deeply and regularly.

❖ Purchase a Neti Pot and use it regularly to help increase your quality of breathing.

Shallow breathing:
If you fall into this group; you may have been living with this experience for quite some time. Some people even remember a time when they became shallow breathers. Again, there tends to be a big sliding scale for this group. So no matter where you are within the shallow breathing space; there are things that you can do to deepen your breath work.

One of the priorities for this group involves creating a living environment which supports the air that you are currently breathing.

❖ Make sure that the air filters within your home are changed regularly. You may want to purchase the filters for people who experience allergies. These filters tend to grab more stuff in the air. You may also want to have the duct system within your home cleaned by a professional on a regular basis.
❖ Bring outdoor air into your home on a regular basis. Even if you can only open your windows for a few minutes a day; do it. The clean air will move the old stagnant air out of your house allowing you to breathe fresh and clean air. Stagnant air contaminates the lungs while fresh air helps to oxygenate and clean them.
❖ Bring air filtering plants into your home. You can find these plants at big box plant stores and they are clearly marked on their labels as air purifying plants.
❖ Some people find that they breathe differently depending on where they live. (Ocean air vs Desert

air) You may do better breathing in moist air. You may want to practice using a humidifier to see if moist air is easier for you breathe. The opposite is also true. If you have trouble breathing in a moist living environment, perhaps dry air is better for you. You can use a dehumidifier and see if that helps.
- ❖ If possible, remove any carpeting in your home. Changing out carpeting for flooring helps to reduce chemicals that seep into the air which can negatively impact your air quality and your breathing.
- ❖ If possible, have your home checked for black molds which could contribute to poor air quality and breathing challenges.

Working with a professional who is trained to help you will also be a huge support system. There are numerous professionals who understand the importance of increasing and deepening the quality of breath. Working with a trained professional will allow you to learn breathing techniques while simultaneously strengthening your lungs. Like any strength training program; this allows you to increase strength over time. Everything you do will add up to big change.

- ❖ If you have limited mobility, for whatever reason, contact a professional trainer/instructor who is certified to support you. Movement, no matter how seemingly small allows for deeper breathing.
- ❖ Work with a breathing instructor to learn ways to increase and strengthen your breathing. Try different kinds of breathing styles and different instructors to find the ones that you enjoy the most.

❖ Purchase a Neti Pot and use it regularly to help increase your quality of breathing.

8.

H2O Power
Drinking | Dunking | Soaking

This chapter is all about the incredible power of water and its impact on the body. So many people that I have worked with over the years have had physical and emotional stress that was shifted by increasing their daily interaction with water. As we have been told for years, water is vital to our physical makeup and is the backbone of our ability to maintain our life force. While many of us know this to be true; I have found that incorporating daily water intake to be challenging for some people. Even if you are someone who carries your water with you everywhere you go; you will still find some benefits within this chapter.

We know that drinking our daily recommended value of water every day allows us to support our organs and physical health. After all the majority of our body is made of water. We need water, not only to survive but to thrive as well. Here are just a few ways that water supports the body:

- ❖ 75% of the brain is composed of water
- ❖ 84% of the body's blood is made up of water
- ❖ 22% of bones are made of water
- ❖ 75% of muscles are made of water
- ❖ Water protects and cushions the vital organs
- ❖ Water cushions the joints

Just looking over this short list, it is easy to see that water truly is a life supporting source for us. So, if we know this to be true, why is it so challenging for so many people to drink water?

The top three reasons that I have found are:

- ❖ Convenience Issues
- ❖ Addiction to Soda and Other Dehydrators like Caffeine and Sugar
- ❖ Taste

I have heard everything you can imagine as to why people do not drink enough water. But at the end of the day; the reasons can pretty much be dropped into the above categories. So, think for a minute about your own water intake and take an honest inventory about your own daily routine.

Some of the issues that show up for people when they aren't drinking enough water can include physical challenges with their organs and body functions. People can also experience things like: headaches, dizziness, moodiness, lack of focus, bloating and inflammation, constipation, and issues with sleeping just to name a few.

I found that when clients increased their water intake on a consistent basis they were able to shift things that were creating challenges for them in their daily lives. One of the big issues that people found when making these shifts was the fact that they had to acknowledge *why* they were repeating this pattern of cutting off their own life force.

For some people, the overall message was about slowing down and re-prioritizing their life so that their health was number one. This issue often shows up for the people who tend to have very busy schedules. This group often reported that they would "forget" to drink water. Many could not remember how many days it had been since they last drank water.

Another big message surrounds addiction issues. This group tends to consume large amounts of caffeine, sugar, and or soda's. This group tends to push past their natural body needs by consuming large amounts of chemicals to keep going. Many clients told me they had been consuming large amounts of these chemicals for years on a daily basis. Some even reported they were afraid to stop because they didn't know if they could make it through the day.

This group could often find other areas of their lives where addiction issues were showing up. Often there was also a timeline where these patterns began. Working through the deeper issues while slowly detoxing off the chemicals created huge shifts for people.

The last group focused a lot on the taste of water as being the reason they avoided drinking it. Many of the people in this group had previously or concurrently been part of the Caffeine, Sugar, and or Soda group. Simply by adding fresh fruits, herbs, and even vegetables to water; people in this group were able to enjoy increasing their water intake on a daily basis. Overtime, this group found that as their pallet completely cleared from detoxing off of sugar caffeine, and soda, they actually began to enjoy the taste of water.

In addition to drinking water, dunking and soaking in water are also powerful ways to support the body in releasing and clearing from stress. Often times when clients tell me that they feel overwhelmed, burned out, and even lethargic; we talk about their H2O exposure.

Our bodies, just like buildings tend to store energy within them. So, as we go through our day to day lives we pick up little things here and there. Think for a moment of a time you were feeling great and then you arrived to work and there was a stressful situation happening. You may remember feeling your body become tense or heavier as you were subjected to the situation. When that happens, the body literally soaks up the situation and it finds little places and spaces to hang out; usually in the places we tend to hold stress. (For example, neck and shoulders or lower back) If we don't clear our bodies regularly, we store that energy up until it begins to show up as stress, pain, heaviness, or lethargia etc.

By getting into water, we can actually shift that pent up energy within our bodies. Things like Sea salt and Epsom salt baths create a huge support system for the body by leaching out that stuff that has been collected throughout the day.

Getting into a swimming pool or swimming in the ocean allows the body to decompress and to clear itself. Think about the refreshed feeling that you experience after swimming. Many people report that they can physically feel the "stuff" from their day just dropping off of them. The reason the stress shifts is due to the clearing of that old stagnant energy from the body. (Similar to wringing out a sponge after using it to clean up a big spill.)

The sound of water is also very soothing for people. Even having a small water fountain in your office or at your desk can help to reduce the impact of stressors in your day. If that isn't an option for you, ocean or water sounds are readily available as MP3's or physical CD's. This is a great way to manage your energy until you can get to a body of water for dunking, swimming, or soaking.

Dr. Emoto's research with water (2) also teaches us about the healing and programming effects that water has; and the impact it has upon our bodies. We can apply this modality to the water that we drink and that we soak in as another layer of support for our overall health and wellbeing.

Breathe Through It:

If reading this chapter has brought your attention to some issues that you are experiencing right now; know you are not alone. Acknowledging some areas where you may need to make some adjustments allows you to get on track again. Like any positive changes that you make in your life; changing one thing automatically impacts all other areas of your life simultaneously. Like throwing a pebble into a body of water, the ripples continue far past the place where the rock hit the water. Take a deep breath, in through your nose and out through your mouth. Good. Repeat if you feel Guided.

Activity:

Start by taking an honest inventory of the amount of water that you are drinking every day. Please do not include beverages like iced tea, lemonade, or things of that nature. Count only the water that you are drinking daily.

Then, take an honest inventory of the caffeinated, sugary, and or soda style beverages you are drinking on a daily basis. This includes things like energy drinks, coffee, caffeinated tea, and synthetically flavored waters.

Once you have your honest list you can then place yourself into one of the 3 categories listed earlier in the chapter. This will give you a better idea as to how you can increase your water intake and reach out for support if need be. You may find that you can fit into one or even all of the categories at the same time. That is absolutely okay and again, if that is the case, you are not alone.

If you find that you resonate with the convenience category; great news, there are tons of water bottles available. In the last 10 years, water bottles made from a variety of products have popped up everywhere. You can begin the healthy habit or carrying your water with you so you can continue to hydrate throughout your day. Like anything new, you will have to make a conscious practice of preparing and carrying your water with you each day. Remember, part of your personal growth and healing comes with reprioritizing your life and making your needs the number one priority within your day, every day. This is a great place to start.

If you find that you resonate with the addiction category, you may want to reach out for support from a 12 step program. You may also want to work with a nutritionist and or a naturopath to support you in slowly detoxing from the chemicals.

For those of you who resonate with the taste issue; begin experimenting with water infusions. Choose fresh fruits, herbs, and vegetables that you enjoy and place them into your water bottle. The flavors from these foods and herbs will infuse into your water providing you with a variety of flavors. There are water bottles that have a little drop in "infusion cage" which allows you put your goodies in there without them free flowing around. (They look similar to a coffee press.) You can also buy these same kinds of things to place into large water pitchers or the fancy serving pitchers you find at garden parties. You do not need to use these to infuse your water, but they are available for convenience if you choose.

In addition to getting clear about how to increase your water intake and hydration; taking some time to clear your body with water will support you in many ways. Even if you aren't a "bath person," you can still benefit from a salt treatment. The best salt treatment available hands down, is to swim in the ocean. If you live near the sea, get into the ocean and play, swim, and dunk your body. (Including your head.)

If you can't get to the sea, no problem create a sea salt bath to experience the same kinds of benefits. You can find Epsom salt and Sea salt at your local health food store. Often times, you can find both of these salts in the bulk section, so you can purchase the amount you want; without paying for all of the packaging. Add about a cup of each to your bath water and soak for about 20 minutes. When you get out of the bath, you may notice a gummy film on your tub. This is the residue that was released and detoxed from your body during your salt bath. Simply wipe it away and rinse it down the drain. Many people notice that they feel lighter, more like themselves, and that they have a sense of calm after a salt bath. The more you can incorporate this treatment into your weekly routine, the more easily you can manage your physical energy.

Don't have a bathtub at home? That's okay too; you can still benefit from a salt treatment. Pour your salt mixture into a bowl; and bring it into the bathroom with you. After you get into your shower; take a little bit of the salt mixture in your hands and lightly, beginning with the bottoms of your feet and moving upward begin to gently exfoliate with the salt. This will allow you to receive the clearing and restorative treatment from the salt.

If you work in an environment where there is a great deal of tension or stress and you have a little nook that is all your own; get a small fountain. You can find small water fountains at big box stores; especially at back to school time and also around the holidays. They are very affordable and they don't take up much space. The soothing and relaxing sound from the water makes a big impact on the way you will feel throughout your work day. You may want to get one for your home as well.

If it isn't possible to bring a fountain to work, listen to water sounds to help decompress you throughout your day.

Any time that you can spend near, or in the water, you will find that you will reap benefits. This doesn't need to be something that takes up a great deal of time within your schedule. However, you will find that by increasing your exposure to water (and increasing the amount you drink daily) that you will physically feel better and you will also release that built up pressure and stress that you have been carrying around with you.

Cheers to you and to your new renewed connection with the magical elixir we call, Water.

9.

Sound Therapy

The sounds that we hear create a powerful impact on the way that we think, feel, behave, and experience our lives. Many times we can "tune" out background sounds and noises that are happening around us, however this does not change the effect that they have on our senses.

If you think about a time when you were standing next to a river or the ocean; you may be able to hear the sound of the water in your mind. As you connect with this memory, you may also be able to feel your body relax and release as you connect to the memory of the sound of water. Now think about a time you were next to a car whose car alarm wouldn't shut off. Again, you may be able to hear the sound of that particular car alarm in your mind. As you remember this sound, you may also notice your body tightening up as you connect to the abrasive energy of the car alarm memory. These are just a couple of examples of the power of sound and how it impacts us within our day to day lives.

Sound therapy is a tool that can be used to help people reduce tension in their minds and bodies as well as to increase creativity, thinking, meditation, and happiness. This therapy can be folded into the fabric of our lives easily by making some gentle yet effective shifts in our daily patterns.

Many clients tell me that they have a hard time focusing or that they feel they have trouble unwinding or letting down. If you resonate with this experience; sound therapy can be a powerful support tool for you. Some of the first things to pay attention to when teasing out where "invisible stress" may be coming from is to Look, Listen, and Feel as you walk through the rooms of your home. (This technique can also be applied to your professional work space.)

Carve out some time in your day; usually it's most helpful to do this after work. It doesn't matter if you work from home or you work in a physical location away from your home. By waiting until you are finished with your work day; it is easier to employ the Look, Listen, and Feel Technique.

Grab something to write with and something to write on and then take 3 deep cleansing breaths to help set up a new energy, one separate from your work day. Then begin to slowly and mindfully walk through the rooms within your home. Note what you see, hear, feel, and know as you move through each room. For example, if you see the television on in one room and a laptop on and something is streaming through it while cell phones are also being used to text, surf etc. document that. Go into the next room and the next until you have finished every room in your home. Include the sounds of appliances and other electronic items, as these all contribute sounds to your home. Then, step into the outdoor spaces around your home and document what you see, hear, feel, and know.

Once you are finished go into a quiet place in your home and really allow all of the sound data you've just collected to sink in. You may be surprised at what you find; most people underestimate the amount of sounds that are happening within their living spaces. As you look over your list, make notes about the quality of those sounds.

- ❖ Which sounds are soothing for you?

- ❖ Which sounds are challenging or ingratiating for you?
- ❖ Which sounds are neutral for you?

This list will give you crystal clear insight into the amount of invisible stress being pumped into your home just by sound alone.

Breathe Through It:

Now you have your list and you have a very clear understanding of the kind of sound that is happening within your home. You also have a good idea of the rate that these sounds are happening. This is good news, you now have a baseline. This means that you can now begin to make some subtle yet powerful shifts to increase positive sounds and to use sound therapy to support you and your household.

If you are feeling uncomfortable or uneasy about how you will be able to make changes, stop for a moment and breathe. Pay attention to any tension or stress that may be holding space within your body right now. Good, notice if you are holding stress in your stomach, neck, or shoulders. (Or perhaps somewhere else) Release these muscles with another breath, good. Now, notice if the same places that felt tight a moment ago are the places you tend to find stress in your body on a regular basis.

By making some subtle shifts in your home and or office, you can create a more relaxed and supportive atmosphere for yourself and others. This relaxed atmosphere will also allow your body to experience more relaxation as well.

Activity:

By integrating soothing sounds into your home, you create an invisible support system for yourself. So, rather than feeling the tension or tightness in your mind and body when you are in your home; you will feel a gentle and relaxed calm move through you and around you.

You can begin by acknowledging the kinds of sounds that you enjoy. Do you like to listen to the sounds of water? Are you relaxed by the sound of bells or chimes? Does classical music feed your soul? Once you find the recipe of sounds that fits you; begin to bring them into your home.

You can find small desk size water fountains at big box style stores and there are also many places that offer larger water features designed for inside the home. Water tends to be a powerful way to soothe and calm the senses, so if you are someone who enjoys being near water, this could be a powerful sound therapy tool for you. Turn this on when you walk into the room. If you work from home, turn it on first thing in the morning and turn it off when you retire for the evening.

Layer other pleasing and relaxing sounds over one another. So in addition to a water feature, you can also play a relaxing sound file or CD in your home quietly. You can play sounds from nature, classical music, or your favorite band. Bells, chimes, and other things that make sound when they are moved by wind can help to add yet another layer of invisible sound therapy to your home.

Once you've created a strong foundation of sound therapy in your space; it's time to reduce and or remove some of the challenging or ingratiating sounds. If you live with several people in your home; this process may require an open dialog about the overall goal of reducing abrasive sounds and respecting one another's space. This process may open up the dialog for some Time Structuring and Space Structuring around noise making items.

So, if you're a parent, you may ask your children to:

- ❖ Limit the amount of devices that are on at one time in a common space within the home.
- ❖ Agree upon a time limit for screen time so that there is an end point in sight.
- ❖ Or, perhaps ear phones, or mute buttons can be used in common areas while devices are being enjoyed.

Any kind of seemingly small shifts when reducing challenging sounds, create huge changes in the way you and your loved ones will feel within your home.

Once the sound in the home has been shifted, you may notice that you begin to feel lighter and experience clear thinking and focus. You may notice that your body feels more relaxed and balanced as you spend time around the sound therapy you've layered into your home. You may notice that you can more easily let down from your work day; and that you feel more gentle. You may also find that the people within your home feel and behave more gently as well.

If you have children in your home, you may want to support them in doing this activity within their bedrooms so they can implement the sound therapy that resonates with them. By creating this healthy habit and empowering your children to use sound therapy; they are more likely to utilize it as they continue into adulthood too.

Sound therapy has an immediate and lasting impact on people and on our pets too. It is never too late to make some subtle and powerful shifts to the sounds within your home or work place. Once you understand the healing nature of sound, I believe you will find that you employ it in many facets of your life.

10.
Visual Therapy

Visual Therapy is a powerful tool which can support you in gaining more clarity, ease, focus, and relaxation within your home and work place. Many of us don't realize how much we are impacted by the items, images, and overall quality of what we see within our day to day lives. Visual Therapy is another "invisible" yet very visible tool which can create huge personal and professional shifts for people.

When working with clients who feel that they are having a hard time managing stress, tension, and focus throughout their day; I talk to them about this tool and technique. Visual Therapy focuses on the physical items and or lack thereof within your physical space. By understanding the impact that your physical environment is playing within your life, you can make subtle yet powerful shifts to restore balance and homeostasis to your life.

For example; let's say you work or live in an environment which feels lack luster, heavy, depleted, or uninspiring. This overall quality or feeling that is represented within this space will begin to impact you, physically, mentally, emotionally, and spiritually. As time passes, this impact can become magnified which can exacerbate feelings of tension, stress, lack of focus, and even body pain.

Many times clients will tell me that they have become so accustomed to the way things look within their home or work space that they don't even "see" it anymore. This is very common for people; especially if they have been "meaning" to make some changes for a significant amount of time.

For people who have been putting this issue on the back burner of their lives for quite some time, a push pull dichotomy often comes into play. Clients notice that they feel off, like something is missing, and that they feel over stressed. These same folks notice that when they come into their home or office they feel frustrated by what they see. However, because of their level of exhaustion, level of acceptance, and choice not to make time to deal with the situation, it becomes shelved, yet again. Due to this avoidance pattern and level of acceptance of the situation; these clients continue to be impacted by the heavy nature of the energies within their environments; which contributes to and fosters the cycle again. As you can imagine this can become very frustrating and overwhelming for people over time. Many clients reach a place where they believe that it will always be this way. This is absolutely not true.

Visual Therapy can be used in any space where you feel something is off or creates stress for you. With some simple yet effective changes, these challenging experiences can be reduced and even eliminated within any space.

I have found that people across the board benefit from using this technique to shift their spaces. However, I have found that highly sensitive people and children tend to have an even more visceral response to the changes once they are implemented. Behaviors, physical feelings within the body, and people looking younger are only a few of the immediate and lasting changes that I have seen happen for clients. Better studying habits, improved grades, positive communication, improved sleep, increased clarity and focus, and overall happiness are also things that clients have experienced from making these shifts within their homes and work environments. The most common feedback that I've received over the years is that people didn't realize how much they were being impacted by their environment until they made these simple yet effective changes.

Breathe Through It:

If you find that you resonate with this experience; just know that it means there is an opportunity for positive change. If you find that you feel uncomfortable or overwhelmed when you think about a space or place that could use Visual Therapy within your home or office; breathe. Any tension or stress that may be holding space within your body at this time is showing you that you are very sensitive to your surroundings. This is a powerful message from your body letting you know that as you make these subtle changes, your body will be positively impacted.

Activity:

Some of the first things to pay attention to when teasing out where "invisible stress" may be coming from is to Look, Listen, and Feel as you walk through the rooms of your home. (This technique can also be applied to your professional work space.)

Carve out some time in your day; usually it's most helpful to do this after work. It doesn't matter if you work from home or you work in a physical location away from your home. By waiting until you are finished with your work day; it is easier to employ the Look, Listen, and Feel Technique.

Grab something to write with and something to write on and then take 3 deep cleansing breaths to help set up a new energy, one separate from your work day. Then begin to slowly and mindfully walk through the rooms within your home. Note what you see, hear, feel, and know as you move through each room. For example, if you see piles of paper, things that need to be put away, damaged furniture or partially finished projects etc. document that.

Really pay attention to the way each room makes you feel. Look at each item and thing within each room as if you are looking at it for the very first time. Be honest about what you see and how it makes you feel. Listen for any messages that you may hear as you collect your data. For example: Messy, unkempt, procrastination, just like when I was living at home, one day, empty, cold, cluttered etc. Go into the next room and the next until you have finished every room in your home. Take your time and really look, listen, and feel so you can get a deeper understanding of what is happening within each space. Then, step into the outdoor spaces around your home and document what you see, hear, feel, and know.

Once you are finished go into a quiet place in your home and really allow all of the data you've just collected to sink in. You may be surprised at what you find; most people underestimate the amount of things which don't feel like a fit within their living spaces. As you look over your list, make notes about the quality of your surroundings.

- ❖ Which spaces are soothing and supportive for you? Why?
- ❖ Which spaces are challenging or ingratiating for you? Why?
- ❖ Which spaces are neutral for you? Why?

This list will give you crystal clear insight into the amount of invisible stress being pumped into your home just by your physical items, their placement, and their status. (Working, Damaged, Project In Progress etc.)

Now you have your list and you have a very clear understanding of the kind of issues that are happening within your home and of their impact on you. You also have a good understanding of any repeating patterns that you may have continued to play out from your childhood.

This is good news, you now have a baseline. This means that you can now begin to make some subtle yet powerful shifts to increase positive experiences within your home.

Now you will need to take some time to understand what things you want to bring into your home which will support you in feeling more at ease. Refer back to your list so you can remind yourself what you want to release and work backward so you can bring in the things that will help you to achieve your desired outcome.

Making a trip to your favorite bookstore is a great place to start. Grab a big stack of design magazines and venture outside of your comfort zone as you choose them. Take some time to look through your stack and notice what things you are attracted to. Answer the following questions as you move through your stack.

- ❖ What repeating things do you find resonate with you? Why?
- ❖ What kinds of rooms/spaces do you feel represent you? Why?
- ❖ How do these rooms/spaces make you feel?
- ❖ How are these rooms/spaces different from where you live now?

- ❖ What changes do you need to make in order to move closer to the rooms/spaces which you feel represent you?
- ❖ Do you need to ask for help in this process?

After you have answered these questions and found some great inspiration from your magazines; you are ready to move forward.

You may want to work with some professionals as you begin to make the changes needed to bring your space into balance. Being really honest about the challenges that you have within your home will allow you to move through the shifting process more easily. Some people can do all of these things on their own. However some people may find that reaching out for support helps the process to be smoother and allows the changes to begin more quickly.

You may need to contact:

- ❖ Professional Organizer
- ❖ De-cluttering Specialist
- ❖ Someone with a great eye for design and a knack for bringing spaces together. (This can be a friend or trusted family member.)
- ❖ Feng Shui specialist
- ❖ Painter
- ❖ Carpenter
- ❖ Gardener

You may also want to:

- ❖ Have a yard sale with the items that are no longer needed
- ❖ Donate items that don't resonate for you anymore

- ❖ Do a releasing ceremony to cleanse your space before bringing the new energy into your home.
- ❖ Work with a Counselor or Coach to support you in releasing and healing old patterns.

After all of the old has been released and cleaned up; you can begin to bring the new things and energies into your space. You will find that each of the stages of this process creates a huge shift in the way that you feel and in the way your space feels as well. Many people find that a spark of excitement becomes rekindled for them again. As the spaces come together, people find that they undergo a deep catharsis in the releasing, clearing, and rebuilding phases of this Visual Therapy technique. It's really important to understand that this does not need to cost a lot of money. In fact it isn't about the money, it is about bringing your space into congruency and balance.

From the Client Files:

> I want to share an example with you to underscore how applying Visual Therapy can create effective change without costing a great deal of time or money. I began working with a client who had been experiencing a great deal of increased stress in his life due to his work demands.
>
> This client had been working in his field for many years and was in fact a leader within his professional field within his community. He expressed that although his work demands had remained consistent there was an intense increase in his stress, sleep disturbances, neck, shoulder, and back pain, increased feelings of disconnect and the

feeling there was never enough time in his day for "downtime."

As I met with this client in his office for the first time, there were some things that stood out to me right away. First, there was not one thing hanging on the walls within the office; the furniture felt cramped and there was a mishmash of paper work all over the room in stacks. There was also a packing box next to the office door and piles of things behind his desk.

Immediately, I noticed that my shoulders began to hunch over and that my stomach felt tight while being in this space for no more than ten minutes. My client worked one on one with clients in person in this space and I immediately thought about how it must feel for them to sit in here while working with my client.

I noticed that the other offices were decorated and that my client was the only person whose office felt cold, unpacked, and stressful. When I asked how long he had been in this office and why he never hung any pictures. He told me that he had been meaning to make this space feel more like him; however he hadn't gotten around to it in the last 2 years. My client also told me that because of his schedule he hadn't had time to make the changes. He also told me that he spends nearly six days a week in that office and works around 60 hours a week.

We talked about the kinds of things he liked to do outside of the office. Almost all of the things centered around being outside; hiking, swimming, fishing, and traveling to power places on the planet. I found it interesting that someone who works in an office under fluorescent lighting felt so connected to the great outdoors, yet there was not even one sign of nature in his office where he spent the majority of his waking moments every day. My client also mentioned that he enjoyed taking pictures and increasing his photography skills. He happily showed me many images that were stored in his computer. The images were incredible. I noticed that while my client shared these images with me; his face and body language became more relaxed. There was a softening to the way my client spoke and there was a light that turned on in his eyes as well. My client told me that he liked to flip through his pictures when he had time to connect to the memories of the places he has been. He also told me that those outdoor places made him feel more like himself and that he could feel the stress fall off of him while he was there. I thought okay, perfect!

Here were the parameters we had to deal with in his corporate setting:

- ❖ The wall color could not be changed
- ❖ No outside furnishings could be brought into the office
- ❖ Every office must use the exact same furnishings including number of desks and file cabinets
- ❖ No rugs or floor textiles could be brought into the office

85

- ❖ There was absolutely no natural light or window in the office

Additional parameters due to client's needs:

- ❖ Changes needed to be quick and affordable and available in town. (Absolutely no ordering of anything and waiting for it to arrive.)

The first thing I did was ask my client to sit in the chairs where his clients sat to work with him. I asked him to experience what his clients did every day. My client told me that he had never sat in those chairs before and said that he finally saw what his colleagues had been telling him for two years. He realized his office was not a welcoming place to be, for his clients, or for him.

We started with some simple shifts in the placement of the furniture so it was more efficient for work and more comfortable for clients. Instantly the room felt more open and inviting. Then, my client moved the piles of paperwork into file cabinets and got the clutter off the desks. The box next to the door was emptied and recycled. (That in itself helped the space to feel more welcoming and not like someone was in the middle of moving.)

Next we started to bring things into the space that represented my client. I asked my client to choose several pictures from places he had traveled to that made him feel relaxed, peaceful, rejuvenated, and like "himself." He went to Costco had the images printed and then went to a big box store to purchase ready-made frames which included mats. Then it was off to a home store to purchase some hardware to hang the pictures and to purchase a low light plant and a pot to hold the plant.

My client chose to hang the photos around his entire office in a panoramic view so no matter what direction he was facing he could see an image that felt uplifting for him. He also hung images behind him so his clients would also have something uplifting to look at. He chose a combination of ocean, forest, and mountain scenes. It took less than one hour of time prior to work to hang the pictures. He also told me that he was able to print the images at Costco and purchase the ready-made frames in under an hour and a half the night before.

We then talked about bringing in some crystals and some gentle nature sounds to help create Sound Therapy in the space as well. My client purchased a small water fountain at a big box store and a dual CD set with soothing sounds.

When I was invited to see the finished project, I was taken aback instantly. The feeling in the office space felt welcoming, warm, relaxing, soothing, and professional. This space felt conducive of a healthy work environment while also creating a feeling of respite at the same time.

My client told me that with under $200.00 he was able to make the changes to his space. He told me that he noticed a palpable change in his stress level, happiness, and ability to make more time for himself. He realized that he had not carved out the time for "downtime" and that part of the problem was that he felt so overstressed that by the end of the day he didn't have the energy to do anything else. My client also found that he became more efficient with his work because his work environment was healthier; which allowed him to make more time to invest in his life outside of the office.

My client shared with me that his colleagues and clients all commented on the huge difference in his office space. Colleagues shared with him that he seemed happier, focused, and more relaxed. When I asked him why it took so long for him to make the changes, he told me that he just got used to the way his office had always been. He thought it would take too much time or effort and had in many ways given up on it being any different. He also shared with me that he wished he wouldn't have waited so long to make the changes but was glad that he did it. He also told me that the Visual Therapy experience had given him an opportunity to look at the other places in his life where he could apply this technique. He told me that he has been experiencing more work and life satisfaction since our work together.

People often tell me that they finally understand the connection between their environment and their own personal wellbeing after implementing the Visual Therapy technique. When you surround yourself with spaces which feel uplifting, inspirational, and clean; you will find that you simultaneously break old glass ceilings that you had been holding onto within you and around you. You will find that you feel more relaxed and at ease in your home and work environment; but also within all areas of your life.

11.

Home Sweet Om

> Home is where the heart is.
> (Pliny the Elder)
> Home is where one starts from.
> (T.S. Eliot)
> The home should be the treasure chest of living.
> (Le Corbusier)

These are only a few of the many quotes and sayings we have as a human culture surrounding the idea of home. Home is an important place and one that should be honored and cared for with the upmost love and respect. After all, this is the place which rises up to greet you after a long day, after a long sleep, after a good cry, and after a wonderful celebration. Home is a place that envelops you and nurtures you so you can fully relax and release. Home is a place where you can be your true self and feel completely at ease.

So, why is it that so many people are making their homes a low priority within their lives? This is a question that I have asked myself many times when working with clients. I have found some overall themes or umbrellas for different groups of clients who tended to have similar issues within their homes. The bottom line across the board is that the way we treat and live in our home sets up our personal glass ceilings as we move into all areas within our world. Financial security, healthy relationships, physical health and wellbeing, life satisfaction, life purpose, career, happiness, mental and emotional health: all of these life areas are directly impacted by the state of our home.

Some people repeat unhealthy habits that were taught to them due to their family of origin. Some people procrastinate working on their home and create excuses about why they can't get it together. Others genuinely need help understanding how to create a living space which reflects them and they feel unqualified or afraid of learning how to do it. And on and on, there is a large sliding scale of reasons why the investment in one's home and the respect of one's home is not valued.

I have spent many years going into people's homes whether it has been within my private practice or during my work in the field. I can tell what is happening for people emotionally, professionally, physically, and within their relationships just by stepping into their homes. Often times, I can get a lot of data just by looking at the home from the outside. I think it is really important to preface this by saying that this chapter is not about investing a large amount of money into making a shift. The truth is that the shifts come both from those living in the home and from physical changes to the home. It doesn't take a lot of money to increase the overall value, care, and health within a home.

The first thing to be clear about when working on this area is to be honest about what your home currently looks and feels like. It is important to be honest about the kind of lifestyle that is being nurtured within your home. Here are some questions to consider when you think about your home.

- ❖ What kind of relationships, language, and activities happen within my home?
- ❖ How do I feel in my home?
- ❖ Do I avoid being at home? If so, why?
- ❖ How do guests feel in my home?

- ❖ Do I feel uncomfortable having guests in my home? If so, why?
- ❖ How would I describe my home?
- ❖ How do I want my home to feel?
- ❖ What changes do I need to make within my home so that it matches how I want it to feel?

After you have answered these initial questions you will have a better understanding of your personal home situation.

Breathe Through It:

Connecting to the energy of Home and all it entails can be very emotional. Many times people are reminded of specific memories and people as they think about what home means to them. Sometimes the memories of home can elicit an understanding of patterns that have been carried out from one generation to another. Sometimes people feel a heaviness around home because they don't feel a sense of home in the place where they are currently living. Some people feel a great deal of happiness as they connect to home because they do feel supported and nurtured within their home and they want to increase that experience even more.

No matter where you are within the sliding scale of shifts on the home front; know that you are not alone. As you make any change, no matter how seemingly small, you will yield huge benefits. The home is a powerful metaphor for all areas of our lives. As we clean up the issues within the home, we simultaneously receive the opportunity to clean up the underlying issues at hand. I have found that clients who committed to making changes to their home experienced positive outcomes.

Activity:

The next piece involves being really aware of your home in its current state. Some people may feel guided to ask a trusted friend to do this with them. Sometimes it is easier to see what is happening and what needs to be shifted with fresh eyes.

With a camera and some paper and a pen (and with your friend if you have invited someone to support you) stand in front of your home. It does not matter if you live in a single family home, an apartment, a brownstone etc. Go outside and look at where you live. Take a picture of the front of your home. Write down any things that stand out to you right away. Ask your trusted friend for support. You are looking for anything that does not rise up to greet you. Here are some things that may be on your list.

- Broken Items including windows or porch railings
- Dirty front door or stoop
- Furniture or things that do not belong in front of your home
- Overgrown shrubs
- Planters that need to be maintained
- Vehicles that are not clean or maintained that are parked in front of your home
- Garbage
- Lawn care items that were never put away
- Partial Projects that haven't been finished or cleaned up properly

Try to resist the urge to make excuses or to tell stories to yourself or to your friend about why things are the way they are. Document what you find and try to be as honest as you can.

Now, go inside your home and walk through every room. Take a picture of each room and write down everything you notice that is not representative of a home which rises up to greet you. Take your time, and if emotions come up for you, allow yourself to feel them. If you have a support person with you, feel free to share with them what you are thinking and feeling as you do this important work.

Here are some things that may be on your list:

- Clutter
- Broken Furniture
- Structural Damage
- Dirty
- Walls and Moldings are damaged
- Dark
- Smells Unpleasant
- Broken Appliances
- Broken Dishes, Kitchen Ware, Utensils
- Closets/Pantry overflowing and a mess
- Rooms are not accessible due to piles of stuff
- Partial Projects that haven't been finished or cleaned up properly

Now go into any out buildings like garages, sheds, barns, or your basement and continue the same process.

No walk around your home and look at open spaces like back yards or patio areas and continue the same process.

When you are finished you will have a lot of important information to tell you where you are now and what needs to be done to move forward.

- If you are someone whose home is immaculate and there aren't any issues that need to be attended to, yet you still feel your home doesn't rise up to greet you, have faith. There are many people in this group with you. I will talk more about how to make some shifts for you in a bit. Hang tight.

For those of you with some things on your list that require physical changes and elbow grease; it is time to ask for help. Enlist support to help you make the changes on your list. The truth is that if you have things on your list that have been there for a significant amount of time, you probably need to ask someone to help you to make the changes because you haven't taken action on it up to this point. Hiring someone to support you will be imperative in making the changes in a timely matter. *If you find yourself thinking, "Oh I can do it, I'll do it this time, now I'm ready to make a change." I implore you to ask for help. I also encourage you to work with a professional counselor who understands the connection between one's home and self-worth issues.

When people reach out for help within this group they can make huge change that is both immediate and lasting. People in this group find that a lot of the procrastination issues lead back to worthiness issues. There is often a lot of family of origin issues happening within this group which a trained counselor or therapist can help you with as well. I've seen people make radical change by physically having the work done within and around their homes but also by understanding that they are worth living in a healthy, high functioning home which honors and rises up to greet them.

I have found that those clients who reached out for support right away were able to effect the greatest positive change.

Those that procrastinated found that they continued to foster some of the same patterns which led them to their current situation. This is why reaching out for help on the physical and mental and emotional front are equally important for this group.

For those of you who live in immaculate homes yet still feel that there is something missing; you are not alone. There are many people who experience this sense of disconnect within their homes and aren't really sure how to make a change.

There are usually two different groups of people who identify with this experience.

The first group tends to report that they don't have enough time to make their home a place which reflects who they are and how they want it to feel. Often times, people in this group know exactly what they want and they understand what styles, colors, and design matches them, they just don't have the time to do the work themselves. If you resonate with this experience, then this is a great opportunity to work with professionals who can support you in making some shifts to help you feel like your house is now your home.

You can work with a variety of professionals depending on the type of changes that you want to make. These professionals can also be friends, family members, or even colleagues who have a natural gift for bringing spaces together.

Here are some professionals that may be able to support you in tying everything together:

- ❖ Personal Shopper

- ❖ Interior Designer
- ❖ Feng Shui Specialist
- ❖ Professional Organizer

The second group tends to include people who don't really know where to start. This group can feel frustrated when trying to figure out what looks good, how to place furniture, what colors to bring into the space, etc. This group tends to know what they want their home to feel like and can easily express words to describe their dream home. This group can also pin point what they like in someone else's home and they know it when they see it in a magazine; but they don't understand how to integrate it into their own lives. This group also tends to need support in understanding how their personal style ties into the looks or themes they may be attracted to. Many times when people in this group try to incorporate things into their home, they feel like something is off and this contributes to more frustration so they can tend to give up on the whole thing. This just perpetuates a vicious cycle because their home doesn't feel like a home and so the process to fix it begins again.

This group would do well working with someone who understands the process of building a space. This group does well being really involved in the process so they can learn how to work with design elements to create a space which reflects them. Finding a professional who loves to work with their clients like a coach is a great fit. Working with someone who want to do the job without communicating the process with people in this group is not a fit. Being a part of the team and gaining a skill set that can carry over to other projects and spaces is a great fit for this group. This style of mentoring is empowering which allows people in this group to learn as the process unfolds.

A big key here is finding the right professional to support the people who resonate with this group. Here are some things to focus on when looking for the right support person.

- ❖ It is important to find someone who you like
- ❖ It is important to find someone who you feel comfortable with
- ❖ It is important to find someone who you feel is easy to talk to and open and receptive to your ideas.

Remember this can be someone that you already know and trust. Interior Design students are great candidates for the job because they are often looking for clients to help build their resumes while they are still in school. Interior design students often have a more affordable fee than those who have been working with clients for many years.

No matter where you are within the shifting and upgrading of your home experience; know that you are worth it. As you read and worked through this chapter, I hope that you received some important information about ways that you can increase the love and nurturing within your home. I hope that you also have a better understanding of the importance of investing in a home which rises up to greet you. I am wishing you a wonderful Home Sweet Om experience.

12.
Space Clearing

This is an ancient tool that people have used all over the world to create spaces that not only rise up to greet them, but which also allow for a high vibrational frequency to move through the spaces as well. If you are wondering how on Earth you will be able to access and apply this method; don't worry it is easier than you think. In fact, many people employ this technique without realizing that they are doing it. Most people can feel the impact of this technique when they are in the presence of it. For example; think back to a time when you walked into a home or office where you felt taken aback by the warmth, inviting quality, and comfort that you felt as soon as you crossed the threshold. Good, now that you can remember that feeling and experience, you have a great understanding of the importance and impact this method provides.

Some people confuse Space Clearing with Clearing Clutter and in some ways they are very similar. Clearing Clutter refers to cleaning out closets and donating or recycling items that are no longer being used. Clearing away the old allows spaces to feel lighter and creates space for the new to enter. Space Clearing refers to clearing away any heavy or dense energy that could be hanging around within a particular space. So in a way you could say that this technique allows for any old, stale energy to be mucked out of the space to create room for the new brighter energy to be welcomed. You might even call this the energetic equivalent to Clearing the Clutter.

You may wonder why this technique would be needed or considered important. You may feel that cleaning your space should be sufficient enough on its own. Cleaning and clearing clutter are powerful shifts; this just helps to bring that work to the next level. Think back for a moment to a time that you walked into an office or into a home where you instantly felt a heaviness, or a feeling of something being off, or even an icky feeling. You may have thought to yourself, hmm, I don't care for the feeling in this room but I'm not quite sure why. You may have even looked for reasons why it felt uncomfortable for you; such as: the décor, the cleanliness, the organization, the furniture placement, etc. After running those thoughts through your head and saying no, that's not it to each of them, you may have still felt stumped. The reason for that feeling comes back to Space Clearing.

Physical buildings (and physical spaces, including vehicles) hold energy within them and when they aren't cleared regularly the energy, air, and overall imprinting within that space begins to create build up. This build up, (similar to an energetic debris, dust, or film) overtime can leave spaces feeling heavy, unpleasant, depressing, unwelcoming, and stagnant. If you have ever been into an attic or a basement that isn't used very often you can get a clear understanding of what spaces feel like that aren't used or cleared very often.

Rooms and spaces that feel unwelcoming and heavy tend to be avoided because the feeling is not pleasant for us or for pets. This avoidance can create a cyclical effect which only intensifies the heavier feelings of a particular space. This can lead to challenges for homes or places of business if people don't want to be around that feeling. In some cases this heavy and dense energy can lead to physical and emotional challenges.

In addition to energy not being able to move which can create the heaviness or stagnant feeling within a space there are other contributors to dense energy. Spaces where there has been arguing, addiction behaviors, trauma, and other intense situations create an immediate impact on a space and can create a lasting imprint over time if the behaviors continue consistently without intervention and clearing.

Often times when homes have endured a great amount of trauma within them they tend to stay on the market when the owner is trying to sell. Potential buyers can feel the heaviness of the home and are repelled by it; thus choosing something that feels healthier and brighter. The buyer is instinctively reacting to the energy imprint within the home. So while some people are not able to see the impact of space clearing with their eyes, most everyone can feel the impact of this technique instantly.

- o If you are a real estate agent and you have a tough home you are trying to sell; often times using Space Clearing can help you move your clients' home. If you have done all the traditional things and people are still feeling pushed away by the home; there are likely some things that need to be energetically cleared away that are still lingering. Great methods to employ in this situation is Smudging combined with House Blessings and Clearing. I have seen tough homes move with these techniques many times.

When a space is consistently maintained by using Space Clearing techniques the people and pets who interact with the space reap big rewards. Increased energy, clear thinking, a positive sense of self, feeling light and bright, being open to possibilities, better breathing, optimism, gentility, and positive communication to name only a few of the common experiences reported.

Here are a few of the many methods available to you when Space Clearing your home, office, or other space.

Feng Shui: This is the ancient practice of arranging furniture and spaces allowing for a balance between the masculine and feminine energies. This treatment brings balance to all aspects of one's life and creates harmony within the space. This is a very thorough application of space clearing and space blessing.

Smudging: This is an ancient Native American practice of burning sage to clear away heavy or dense energies within spaces and from physical objects. This is a powerful way to shift the energy and to clear away the old and make room for the new. This is a sacred practice.

House Blessings and Clearings: This is an ancient practice that people all over the planet have been using across cultures for millennia. This practice allows for a blessing to be said and infused into the space while also clearing away any old or residual energies that could have been lingering there. Often times House Blessings, Clearings, and Smudging are included in one ceremony; especially when someone moves into a new home or a new professional office.

Archangel Michael: Working with Archangel Michael to clear a space is a powerful way to remove anything that is no longer wanted and to bring a space into a very high vibrating, safe, and powerful place. Anyone and everyone can work with Archangel Michael as he is a nondenominational angel who is available to anyone who calls on him for help. Archangel Michael is known as a protector angel who helps to clear away anything that is no longer needed or anything that is not of the highest integrity or vibration. You do not need to be an angel expert to work with Archangel Michael or any angel for that matter.

Plants: Bringing plants into your space is a fantastic way to clear energy and to raise the vibration within your home or office. Plants absorb dense heavy energy and they transmute it while simultaneously creating oxygen for us to breathe. There are many plants that are NASA certified due to their air purifying qualities. You can find these plants clearly marked on their tags in any place that sells indoor plants. Bringing the outdoors in allows for you to have grounding and earth elements within your space which helps to create balance. Bringing living breathing elements into your space will also help to support the air and energy circulating process.

Each of these methods can be conducted by you. Yes, that's right, if there is a particular method here that you feel gravitated toward; there is a lot of information available about how to apply these methods on your own. Some may feel guided to contact a professional to help them with the method or methods that feel best for them; that is great too.

If you feel guided to work with a Space Clearing Professional, here are some things to focus on when looking for the right support person.

- ❖ It is important to find someone who you like
- ❖ It is important to find someone who you feel comfortable with

- ❖ It is important to find someone who you feel comfortable having in your home or office
- ❖ It is important to find someone who you feel is easy to talk to and open and receptive to your information and insights into what is happening within your space.

Breathe Through It:

If this information is new to you and you aren't quite sure where to begin, it's okay. If you are wondering if you are going to be able to apply the methods correctly in your space; I assure you that you can absolutely apply each of the above mentioned techniques on your own. {Or with the help of the internet.}

Space Clearing simply allows you to bring your beautiful space to an even higher functioning place. It is not one more thing to add to your list of things to remember to do; but rather it is a tool that will allow you to maximize and yield many benefits.

Activity:

Pay attention to the types of Space Clearing that seemed to resonate with you right away as you were reading through the list. You may have felt a gut reaction to one or more or you may have thought, oh I like that idea, etc. These are the techniques which resonate most with you which means they will resonate most with your personal space.

If you aren't sure which techniques feel like a fit for you, simply re-read the list of space clearing techniques above and find which ones feel most like you.

Now that you know which techniques you would like to implement; I invite you to get a little more information about each one. Simply Google or browse your favorite bookstore to get some more details about the techniques that you would like to apply. You will find that there is a lot of information available to support you in maintaining a Space Clearing practice on your own. My little piece of advice is to find techniques and information that feel like a fit for you. It is important to find your own style of implementing space clearing techniques. There is no "one way" or "right way" of doing these things; it really comes down to finding the ways that are right for you. {This can change, depending on how you are feeling, which is great.}

If you feel guided to hire a professional to support you in your Space Clearing make sure you focus on the right person for you. This person will be spending some time in your home or office and you want to make sure that they are the right fit for you and your space. If you have a trusted friend or colleague who offers Space Clearing services, start with them. If you don't know anyone who is offering this work in your area; ask your friends and colleagues for a referral. Local magazines that focus on natural healing, wellness, and the like also tend to have advertisements for people who offer Space Clearing services.

I hope you will enjoy learning more about this technique as you apply it to your own home or office. I hope you enjoy the shifts and benefits that come from making Space Clearing a healthy habit you enjoy for years to come.

13.

Workplace Wonderland vs. Workplace Woes

Right away, your first reaction to this chapter will give you a pretty great insight into how you feel about your current work situation. Work is such a huge part of our lives and completely folded into the fabric of how we feel about ourselves, our contribution to the world, and our overall autonomy. People will often will tell me that they don't see work as being integral to their overall happiness and well-being; but as we begin to dig a little deeper, low and behold they realize how much work plays a role in their lives.

No matter what kind of work you do or where you work, the truth is, your work matters. Not only does your work matter to the people that your work helps to serve; but it also matters to you and your loved ones. We spend so much of our time investing in our work and so the world we work within becomes a world that we are heavily invested in too. This work "community" {whether you work with other people, or are working with your business partner, the internet, or you are a full time high consciousness parent} tends to receive more of our time than the other people and groups that we are connected to. This can create a situation where people are spending more time with their work community than anything else. So, it is important that you feel good about the work you are doing, the people within that community, and while working in whatever space or place where you do your work.

This is not a chapter about how one kind of contribution is better than another. This is about connecting to the heart of the work that you are doing now to make sure that it is the work that speaks to your soul. Sometimes simple shifts are all that are needed to move from frustration or dissatisfaction to a place of joy and excitement about your work. As you move through this chapter however, you may find that you are being guided to make bigger shifts and changes which is also very exciting. When moving toward work that resonates with you; you open doors to more happiness, autonomy, and life satisfaction. Okay, let's dig into this whole work thing a little bit more.

Breathe Through It:

If you feel any tension in your body as you think or read about work scenarios; it's okay, take a deep breath in through your nose and out through your mouth. Good. If you are feeling like you need to make a list of all the reasons things aren't moving forward the way you want them to and the reasons why; take a breath. No one is going to make you feel bad about your current work situation. Everything is okay. If you feel like all you want to talk or think about is work and admitting that out loud or to yourself makes you feel a bit self-conscious; it's okay. No one is going to make you feel bad about being excited about your work.

Talking about work brings up a lot of emotional reactions for everybody. We are emotionally connected to our work because work impacts all areas of our lives. Our work does not define who we are; but it does make a large impact on our day to day lives. By getting into alignment with what feels good to us within our work we can then create more ease and joy within our day. By increasing joy within our day to day life, we create a win win for everyone, beginning with us. When we feel happier and more fulfilled, our loved ones get to connect with a happier and more fulfilled us. (yay!)

Activity:

You will need to take out some paper and a pen or open a new document on your computer or tablet. It is really important to take the time to actually write the answers as you move through this exercise. You may think that just answering in your head will be enough; but I really encourage you to write your answers. This will help to connect you to a lot of insight and wisdom from your higher self. You will find a lot of great insights and takeaways as you move through this experience that you can refer back to at a later date.

First Impressions:

Write down a list of everything that you have in your work space. Try to refrain from leaving out the things that you are meaning to clear away and fix in some way or another. No one is going to see this but you. {Again it doesn't matter where you work, or what kind of work you do, there is always a work space.}

Ask Yourself:

- How does my workspace make me feel?
- What things do I love about the place where I work?
- What things create distractions, stress, or feelings of frustration or overwhelm?
- What things make me feel like myself while I am in my workspace?
- Is my workplace efficient for my needs? If so, in what ways? If not, why?
- What changes would I like to make to my workspace?

Sometimes, the first way to make a big impact on the way we work and how our work impacts us begins with the physical environment. Taking some time to really get clear about the things that can be changed or shifted to create an environment which rises up to greet you can make all the difference in the world.

If you have been meaning to replace items that are broken or no longer work but just haven't gotten around to it; ask for help. I find that people who have a lot of these kinds of issues in their work space have great intentions to take care of the issues, however they procrastinate taking action. Over time, more and more issues build up in the work space. What happens is that the person doesn't even realize how distracting and heavy their workplace has become because they have gotten used to it. This kind of situation not only creates undue stress for the people who have to be in that space but it also creates energetic blocks to forward motion. Think of a garage or a basement filled with stuff that isn't being used. A place for cars and a cool basement game room are completely off the table when the spaces are filled with things that shouldn't be there. The same thing is true here.

Working with a professional who can support you in physically removing the items that are no longer working will make a huge difference in the way you think, feel, and work. (I've even seen clients lose weight and reduce signs of aging in their faces by clearing out the stuff that is no longer working.) Please don't get trapped into the circular thinking that you will take care of it at a later date and that you don't need to hire someone to help you. That is exactly how you got into this situation to begin with. Investing in your overall well-being by working with a professional organizer will be well worth it. I promise.

Sometimes, working with someone who understands how to place furniture and maximize space is all that is needed to make a big impact on your work space. If you feel like your work space is challenging and not efficient for your needs; ask for help. If you find that you just don't know how to maximize your space and you feel frustrated when you are in your work space; ask for help. These kinds of frustrations can lead to undue stress and distractions which can make your work day feel uninspired. Again, this doesn't need to be a huge expense and can often be accomplished in one or two sessions. The benefits you will receive will be well worth it. This can also be someone you already know like a trusted friend or family member.

Here are some important things to remember when hiring someone to help you with any of your spaces or places:

- ❖ It is important to find someone who you like
- ❖ It is important to find someone who you feel comfortable with
- ❖ It is important to find someone who you feel is easy to talk to and open and receptive to your ideas.

Okay now that your physical space feels like a fit for you, let's look at some other aspects of your work environment.

- ❖ What kind of work do you do?
- ❖ How do you feel about your work?
- ❖ Do you feel passionate about the work that you are doing?
- ❖ What is it that makes your heart sing about your work?

- ❖ What part of your work feels uninspiring or unfulfilling?
- ❖ Do you feel like you are ready for a change within your work? If so, why?
- ❖ If you could change anything about your work what would it be?
- ❖ Do you feel like you have enough support which allows you to do the best work possible?
- ❖ What kind of additional support do you want or need?

As you look at these questions and answers you will find that this goes straight to the heart of the issue. The big issue is always, "Am I doing work that I am passionate about and am I being fulfilled by this work?" As you answer these questions you will be able to find the areas that are asking you to make some changes which will allow you to move more into alignment with your true self.

Sometimes, you will also find that what you need is additional support. When clients up level the amount of work they are doing, they can sometimes feel overwhelmed and begin to blame themselves. They may feel that something must be wrong with them because they were once able to do everything all on their own; but now it is more challenging or even draining for them. If this rings true for you, you may need additional help. This help can come from brining on a staff member to help you, giving your children chores, or hiring someone to code better features into your website so you can have more time.

In addition to understanding if you are doing the work that matters to you, and having enough support, some people also find that this brings up issues of feeling unfulfilled or bored by their work. If you are feeling bored by your work

111

there are a couple of things that can be issues for you to investigate further.

The first area is called: I Can Do This With My Eye's Closed

If you enjoy your work but feel like it is no longer very challenging for you; it can lead to feelings of boredom. Often this is a good time to begin a new project or ask to have more responsibilities if you work in a group environment. If you are self-employed, it may be time to get clear on what you need to add or shift to feel passionate about your work again. Focus on getting back to a feeling of joy and excitement; this will help to ignite your creativity and idea formulation. You may find that it is time to let some things go to make room for others. Changing things up can be the catalyst to reigniting your passion and to creating positive change for your clients as well.

The second area is called: Been There Done That

If you feel like every day is the same as the day before and you are genuinely not feeling fulfilled by your work in a way you were before; it may be time to look for work that resonates with where you are now. If you feel heavy and uninspired by your work, it could be that you have gotten everything that you could from it and it is time to move forward to something else. This can sometimes include applying for a promotion or moving to a department that you are excited about. Other times, it can mean that it is time to close one chapter and open a new one.

If reading through your answers leads you to a place where you realize that you aren't being fulfilled by your work and that your unhappiness is impacting other areas of your life, that's okay. Realizing this and accepting it as your personal truth is very powerful. This kind of understanding about your current situation leads to big positive change. This means that it is time to connect with a professional to offer you further support.

Here are some professionals that can support you in moving forward with work that resonates for you:

- ❖ Life Coach
- ❖ Business Coach
- ❖ Career Counselor
- ❖ University Advising (It may be time to go back to school)
- ❖ Therapist Specializing in Career Changes

Some people find that after reading through their lists that they want to go back to work after taking some time off, but feel intimidated. If this rings true for you, take a breath and know you aren't alone. Meeting with the professionals listed above can help you to prepare to take that next step in your professional work life.

The truth is that it is never too late to choose a new path for your work. If you feel guided to do something brand new, great, go for it! The most important aspect when looking at our work always comes down to the way that it makes you feel. When you invest in work that you believe in and that makes you feel good about yourself, you will find that every area of your life benefits. Taking the time to shift the areas that are ready for change allows you to yield big benefits. I promise, you are absolutely worth the investment. As a side bonus, when you invest in yourself, your work and all of your relationships improve as well. I call that a win win!

14.

Who Am I? Where Am I? How Did I Get Here?

Have you ever felt like you didn't know how you arrived at a certain place within your life? The feeling is somewhat similar to the feeling of arriving home after driving on the freeway, but not really remembering the "driving" part. So often I work with people who feel this way at some point in their lives. I have found these moments of awareness to be powerful catalysts for change for my clients.

Perhaps you haven't had this experience in an intense way but have had moments where you realized that it was time to get things realigned so they matched your vision for your life. No matter where you may fall within the spectrum of this life experience, I believe that shaking things out and getting clarity is always a great support system.

For those of you who have had an experience of feeling like a visitor within your own life; I want to share with you that you can absolutely make a change and take control of your life again. So many of my clients have told me very similar stories over the years where they have veered off course. These stories tend to have a deep theme of a knowingness of what they want within their lives, however they have been sidetracked along the way. The ways clients have been sidetracked have varied from family pressure, personal fear, relationship issues, stress, addictions, and many others.

What I know is that throughout the time frame of being off course; the desire and calling of our hearts does not go away. There are ways to make that calling become more dimmed or feel more distant however it is always there.

When we come into this world, we bring with us what it is that we are called to do while we are here, along with our personal gifts, joys, interests, and the like. So when we set those dreams and callings down it can lead to a great sense of separation from our own selves. This separation or a deviation from our inner guidance can create a lot of challenges as people work to find their way back home. For some people it can be a simple shift; for others it can take a significant amount of time. In the end; the only thing that matters is that we heed that calling and take action accordingly.

Breathe Through It:

This chapter can bring up some very strong feelings and emotions. You may find that memories, scenarios, and past decisions may be coming up for you. If you find yourself having an emotional response to these thoughts and feelings, give yourself permission to let those emotions come to the surface. Take some nice deep breaths; and do a little bit of gentle stretching. You may find that your neck and shoulders feel tight and that your stomach is clamped down. Do a quick scan of your physical body and relax your muscles. This chapter is in no way trying to drudge up challenging chapters from your life; but rather to support you in moving forward.

Activity:

Carve out a little time where you can make sure that you won't be interrupted. You won't need a lot of time, 20 minutes of alone time will support you in this activity. You will need something to write with, a notebook, or a new document on your computer or tablet.

I call this activity, "Where did I set down my bags?"

Below you will find an activity to help you clarify some key moments in your life. You will find that there are things to read through and to recall within your own life and some questions to answer. Many people find that what shows up for them is extremely powerful and they find a lot of important information to support them in moving forward. Just relax, breathe, and allow yourself to recall and experience everything that shows up for you. I encourage you to write down any thoughts, information, wisdom, and memories that come through. Please don't worry about grammar or sentence structure, just write. This exercise is for you and no one else is going to see it.

In the quiet of your space think back to the time of your life where you knew what it was that you wanted for yourself. Not what you wanted in relationship to others within your world, but what you wanted for you. You may see an image of yourself as you think back to this memory.

- ❖ How old are you?
- ❖ What other feelings or emotions are connected to this time of your life?
- ❖ What dreams, desires, and goals did you have for yourself?

Now picture yourself at the age that come up for you and see yourself holding a piece of luggage in each hand. Inside of this luggage you have packed all of the things that you will need to move forward with your dreams.

- ❖ What does your luggage look like?
- ❖ What color is it?
- ❖ What is packed inside of your bags?

Picture yourself standing on a road and then see yourself begin to walk down this road. This is the road of your life.

- ❖ What does your road look like?
- ❖ Do you recognize the place where your road is located?
- ❖ Are there any other people on your road?
- ❖ How do you feel walking down this road?

As you continue walking down this road of your life you may notice that it has twists or turns. You may notice that the road changes from one material to another or from smooth to rocky. You may also notice different feelings in different places along your road. You may also find people, situations, or life experiences show up along your path. As you move down your path; you find yourself setting either one or both of your bags down on the ground.

- ❖ At what point as you move down your path do you set down your bags?
- ❖ Did you set both of your bags down together or did one get set down in one place along the road and the second in another place?
- ❖ Did you set down only one bag?
- ❖ As you look back at the places where you set down your bag/s; what life issues were prevalent at that time?
- ❖ How do you feel as you think about setting down your dreams at different places along the road of your life?
- ❖ How have things changed in your life due to this choice to set down your bags?

See yourself going back to the places in your life where you set down your bags. Look at your younger self and give yourself a hug.

- ❖ What would you say to your younger self?

Now see yourself pick up those bags and begin walking down the road of your life again until you come back into the present time and space. You may notice that your younger version/s of you walk with you or follow you for a while but eventually they "disappear" because your dreams and goals are back in your hands again.

Now that you have finished this exercise you have opened yourself up to some important information about what you are being asked to do. You may have also found that you felt a deep warmth or reconnection within your heart as you consciously reconnected to your dreams and desires. If this exercise felt emotional for you; that's okay. Our dreams, desires, and life purpose are very personal so it is natural to have a strong reaction to any deviations you may have encountered along the way. You may want to take a little breather for a minute or drink some water.

Now that you have reconnected to your personal calling and desires, it is time to reach out for support to begin moving forward. If that makes you feel a little bit (or a lot) nervous, that's okay, breathe. There is so much support available to help you move forward with whatever it is that is calling to your heart. For every calling there is someone who can help guide, support, mentor, or sponsor you along the way.

You don't need to have all of the answers figured out to begin. Take one step to move forward on your path and then you will be given another one and so on. I have found that reaching out for support is a HUGE benefit because someone else, especially someone with experience in your area of interest knows how to help you move forward. Plus having someone else in your corner who understands what it is that you are doing creates a built in camaraderie which creates a complete win win.

Clients often tell me that they feel it is too late for them to move forward with their deepest desires. They fear they are too old or have missed their window of opportunity. What I know for sure and have seen time and time again with clients and within my own life is this: the yearnings of your heart will never be quenched until you take action. It is the action that allows your soul to rejoice and you in turn will feel the release and excitement from moving forward. It is in the procrastination or pretending your dreams are no longer there that creates the ache or pressure you feel within you and around you.

It is never too late to begin something you know you are called to do. You will increase in age every day no matter what; so please take action in direction of your dreams. You are absolutely worth it and you will be so glad that you did. You can do it. You are called to your path because you are the only one who can fulfill your purpose. We need you to honor your purpose. When you honor the wisdom of your heart, everyone wins.

15.

The New You

For so many people that I have worked with professionally and with people that I know personally there comes a moment where there is a disconnect with who they are and how they are living. This experience can create feelings of sadness, confusion, and even feeling like the spark or magic of life has gone away. Have you ever thought that there was something off in the way that you feel about yourself but you just can't quite put your finger on it? Have you ever felt that who you are isn't being represented in your day to day life? Have you ever looked into the mirror and thought that you didn't recognize yourself? These are a few examples of some of the experiences that people have when they find themselves in a time of their lives where they are being guided to make some changes and updates.

For some people it can feel overwhelming to think about making changes to their lives. Some people who are in this group actually choose to continue feeling and living the same way because they don't want to take the time to make changes. In truth, we come to change when we are ready and not a moment sooner. But for others who are experiencing this very specific call to change; they realize they don't want to continue to feel this way and are ready to find ways to get back to who they really are. I find that some people are in between these two groups; they don't like how they are feeling and want to feel more like themselves again; yet they aren't really sure where to start and so they find themselves knee deep in overwhelm. So, no matter where you are when it comes to this issue; there is always something that you can do to begin moving toward the new you, which in truth is the real you.

Breathe Through It:

This topic can bring up a lot of emotions for people. It can also bring up a lot of memories from the past where you may have felt like you didn't feel comfortable in your own skin. Sometimes, people find that there are memories that show up which are connected to parents or other authority figures. You may also notice that there could be some tension or tightness in your body as you think about this. Take a moment to breathe and let any emotions that are surfacing come up and out as a method of support for you.

Activity:

You will need something to write with, a notebook, or a new document on your computer or tablet.

You will also need to carve out some quiet time to work through this activity. 25-60 minutes depending on how quickly you work. You may find that you want to do this activity more than once on different areas of your life.

Some people find that bringing a support person in during this activity is helpful.

- ❖ If you find that this is a fit for you make sure you choose someone who is supportive, kind, and committed to lovingly help you move forward.
- ❖ Don't choose someone who is going to be distracted by their phone or not fully invested in supporting your process.
- ❖ If you choose to work with a friend; please do the writing exercise prior to them coming over to your home.

With your notebook or computer spend 5 minutes writing down what things or situations no longer feel like a fit for you. You don't have to understand why they no longer feel like a fit, just use the 5 minutes as a free write to get it all out onto your page or pages. Please don't censor yourself or worry about grammar or sentence structure. This writing exercise is just for you and no one else will see it.

Once you are finished writing give yourself permission to read over it. You may be surprised by some of the things that showed up and not so surprised by others. This free write will give you a road map to the areas of your life which are asking to be shifted, changed, and updated so they resonate with who you are right now.

Based on the information you collected you will begin to work through your list. If you are working with a friend; this is the time to work through your list together.

For Example: You feel that your clothing no longer represents who you are. In this situation you would work with your friend or alone to pin point what style or feeling does represent you and how you want to feel. (It's okay if you aren't sure what resonates with you at first.)You may want to look at images on Instagram, in magazines, or websites that resonate with you. Then, go through your closet and remove everything that no longer fits what you are working to accomplish.

The reason you may want to have a supportive friend with you is to help you when you begin to override or create excuses about why you should hang onto things that no longer match who you are now. This can sometimes sneak up on people and can also lead to a lot of emotions and grieving as you work through releasing the old. I have worked with people who have argued that keeping clothing that is ripped and no longer fit them should be kept in case they may need it one day. These kind of thought patterns are ways to keep you stuck and while they are uncomfortable you can work with your support person to let them go.

While working through your closet, release anything that is:

- ❖ Ripped, torn, stained, or damaged in some way
- ❖ No longer fits you
    - o Including clothing you have in case you gain or lose weight again.
- ❖ Has lost its other pair, such as missing a sock
- ❖ You've been meaning to have altered for the last several years
- ❖ Might wear one day but haven't ever worn it in the last 2-10 years

If you are going to work through your closet, remember that you can sell or donate clothing that no longer resonates for you and know that you are helping someone else at the same time.

Once you have cleaned out your closet; take the items to be donated or sold immediately out of your home. This will help to prevent you from bringing them back into your closet, "just in case" you might need them again. Then go with your friend to find some clothing that matches the style and look that resonates with who you are now. Make sure that as you are shopping you both stay focused on the new looks you want to wear. If you find yourself gravitating toward older styles out of a habit gently ask your friend to help you refocus.

Here are some of the top areas for people to update when they are working through this realignment:

- ❖ Clothing including under garments
  - o Give yourself permission to purchase new bras, underwear, undershirts, camisoles, or tank tops, tights, leggings, and socks.
- ❖ Accessories
  - o New handbag, work or computer bag, wallet, and shoes

- ❖ Make Up/Grooming
  - o Make Up has a shelf life so you may need to get rid of anything that has been sitting around for too long.
  - o Purchase new razors, creams, hair products and other grooming tools.
- ❖ Hair Cut
  - o Maybe it is time for a new hairstyle or subtle change especially if you have been wearing your hair the same way for a long time.
- ❖ Bedding and Towels
  - o Release torn or damaged linens and bath towels and check out some new options at a local White Sale or big box shop.

In addition to the emotions that can come to the surface for people as they begin to release the old; it can also feel overwhelming to see all of the "damaged" goods that have been kept around for so long. Often people will realize for the first time that they have settled for broken or damaged items in many areas of their lives without realizing it. Broken and worn out things or things that we have simply outgrown all have an impact on the way we feel about ourselves. These items contribute to personal glass ceilings and upper limit thinking which can keep us stuck.

What people realize when doing this exercise is that as they release the old they simultaneously feel lighter and more like themselves again. This does not have to cost a lot of money at all. There are so many great shopping choices for every budget. Cost should not be used as a reason not to do this exercise. If you find that this reason is creeping in for you, please work with a support person and go out to do some window shopping with them to see how doable this really is and then dive in.

I have found this exercise to be a powerful catalyst toward change for clients and friends. I have also seen how this contributes to a new lease on life, more energy, and more confidence for people. I have watched people find that spark or magic again because they physically, emotionally, mentally, and spiritually feel more aligned with who they are and it translates to all areas of their lives.

16.

Write

Yes. Write. For some of you, reading this will feel like a huge relief and it will resonate with a place inside of you which feels like coming home. You know that it is time for you to write and you can feel that deep call within you to get back to your writing. For others, it may make you want to turn to another chapter or think of other things you could be doing right now. However, no matter where you fit within these two examples or perhaps you find yourself somewhere in between; I promise you this chapter applies to you.

It doesn't matter what kind of relationship that you have with writing or what kind of relationship you have had with it in the past. The truth is that writing is powerful and healing and it doesn't take a lot of time to glean support from this act. No matter how busy your schedule is and how much running around you do within your days, weeks, and months, this act of writing is something that you can create time for and will benefit from. Yes, even if you dreaded high school English class. You see, writing is personal and unique for every single person. Writing is for you. Yes, it is true that some people write to share with others; however it is not necessary to write for others to receive the benefits that come from writing.

Writing allows us to get to the heart of what we are feeling, thinking, and experiencing. There is a powerful connection between writing and unlocking wisdom from our higher self. Writing can help to provide insights to situations, problems, and even hone in on some things that could be changed allowing for a happier and healthier life. Writing also allows people to get into that quiet space within where you can hear your thoughts and become quiet. Writing can create a pathway to your inner wisdom and can support you in increasing your ability to connect with your higher self and inner truth.

You don't have to spend a lot of time or create formal spaces or experiences to write. That is the wonderful thing about writing, you get to choose the way or ways that are right for you. Your relationship with writing is yours and yours alone and as you foster this relationship you will find that you gain a great deal from it.

Whether you decide to keep a gratitude journal, a memory jar, or a value list; the choices are endless. What matters is that you write so you can connect to the place inside of you that is asking to be fostered. (You wouldn't have turned to this chapter if there wasn't something here for you. If you are reading this book cover to cover then there is something here for you too.)

Breathe Through It:

Writing can elicit a lot of really strong emotions for people. Notice how you are feeling right now. Do you notice any tension holding space within your body? Are you holding your breath? If so, take a moment to release any tension or tightness and take some nice long deep breaths in through your nose and out through your mouth. Good.

If you find yourself thinking about past memories where you experienced stress about writing, allow them to move through you. These memories are coming up as a way to help you clear the old intensity that you have around this issue. If emotions surface as you move through these memories allow them to come up as a part of the healing and clearing process.

Some of you may feel like this message is confirmation about you recommitting to your writing calling. I am here to tell you that yes, it is. If you find yourself feeling fidgety, or thinking about all of the reasons that you don't have time to get back to your writing routine or schedule; please stop and breathe. It is okay that you feel the writing discomfort coming over you; however the truth is that the only thing that will quell that feeling in your stomach, neck, and shoulders is actually writing. I know. You know. It is the truth. As you let the procrastination lists and thoughts move on by and you allow yourself to get back to a centered place you will feel the truth within you. Those who are called to write as a part of their life purpose quiet their anxiety by writing. It is time to make the time to recommit to your writing. Breathe. You can do it.

Activity:

You will need to take a little bit of time to decide what kind of writing you are being called to participate in at this time. Remember you don't have to choose only one thing. You can choose something right now and then try something else in a few days or a few weeks to feel out what you like best. Or, you can try a few different things all at once and see how that feels to you. Your choice.

Here are a few different ideas to get you started:

Gratitude Journal:

This is a pretty popular writing technique that made its way into the main stream when Oprah Winfrey talked about the power of a gratitude journal on her show in the late 90's. A gratitude journal allows you to spend a small amount of time daily jotting down things that you feel grateful for from your day and why. Not only does this method allow you to focus on the good that you have in your life right now it also allows you to shift into a space of gratitude, grace, appreciation, and love. Those are some pretty powerful benefits right there. In addition to those benefits focusing on gratitude allows the Law of Attraction to begin working for you as well, which brings even more for you to be grateful for. This type of writing creates such a powerful win win because you don't have to spend a lot of time writing yet you receive so much from the experience.

Some clients have told me that by participating in a gratitude journal they found they were able to release old anger, grudges, and heaviness because they were consciously focusing on the good within their lives every day. Many told me that they didn't realize how much old stuff they were holding onto until they began to shift their focus with only a few minutes a day.

If this feels like a fit for you; find a journal or a notebook or simply open a new document on your computer. It doesn't matter what you use as your journal so long as you enjoy it. You may want to keep this next to your bed or a place where you like to wind down in the evenings and choose 3 things that you are grateful for and why. You may feel guided to connect to your feelings and emotions to really help connect with your experience of gratitude but you don't have to do that. The most important thing here is to find the way that you want to work with this energy of gratitude. Try to work with your gratitude journal daily and watch how your life shifts in the process. This can take as little as 2 to 5 minutes. There is no right way to do this, just your way.

Memory Jar:

You will need a jar with a lid, canning jars are great for this one but any jar will work. You will also need some paper and something to write with. I like to use colorful paper so I can see lots of different colors through the jar but you don't need to.

This writing activity is really fun because it allows you to review your day as you are winding down. Find a place that you can have a few minutes to yourself and think back over your day. Find a memory from your day that touched you in some way. It can be something funny, happy, lighthearted, or anything that you want to focus on. Then, on a piece of paper write the memory and the date. Simply fold it up and place it into your jar. If you are using a jar with a lid place the lid on top and place your jar somewhere that is special to you.

Create a memory for your jar daily if you can; or simply feed your jar when you feel inspired. There are a lot of great things about this writing activity. One of them allows you to relive a memory from your day that really touched you. This gets you into a place within that feels good to you; it helps you to get quiet and to move into a reflective space while also moving you into a state of gratitude, grace, joy, and love. This also creates a physical memory bank for you and you can watch it fill up as the days go by. There is something special that happens when you know that inside of your jar you have special memories written down. When you feel like you need a little pick me up, shake up your jar, open it and pull out a memory. It is amazing how the memory that you choose will be exactly what you needed to read at that moment. This exercise also creates a time capsule of sorts as it documents a specific year for you.

You can create them for yourself as well as for your children, partner, or parents. Not only do you benefit from doing the exercise but this would be a really beautiful gift to give to your loved one.

Adding Value List:

This exercise is a powerful one especially for people who need to be reminded about the positive contributions they are making in the world. For this exercise you will need something to write with, a journal, or a new document opened on your computer.

This is a practice that allows you to shift into a space of appreciating yourself and having a better understanding of the contributions you are making to the world. This exercise is another one that works well when you are winding down for your day. Find a quiet place to reflect on your day and write down 3 things that you did to add value. You could include things that you did to add value to your day, to others, or to the world.

In the beginning it may feel hard to think of things to write down; not because you haven't added value but because you aren't used to acknowledging the value you bring to the world. This is a powerful exercise because it allows you to make a huge personal shift in the way that you see yourself and your value.

Many people have told me that this exercise helped them to see themselves for who they really are and increased their self-esteem and self-worth in the process. This exercise can also help you to increase your ability to receive. Often times' people who have challenges understanding their value can also have challenges with receiving too. Many people who see their value as "normal" or "something anyone would do" can have trouble feeling like they deserve to receive. Receptivity can include compliments, gifts, healthy relationships, and even finances.

If you find that this receiving issue resonates for you; you can also include 3 ways that you received during the day. By acknowledging your receptivity you will help to open it up further. Things like allowing someone to open the door for you, receiving a compliment without undermining it, allowing someone to buy you a cup of tea etc. all count as receiving. This combination of how you added value and how you have received during the day helps to create a healthy balance in the way you see yourself and increases confidence as well.

This exercise helps to provide a better understanding of how you make the world a better place just by being you. It really does offer some deep shifts as well because it changes the way you look at how you move through your world and helps you to see how valuable you really are.

Writing for Yourself:

If you resonate with this activity then you may be someone who finds great comfort in connecting to that quiet place inside as you connect your inner wisdom to paper or computer document. You may write for yourself, for your loved ones, or for both. You may find that writing for yourself touches the core of who you are and that you are able to connect to a place within that waits for you to write. You may revel in the connection you have with your inner author, bringing your life to the pages and allowing you to feel your experiences all over again in the written word.

If this is the writing that you love and feel called to do, wonderful! Make time to sit down and connect with that space inside and allow your words, thoughts, feelings, inner guidance, and wisdom to connect with paper or document. Your writing is not only important to you but if you should feel so inclined to share it with your loved ones, it will most likely be very powerful for them as well.

As you continue to foster your writing you keep a log of the things, situations, life experiences, and wisdom that have been integral for you within your life. This not only allows you to gain a great deal from the writing experience but allows anyone who reads it to connect with you in a new, deep, and incredible way. Keep writing. Find the time or times that you enjoy writing and continue to foster this special relationship you have to your inner voice.

Writing for Work:

If you are someone who writes for work whether that includes articles, short stories, lectures, speeches, songs or books; it is important that you nurture your regular writing practice.

Those who are called to write for any kind pf professional work whether you are being paid greatly for it or not so much have a deep drive to write. It is hard wired within you. When writers get away from their writing practice a feeling of discomfort, uneasiness, and even anxiety can creep in. (I often feel a heaviness pushing down on me, particularly my shoulders.) Often times this is when the procrastination or "organization" tendencies can creep in. Whatever your experience may be when you get away from your writing schedule; the only way to get out from under that experience is to write. It can seem like the writing is what is creating that feeling of uneasiness however it is the lack of writing which is actually creating it.

Find ways to create spaces where you can easily sit down to write. Sometimes, simply having your manuscript, speech, power points etc. opened on your computer can make all the difference in the world. It is in the getting started that can create challenges. So, create ways where all you need to do is begin writing.

Setting up time limits can also be very helpful. You can work with 20, 30, 45, or 60 minute segments so you don't feel so overwhelmed. Instead of thinking about writing an entire chapter, lecture, song etc focus on writing for the predetermined time and set a timer. When the timer goes off, give yourself permission to either choose to keep writing or stop. This small segment writing style can really allow you to make great progress on your work without feeling overwhelmed or under too much pressure.

Cultivate your writing style and your writing sweet spot. Are you a morning writer? Evening? Late night? Work with your own natural rhythms and do what feels right for you. Set up a schedule and honor it; if you need help ask a trusted friend to support you in keeping your schedule. Treat your writing the same way you would treat any other appointment you had with someone else.

Enjoy your writing, allow yourself to sink into it and have fun. Take time to write just for you again even if it is only here and there. Remember that as you honor your writing you will simultaneously release the tension, pressure, heaviness, or anxiety that could be holding space within you. The writing is what sets you free from the pressure you feel. Writing unlocks the pressure and allows your creativity, wisdom, insight, and words to flow. Keep going. You do have what it takes. Honor and respect your writing. Honor and respect you.

I hope that this chapter will inspire you to honor the writing that resonates with you. I hope that you will also create different ways to include writing in your own life. Remember there is no one way or right way to write, there is only the way or ways that are right for you.

17.
Creativity

Creativity is a powerful and beautiful thing. It tends to elicit two very strong reactions; either overwhelming enthusiasm or that moment when there is an awkward silence and a feeling of disconnect. Of course there are lots of variations in between, but for the most part when creativity comes up in conversation there tend to be two camps. Tune in to how you are feeling right now as you read this. Are you someone who enjoys, fosters, and nurtures your creativity on a regular basis? Or do you find yourself feeling like you aren't creative and feel uncomfortable when trying a creative endeavor. Does creativity make you think of great memories where you spent hours learning new techniques, or do you find yourself thinking about times where your projects left you feeling less than enthusiastic?

No matter where you find yourself on the creativity scale, everyone is indeed creative. You may feel like you are the one person who isn't creative but I promise you that you are a creative person. Creativity is a natural part of who we are. Creativity is something that moves through us but often times we may not realize that we are experiencing it. (If you feel like you turned to this chapter by mistake, please keep reading. I promise you that you are indeed creative and that you are reading this for a reason.)

I find that many people get confused about creativity as a whole. For some people they may have grown up in very creative families and the kinds of arts that were fostered within their home didn't resonate with them so they felt out of place and like they weren't creative. For others they may not have had many opportunities to experience the bandwidth of creativity that is available so they aren't sure what types of creativity are a fit for them. Others may feel that the kinds of creativity that they were exposed to weren't very fun for them and so believed that they weren't creative at all.

In these situations what I find is that the people in this group are very creative. These folks tend to overlook the areas within their lives where their creativity is being nurtured and feel like it is just "normal." For example, I have worked with a lot of clients who have told me point blank that they were not creative at all, in any way. However, they were amazing cooks and gardeners. Some had a natural gift of putting clothing and outfits together. Others had the ability to understand how spaces should be used and could make any room feel welcoming, beautiful and like a home. (No matter what the budget was, including not purchasing new pieces but simply moving current pieces into different places.) Others were great story tellers and could make children and adults alike long to hear the stories they thought up and shared over the years. These are only a few examples of the ways people overlook their creativity.

Because there may not have been someone in their life who explained that these gifts were actually part of their natural creativity, people in this group can tend to feel like their creativity has been on hiatus from day one. However, clearly, that is not true at all. What I find is that once people in this group begin to see what feels "normal' to them as creative, there is this relaxation that comes over them. I have worked with people who have become really emotional at this realization because they feel like something that they thought was missing has come together for them.

The other camp tends to be filled with people who really genuinely love to nurture and honor their creativity on a regular basis. Many of the people in this group had family members or some other person or people who introduced them to creative outlets that resonated with them. You know these people, they are always working on a project, have a deep love of creating and making things and tend to carve out time to invest in their creativity on a regular basis. Most people in this group report that they not only love their creative outlets but feel that it is a part of who they are and when they don't invest time in their creativity of choice, they feel disconnected from themselves. Some can also experience physical challenges as well, including sadness, heaviness, and even anxiety.

Because creativity is a natural part of the way we are made, it is important for us to embrace creativity in our lives on a regular basis. For some people that will include scheduling time for it but for others it will feel organic and natural. It will feel "normal" and like you aren't expending a great deal of effort to support your creativity.

Honoring our creativity helps us to maintain a place of balance. Creativity is a natural stress reducer and also allows us to open up to new ideas, inspiration, and moving meditation. Have you ever experienced that feeling where it seems like 15 or 20 minutes have passed but when you look at the clock you notice that an hour or more has actually gone by? That is the magic of creativity, when you find your personal niche you can get into that sweet spot where you don't even notice that the time is passing. Creativity can make us feel renewed, restored, and more connected to our true selves. There are endless ways to honor and nurture creativity. It all comes down to understanding what your personal creativity looks and feels like and then giving yourself permission to own it and foster it.

Breathe Through It:

If you still feel like you could be the only person on the planet who is genuinely not creative, please take a breath. Now, scan your body for any places where you could be holding onto tension or stress in your neck, shoulders, or stomach, and let it go. If this topic brings up any difficult memories from a time when someone told you weren't creative or that your work wasn't "right" etc. give yourself permission to let those feelings move through you. This is part of the healing process around this issue. The more you can let these feelings and memories come forward, the more you can clear them.

This is going to be an opportunity for you to explore your creativity and find the things that really resonate for you. Think of this as an opportunity to bring awareness to a part of you that wants to be nurtured. You can do this.

For those of you who feel this chapter is a message for you to make more time for your creative outlets, let me go ahead and confirm that message for you. If you have been shelving your creativity for whatever reason, know that it is time to reprioritize so that you can get back to that place of balance for yourself.

If you have been feeling guided to begin a creative outlet but weren't really sure if it was the right timing for you; let this be a gentle nudge for you.

Activity:

Finding Your Flow:

For those of you who feel that you aren't sure where your creativity lies this activity can help you get a better idea of what resonates for you. You will need some magazines, poster board, a glue stick, something to write with, paper, and scissors.

Contact your friends and ask them to do a big clean out of any back issues of magazines they may have lying around their house. When they ask you what kind of magazines you want, tell them you would love anything that they have lying around. It's important not to limit yourself here since you are opening yourself up to new things.

Once you have a great big stack of magazines, create some alone time where you can really spread out without being disturbed. (You may want to play some music and have something to drink near your workspace.)

Go through each magazine and tear out any images, ideas, words or anything that resonates with you. It doesn't matter why it stirs something in you and the more that you just allow yourself to use your instinct the better.

Once you go through every magazine even the ones you think you would never pick up begin to make a collage of all of your images and words. Glue them to your poster board.

When you are all done, look at the poster board and really pay attention to the things that you are attracted to. With your paper, pen, or a new document open on your computer answer the following questions.

- ❖ What kinds of themes do I notice?
- ❖ Are there any color palettes that stand out to me?
- ❖ How does this collage make me feel?
- ❖ What ideas, images, or insights does my collage bring up for me?
- ❖ Are any of these things connected to something from another time in my life? If so what? How does that make me feel?
- ❖ How can I move toward the things included on my collage?
- ❖ What resources, classes, books, videos, or other support systems could help me to connect with these things more deeply?
- ❖ Was I surprised by what you found? Why?
- ❖ Does this make me want to look into any new creative areas? If so, what?
- ❖ Did this exercise help me to realize that there are already creative juices flowing in my life?
- ❖ How did it feel to embrace this creative collage project?
- ❖ What surprised me the most by participating in this creative collage project?

Creating the Space:

For those of you who enjoy creativity but have stepped away from it for a while; it may be time to reconnect to something you used to do in the past or to try something completely new altogether.

You will need to create a little nook or corner in your home for this activity. Having a space to nurture your creative outlet is often half the battle. So much can get done in small increments of time so long as the space is available to work. If every time you want to work on something you have to spend an hour getting things out and set up it can be a deterrent to getting started. Over time this situation can create a push pull dichotomy where you want to invest the time in your project but it feels like too much work and the inspiration passes.

If you are great with maximizing spaces, take a little time to find a place where you can set up some of your stuff. You do not need a lot of space for this. I have seen laundry rooms, hallways, and even closets turned into great work spaces. Make that space somewhere that when you walk by you can easily access it so you can spend 10-20 minutes or more if you have it on your project just by sitting down. If you aren't great at seeing how spaces can be used, ask a friend or family member to help you.

For many people this simple but significant shift allows them to reconnect to a creative passion they once enjoyed or to try something new because the physical space is available to them. The interesting thing about spaces is that they really do create that *Field of Dreams* situation. If you build it, it will come.

Release the Resistance:

For those of you who feel like you have stepped away from your creative outlets and you feel a heaviness inside of you; it is time to get back to center. While creativity is important for everyone, those who are called to create on a regular basis must honor this call. So, for whatever reason if you have shelved that calling due to other circumstances, it is time to rearrange your schedule.

You may want to work with a trusted friend or family member for this. Having an accountability partner can really help to shift you from feeling disconnected and in the procrastination zone back into your creative flow again. It is really important to get clear on why you have taken so much time away from your creativity. Often, getting clear on that allows a big part of the shift to happen.

With a pen, paper, or a new word document open answer the following:

- ❖ How long has it been since I have been working on my creative outlets in a consistent way?
- ❖ Why have I stopped?
- ❖ Why haven't I started again?
- ❖ How do I feel since taking a break from my creativity?
- ❖ Am I experiencing any symptoms such as sadness, feeling disconnected from myself, a lack of inspiration, or a sense of life feeling less joyful?
- ❖ Am I experiencing any feelings of heaviness, feeling bogged down, or even anxiety?
- ❖ Do I feel like something is missing from my life?
- ❖ Does it feel like I am experiencing the same kind of day over and over again?
- ❖ Has the magic or spark of life seemed to dim since taking a break from my creative outlets?

After taking an honest inventory, you will be able to have a deeper understanding of why things have been on hold for you and how it has made you feel. This is often a huge catalyst to making positive changes so you can get back to enjoying your creativity again. If you find it challenging to get started again, take some time to see if your work station is set up and accessible for you. Having your space and tools ready to go can make a huge impact in getting back into your zone.

Connecting with someone you trust to support you in getting back to your projects can be a great help too. Sometimes, just letting someone know that you are trying to get back to a place that feels good to you can help to create a support system for you. Please make sure to choose a kind hearted and non-competitive friend or family member for this role. You want to find someone who is supportive, understanding, and encouraging as you find your rhythm again.

You could also stoke your creative fires by hosting a group project day. If you have other friends or family members who would like to bring small projects over to your home you could participate in a day where everyone works on their own individual projects allowing for a light and fun group event. (Adding snacks always makes things even more fun, wink.)

Any way that feels right for you to get back into balance with creativity is what is really important here. It isn't so much about how you do, but that you do it. As you know, your creative call comes from deep inside of you and needs to be nurtured on a regular basis. You will find that as you allow yourself to honor that calling, you will feel much better, more like yourself again, and that things feel more joyful within your world.

Pass on the Passion:

It may be time for you to pass on your passion to someone else within your world. Do you know someone who admires the creative outlets that you love? Perhaps it is time to step into a teaching and mentoring role. Think about the person or people who helped to introduce you to the creative outlets that stir your soul. You could be that person for someone else too. You don't have to have a background in education or a graduate degree in advising to be able to teach someone about the art you love. Opening the door for someone else to a world that has brought you so much joy can be a very rewarding and fun experience. Passing on the passion can also rekindle your own joy and excitement at the same time which can create so much fun all the way around. If you feel there is someone in your world who would love to learn from you and you feel guided to support them, maybe it is time to honor that calling.

I hope this chapter about creativity has helped to inspire you to step into your creative space with excitement. Since we are all creative beings, creativity is a natural state. No matter where you find yourself within the creativity sliding scale, I hope that you will take some time to invest in your creative outlets, old and new. Watch how introducing this powerful thing we call creativity changes your life for the better; while providing you with hours of fun.
Happy Making.

18.

Learn Something New

This one can create such a positive shift for people when they give themselves permission to truly Learn Something New. Have you ever had that feeling where things can start to feel ho hum in your day to day life? Have you noticed that you begin to feel like your days, weeks, and months take on a pretty similar pattern or feeling? Does this make you feel a little bit disheartened or even bored? Many times this experience comes from doing the same things over and over again for a long period of time.

Having a routine can be helpful in creating stability, normalcy, and balance, however it can also create a feeling of being stagnant. For many people once they have find their niche and have for the most part mastered it whether that is in a job outside the home or while working inside the home it can be easy to stop learning new things. You may learn new things within your realm of expertise, however what I find is that many people stop learning new things outside of what they have been doing for a long time.

For some people this can be a somewhat conscious choice but for others, I have found this situation to creep up on them when they weren't expecting it. After formal education is over, many people don't seek out additional courses, learning, or things outside of their day to day realm. So over time, there can be a quality of routine that can create a sense of life feeling dull or less exciting than it once was.

Here are some of the things that clients have told me over the years in relationship to this feeling or experience.

- *I just don't feel excited about my life the way that I used to.*
- *While I enjoy what I do, it all feels the same to me somehow.*
- *I used to get excited about the unknown parts of my life, and now things seem to be pretty set and feel like there aren't any more exciting changes on the horizon.*
- *I feel like I am missing out on things that are happening, almost like a generation gap, but I'm not even that old.*
- *I enjoy feeling like I know where my life is going professionally since I've been doing the same work for so long but I miss the options that were once open to me when I was younger or just starting out.*
- *I feel like I have to force enthusiasm or excitement and I didn't feel like that when I was younger. Is it me or is this just a part of life that I have to accept?*
- *It feels like my passion or edge is gone or at least dulled and I am not sure if I am becoming jaded or if maybe it was never there to begin with.*

Do any of these things feel familiar to you? If so, how long have you felt this way? You are not alone in this experience and there are some things that you can do to shift into a place that feels more uplifting, exciting, and inspiring for you.

Depending on your personal situation, there are some tweaks that you can make to help take you from feeling drab, stuck, or uninspired to feeling more like you again. Here are the main groups that I find for people who are experiencing this lull in their world.

At the Top of My Game, Now What?

This tends to be one of the biggest groups of people that I work with. It is also one of the most challenging situations to be in for most people. Here is one of the most common things that I hear from people within this group.

> ❖ *I've been able to do everything that I wanted to do professionally. I worked so hard to get where I am and to be honest, I don't even know if I like doing it anymore. The problem is that I will be working for at least 15 more years; I can't imagine feeling like this for that long. Is something wrong with me? Should I just buck up? Shouldn't I feel more excited about my work? I believe in what I do but it just doesn't feel the way it used to.*

This group tends to be filled with self starter's over achievers, and people who are very driven to not only do the best they can but in a very small window of time. So you may see these people being in high level administration positions and other various successful positions at very young ages. These are leaders in their fields whether they work for others or for themselves. These people tend to be at the top of their class so to speak throughout their entire lives and fuel their passion with hard work, focus, and the ability to see the bigger picture for themselves and their goals.

When people in this group have not only attained their big picture goals for themselves but have also mastered that work they can begin to feel like something is missing. Because this group is naturally driven to learn and to make forward motion, once they have reached their "top level" there can be an experience of their life feeling dull or uninspired. There can also be a feeling of things slowing down which is also something that tends to feel foreign or unenjoyable for people in this group. People here can find themselves in a challenging position because they usually believe in the work they are doing so they feel compelled to continue doing it yet they don't feel as fulfilled by it as they used to. People in this group can then begin to internalize these feelings and try to push through them by telling themselves that they should feel better because they received everything that they worked so hard for so they try to ignore their feelings. This creates a cyclical effect which over time gets to be a heavy burden to bear.

Empty Nest, Not What I expected

People in this group can often be put into two different groups. Sometimes these two groups overlap but for the most part people usually move into one of the groups and identify with it more than the other.

I feel Sad, Lonely, and Heartbroken

This first group tends to find nearly all new Empty Nesters hanging out in it for a while. It is hard to have your adult children move out to begin the next chapter of their lives even though you are proud and excited for them. This group feels a push pull dichotomy and it creates a genuine heart ache and sadness because your little ones are growing up and things won't go back to the way they were again now that they have left home.

Many people in this group feel overwhelmed with the feeling of emptiness that the home has now that the other person is no longer there. Memories of all the great times may play over and over for those in this group. Often there is an adjustment period for markers in the day that used to hold meaning. For example, if your child used to come home from their part time job at the exact same time every evening and you would visit about their day; you may find that you still wait for them to come home unconsciously when they first move out. This kind of experience can bring on the sadness and emptiness feelings all over again. It takes time for these kinds of markers or triggers to become quieter. Even passing their old bedroom may be challenging because it feels like a daily reminder that they aren't there any longer.

These heavy feelings and longing can contribute to feeling uninspired, disconnected, and not like your true self. These feelings can lead people to feel like the spark, happiness, and joy has left their life.

I don't Know What to Do With Myself

Those is this group tend to find that after the sadness begins to subside they feel a bit lost in their new day to day life. Like all transitions and changes, things take time to adjust. It is important for people in this group to not only acknowledge that they aren't sure what to do but to open up to the opportunity to capture the extra time that's available and to use it in a way that inspires, honors, and supports them.

Retired, Nothing But Time, Not Sure What To Do With It

I work with a lot of people who have recently moved into retirement and find themselves feeling unsure what to do with their spare time. There is a realization that on one hand people in this group feel like:

- ❖ They have nothing but time but on the other hands.

- On the other hand they feel like their days pass quickly and can't seem to understand why they aren't getting as much done as they thought they would.

This can create a combination of frustration and stress for people in this group. All of a sudden there is an understanding that time really does move and stretch based on our schedules. So, when a schedule is in many ways downsized, the feeling of time getting smaller is very palpable. Days quickly pass into weeks and it can feel unsettling for people in this group. I often hear stories about how many things people in this group used to do in one day, including commuting, actual work time, family obligations, social time, volunteering etc. and now they feel like it takes all day to do regular day to day things. This is not an unusual experience for people, especially those new to retirement.

The big take away here is yet another life transition which means that there will be an adjustment period and an opportunity for change. This is a time of restructuring, reprioritizing, and rebuilding. This is an exciting time just like any other large life change, it is just about creating the space and accessing the support to transition smoothly into retirement so it feels enjoyable.

I Don't Like What I'm Learning/Doing, Is This Normal?

People in this group can include professional students, both undergraduate and graduate and young/new professionals. This can feel like a really confusing time for students and those new to the professional workforce. Because these are two groups, although closely related it is helpful to look at them individually. I've worked with professional students for a long time both as an academic advisor at a University and as a Faculty member and in my private practice. I've also worked with a lot of young/new professionals as well and this feeling of being in the wrong place is definitely common.

Professional Students:

Students can come up against a feeling of being in the wrong discipline throughout their academic career for a variety of reasons. Sometimes, students feel the work they are doing which they were once very interested in is no longer appealing to them. There can be a fear that they have made the wrong choice and are now too invested in their coursework to change direction. This very idea that they have no recourse can create the feeling of being like a deer frozen in headlights. In nearly every situation, there is an opportunity to change direction without a cataclysmic outcome.

Some students however, are indeed in the wrong discipline and they know it but feel fearful of making changes accordingly. Some of these reasons can include feeling pressured by family expectations, wanting to finish what they've started, or trying to prove to themselves or others that they can do it.

Other students may feel overwhelmed and think they are in the wrong discipline but in reality are just completely overwhelmed. Perhaps they are experiencing an extremely challenging semester, undergoing additional stressors away from school, or just a heavy sense of pressure knowing that the choices they are making while in school will create a pathway to the next chapter of their lives.

All of these scenarios are a natural part of the academic experience and it is in better understanding where the student is feeling unfulfilled which will lead to the next course of action. Once the situation is identified, a support system and solution can be put into place to help reduce or even eliminate the feelings of being in the wrong place and not enjoying the work.

Young/New Professionals

This group often carries the jitters from finishing their degree with them into their new field of interest and expertise. Like all new jobs, there is a sense of excitement and nerves all rolled into one. As a new professional, there is the added element of wondering if you have what it takes to make it in the field and out of the classroom and if your hard work at school will really provide you with meaningful and fulfilling work.

Sometimes there is a let down experience for new professionals because the feeling they hoped to have from entering the professional work force may not be as pronounced as they hoped. Oftentimes doing entry level work doesn't feel as satisfying as the image they had for their new professional life. There is an adjustment period like all new life changes and this one can bring on some unexpected blues. For years students dream of graduating so they can be finished with school and get out into their field of choice. Then, when that day finally arrives, many of these new professionals want to go back to school and become students again.

For some new professionals there may be a realization that they are indeed in the wrong profession; however most will just need to find their right fit within their professional calling. Many who find they are not in a field that connects with them on a personal level chose not to make changes in their field of study while in school for some of the reasons mentioned above. (Most professionals in this situation report knowing they chose a discipline they didn't like and hoped the work would be a better fit for them once they graduated.) But, if this is in fact your situation, there are always options and ways to make changes.

Breathe Through It:

This chapter can bring up a lot of intense feelings, some that you may be conscious of and others that may have been resting right underneath the surface of your skin. If this has brought up some stuff for you as you read through the beginning of this chapter, take a breath. Tune into your neck and shoulders and notice if they feel tight or up around your ears. Roll your shoulders, relax your body, and release any tension or tightness in your stomach. Sometimes this chapter can open up a floodgate of memories of family members who have experienced some of these things and how they impacted you at the same time.

Activity:

At the Top of My Game, Now What?

If you find yourself in this group, it's important to remember that the passion that brought you to where you are is a part of what makes you who you are. Passion and forward motion are part and parcel for you and keeps you feeling like your true self. You may want to see if you can find ways to take your knowledge and either open new doors or begin a project on the side which will help to fuel that passion within you again.

The challenge for those of you within this group is to find the balance between forward motion and enjoying life. However, if you feel weighed down by things being the same all the time then it may be time to see where you can add some passion back into your life again. Take some time to take an honest inventory about what makes you feel excited, interested, energetic, and alive again. It might be something that has nothing to do with what you are currently doing for work, that's okay.

You may be guided to learn or begin something new that is completely different from anything you have done in the past. You may start something new that is just for you and not for your company, clients, or colleagues. You may be guided to start a passion project that fulfills your personal needs and that is more than okay. Remember not to place so much emphasis all the time on making everything you do about other people and know that it is okay to stoke your personal passion and that when you are inspired everyone in your world wins.

This is not to say that by beginning something new you won't open doors to another area of your life completely which could take your professional life in a new direction. Give yourself permission to be open to any possibilities that feel like a fit for you and as always, work with someone who can support you in finding a pathway which provides for a smooth transition from where you are to where you are going if you are guided to make professional career changes.

Empty Nest, Not What I expected

For those of you in this group, it is really important to understand the gravity of this life change and to honor your feelings. If you find yourself having a hard time with the emotions and feelings of loss, you may want to reach out to a counselor or therapist that specializes in empty nest transitions.

Once you have found some healing around the initial transition, it is time to focus on how you want to spend the additional time that you now have. If you have other children living at home, this might not be as much free time as those who have no more children at home but there will be some.

For this Activity You Will Need:

- ❖ A notebook
- ❖ Something to Write With
- ❖ 15 Minutes of Uninterrupted Time

The 15 minutes of uninterrupted time is really key here. So, if you have to let the other people in your home know you need to have a quiet zone, please do so. Turn off your cell phone and the television and computer. You may want to have a glass of water or a cup of tea while you do this.

Make a little nook or nest where you can settle in with your notebook and pen and then for 15 minutes write a list of all the things that you wanted to do in your life. This is Not a list about what you think is possible now because of _____ reason/s. This is an honest list that began from the time you were a child. It is really important not to censor yourself here or to judge the things that were once important to you. If you wanted to be a magician, princess, writer, sticker collector, whatever, just write it down. The more free and honest you allow yourself to be the more that you will receive from this exercise. It doesn't matter if you only have 3 things on your list, you do need to write for 15 minutes even if that means that you write the same 3 things over and over again.

This style of free writing opens up your creativity and allows you to reconnect to that part of you that knows what it is you are being guided to do next.

Once you have finished your free writing session, read over what you wrote. You will find that there are clear themes woven within your list. Once you have found a few things that really hold a special place for you within your heart, it is time to take steps toward making those things happen.

Depending on what the items are on your list you may feel guided to work with a Life Coach, Career Counselor, or Academic Advisor to help you move toward your dreams. Or, you may want to contact a Music Instructor, Art Teacher, or Swim School. The important thing is that you reach out for support from someone in the field of interest that is important to you. When you reach out, and you begin taking action in that direction, you will feel a spark and excitement return to you again. You will notice that as you foster and nurture parts of yourself that have been shelved, you begin to enjoy this new phase of your life and those around you will benefit too.

Retired, Nothing But Time, Not Sure What To Do With It

With the extra time that comes with retirement; this is a powerful opportunity to restructure, reprioritize, and rebuild. This is a brand new chapter where you can create time to do the things that you are passionate about, have been wanting to do, and to learn something new.

The big thing here comes down to scheduling. As mentioned earlier it is imperative to get a hold of your schedule so that you can maximize the hours that you have so you feel like you are investing your time in things that fulfill you. If this is not something you are naturally good at, you may want to work with someone to help you approach your schedule in a new way. Just like a new professional student needs to prioritize their time, so too do you need to do the same thing.

One of the other big things in addition to scheduling is getting out of your comfort zone. Many retiree's may find themselves moving to a new community and maybe somewhere they have never lived before. This opens up a whole new level of change as there may not be friends or family in this new area.

Finding things to do and getting out there into your new community and getting involved will be key to supporting this transition time. Most communities have events, classes, volunteerism and other goings on that may spark your interest. Then, it is about getting out and getting connected so you begin to build a new life for yourself.

You may also find that you are guided to begin a project that has been on the back burner for years, or writing that book, beginning a business or other venture you have been putting off until the right time. Reach out for support or groups that can get you started so you can reconnect to the things that you are passionate about.

A big part of this transition is getting reacquainted with who you are now and the things that are important to you. This is an opportunity to invest in the passions and joys that have been with you throughout your life and to find some new one's too. If you find that you are having a bit of trouble getting going, you may want to ask a friend or partner to attend a class, workshop, event etc. with you to help you get back out there.

Just like going away to college, moving to a new city, or starting a new job, moving into retirement is a transition and a process. Reaching out for support from people and groups that resonate with you will help you to have a more enjoyable transition process.

I Don't Like What I'm Learning/Doing, Is This Normal?

Professional Students

If you are feeling like you are stuck, unmotivated, and not really sure if you are in the right field of study. Don't panic, this is a natural experience for pretty much all students at some point in their academic careers. (Did you know the average student changes their major 3-5 times before graduation?)

What you want to do is make appointments with some key people on your campus. The first appointment will be with your academic advisor who not only understands what you are experiencing but can also give you great referrals and support in moving forward.

You may also want to make an appointment with a career counselor so you can participate in some testing to see if your strengths are in the area you are currently studying. If you aren't in the sweet spot for your academic studies at this time, your career counselor and academic advisor can help get you set up in the right direction without you feeling like you wasted time on earning units. You may qualify for a minor and all units lead to graduation requirements. There is no such thing as wasted time or course work.

You may want to talk to an MFT or Psychologist on campus who specializes in working with professional students. Many campuses have a wellness center where you can get some support. You may be in the exact right field of study but you are feeling overwhelmed and burned out. Some support, comfort, and direction can make a world of difference.

You may need to take some time to do something just for fun. This could mean registering for a fun class without feeling guilty. Maybe it's time to register for a yoga class, pottery, or hiking 101. You may be out of balance with your work load and in need of some inspiration and self care.

You may also just need to slow down a little bit. Take an honest inventory of your schedule and see where you can prune back things that are taxing your time table so that you can not only make progress toward your graduation goals but also enjoy yourself too.

New Professionals

If after beginning your new career in your field of choice you feel a bit ho hum about it, don't fret. There is often a transition period after being a professional student and sometimes that transition comes with a little bit of blues. You may not be in the exact job title of your choice right out of the gate, that's okay. You may not be adjusted to working in the same place all day long, that's okay. As time passes you will begin to feel adjusted to your new professional place and rhythm

However, in the interim you may feel guided to work with a Professional Counselor or Coach who specializes in working with new professionals. Support can help you to feel like you aren't the only one who is experiencing this kind of transition. I promise you that you are not the only one. There are a lot of books about the quarter life crisis which focuses heavily on this exact experience.

If you do feel that you are in the wrong job title, you can work with a coach to support you in finding ways to prepare to move to a job that is more aligned with what you want to do.

I also find that it is really important for new professionals to create time to do things that they enjoy on a personal level. So many years are devoted to preparation for the work force and then once you arrive it can be easy to get swallowed up in long work weeks which can lead to burn out. Take a class just for fun, pick up a personal passion that has been shelved for a while. Join a club, organization, or volunteer group. Make your personal fulfillment as equally important as finding the right niche for your professional outlets. This will support you in not only being a better professional but in finding a deeper life satisfaction and more personal happiness.

I hope that you will give yourself permission to learn something new and start something new no matter where you are in your life right now. I hope that you will go toward these new things with enthusiasm, excitement, and fun. I hope this chapter will inspire you to not only think about what it is that you would like to learn or do next but that you will also take action in their direction. Investing in yourself is always a worthy investment. As you take the time to learn something new, to reacquaint yourself with who you are right now and what excites you; you will find that spark and enthusiasm return to your life.

19.

Move Out Of Your Comfort Zone

Do you feel like you are stuck in a rut or that things feel pretty much the same in your day to day life? Do you find yourself wanting to try new things but then you aren't sure what those things might be or where to look for them or how to get started? Well, then this message is for you. It is time to move out of your comfort zone. There are lots of ways to do that. For some people it may mean a great big leap, for others a step, and still for others a wee wiggle. All movement counts.

Moving out of your comfort zone can bring up some fears, strong feelings, and even negative self talk. Some people find that they really want to try new things and expand their circle but then the thoughts, old memories, or negative messages start to turn up.

Here are a few examples of things that you may experience:

- ❖ Thoughts about not having enough time
- ❖ Convincing yourself that it's really not a good idea because of all the other important reasons that you have decided at that particular moment. Feel free to fill in the blank accordingly_____.
    - o Too much housework, family obligations, professional demands etc.
- ❖ Memories of painful experiences when you tried something new previously
- ❖ Fears of not being accepted or fitting into the new group

- ❖ Fears about not having the courage to put yourself out there in a new group dynamic
- ❖ Feeling to too timid to try something new even though you really want to
- ❖ Believing you don't have what it takes to try something new
- ❖ Believing you don't have what it takes to make changes to your current routine and lifestyle

These are very common experiences and most people experience some level of trepidation in combination with excitement when venturing into new territory. So, if you feel like you are the only person who gets nervous or uncomfortable when it comes to moving out of your comfort zone, I promise you, you aren't.

You have probably heard the old adage that the only constant in life is change. That is absolutely true and when the feeling of being stagnant becomes a part of your experience it's a message to make some changes. The feeling of discomfort is helping you (although it may not feel like it at the time) to make positive change. This feeling is supporting you in taking action steps. When you move with that guidance and take action, you will notice the tension, heaviness, and anxiety begins to lift from you. However, if you choose to stay in the pattern that you have been fostering, those feelings will not only continue but they will become more pronounced.

I have found that when people make a concerted effort to wiggle, step, or leap out of their comfort zones, they experience more happiness, joy, and a sense of fulfillment. Those are some pretty big plusses to moving through the fear, don't you think? You can do this, it is just about finding the ways that are the right fit for you right now.

I have found some repeating themes for clients who feel guided to make changes to their comfort zone. See if one or more of these resonate for you.

- ❖ Afraid to admit (to themselves and out loud) what kind of changes they really want to make
- ❖ Are unsure of exactly what they want to do but know it is something
- ❖ Know exactly what they want to do but have no idea how to get started or are afraid of what they may have to do to get started
- ❖ Have moved into the wrong direction because they feel that is what they should be doing even though they don't enjoy it. (See example one if this resonates for you.)

This is not an end all be all list by any means, but rather some of the main areas that I have seen resonate for people. Some find that one speaks the most loudly to them while others feel they can fit into more than one area. No matter where you find yourself right now, know that there are ways that you can move into a new direction.

Breathe Through It:

Because this topic can bring up so many things for people it tends to be a very sensitive issue. A lot of people feel a tad or even more than a tad uncomfortable with change in general. (Some love change, absolutely, and if you are one of these folks, awesome! Maybe you can offer some support and encouragement to people in your circle who struggle with change.)

Because change can feel uncomfortable and because it can bring up all the moments where changes in the past felt scary, sad, uncomfortable, or uneasy it makes perfect sense why avoiding change can be something that creeps in over time. In addition to the emotional component there is a physical and physiological connection that is also activated by these past memories. The body is so genius that is creates these perfectly imprinted memories that not only include feelings but also physical experiences; so you may remember how your body felt or even how things smelled during a really powerful moment of change from the past.

Right now, take a moment and tune into your thoughts. Are you experiencing any memories from the past that felt uncomfortable for you? Are you thinking about a list of reasons why you won't be able to successfully move out of your comfort zone? Are you wondering if you will be able to enjoy something new? Okay, now pay attention to the way you are holding your body and the way your muscles feel. Have you found and tension? Take a few deep breaths and release any tension or tightness. Good. Now, as you continue breathing release any of those old memories or negative thought patterns on the exhale. Good. If you feel tears forming, allow them to drop. Allowing your emotions to move through you will support you in clearing some of these old painful experiences from the past.

Activity:

Below you will find a Recipe for Success in moving out of your comfort zone. There are only 3 steps and there are lots of different ways to move through them. Just like in cooking, your personal style and tastes will guide you to take this recipe and make it your own. I want to move through each of the three steps to give you some ideas of how to move through them toward your goal. The important thing to remember here is that you not only understand how to move through the Recipe but that you actually do it. Here we go.

Recipe For Moving Out of Your Comfort Zone

You Will Need To:

- ❖ Figure out what you want
- ❖ Get Support that will allow you to move toward what you want
- ❖ Take Action and either wiggle, step, or leap forward

Step One:
Figure Out What You Want

This is a big one, in fact until you do this, you can't move forward with your recipe. This one can be achieved in many ways. Sometimes, you can get the answer to this by sitting alone quietly with your thoughts and something to write with. Getting quiet allows us to tap into that well of wisdom sitting within us that knows what we really want. Sometimes, people know what they want but for various reasons don't want to admit it. Writing about what you want can help to bring it to the forefront which makes it easier to admit it to yourself and own it. Once you do this you can begin to move out of your comfort zone.

If writing about it isn't your cup of tea or you just don't feel like it's helping you enough, you may want to work with a:

- ❖ Coach
- ❖ Counselor
- ❖ Therapist,
- ❖ Academic Advisor
- ❖ Other support professional

An outside perspective and support from someone who works in this realm can offer a magnitude of support, clarity, and insight which can lead you to what you are looking for.

You can also talk to a trusted friend, partner, or family member who you feel very comfortable with. Many times our loves ones who know us really well can support us in pinpointing what it is that we have been avoiding, missing, or afraid to acknowledge. If this feels like a fit for you please make sure you choose someone who is:

- ❖ Easy to talk to
- ❖ Compassionate
- ❖ Will give you their undivided attention

Step Two:
Get Support

This step allows you to take your clear understanding of what it is that you want and to gain insight, information, and resources to implement your forward motion.

So, do you want to join a volunteer group, meet some people who have a common interest with you, increase referral partners, get back into the dating world, go back to school etc?

Conduct some research to find out what groups are available in your area that match your interest. Simple internet searches can provide a lot of information right from the comfort of your own home. You can also ask trusted friends, colleagues, and family members for referrals and feedback. You can also create a group if one doesn't exist in your area.

Step Three:
Take Action

Now that you know what you want and you know how to connect with other like minded people, programs, or groups it is time to make that movement out of your comfort zone. Depending on how comfortable you feel you can choose to do this on your own or you can ask a friend or family member to go with you. If you feel like going with someone else will help you to feel more comfortable, great, go for it. There are safety in numbers and sometimes that safety includes personal comfort and confidence. Again, if you are going to invite someone to go with you, please make sure they are attentive and understand the important role they are playing in supporting you in making a big personal change.

After you have started your process toward change, you will notice that you feel more confident every time you engage in your new realm of exploration. You may also notice that your confidence and happiness increases too. Many people find that they get excited about moving out of their comfort zone and continue to find ways to try new things. Like anything new, the more you do it, the easier it gets. You can do this; just go at your own pace, reach out for support when you need it, and give yourself permission to enjoy expansion.

20.

Go Outside

Your initial reaction to this chapter title will tell you so much about where you are on the indoor outdoor balance spectrum. Some of you may be thinking hooray I am so ready for some dedicated outdoor time. Others may think oh right, outside, yeah I don't think that is going to happen this week maybe not even next week. Hmm, maybe taking out the trash counts so there are a couple of minutes of outside time right there. Others may find themselves smack dab in the middle, wanting to spend time outside but not having as much time as they would like to make that happen.

Due to the state of western lives being mostly lived indoors, many of us have gotten away from our regular connection to Mother Nature. We live indoors, work indoors, and often don't have a balance between indoor and outdoor time each day. Over time this lack of direct connection to nature can take a huge toll on our physical, mental/emotional, and spiritual selves.

Since we are a part of nature and are connected to the natural world, it is important for us to make time to connect with that part of who we are. Nature has a naturally calming, clearing, and healing impact. In fact when we cut ourselves off from time outdoors we can begin to feel sluggish, tired, lethargic, cranky, brain fog, insomnia, and even light levels of depression. Some people find that they experience inflammation from being indoors too long and that their bodies release and calm from spending time outside.

There is also a large body of research that has been published about Earthing which allows you to clear yourself by spending time outdoors. This research talks about the physiological and mental/emotional aspects of this practice. Here are some of the things being shared in professional medical communities about Earthing and Grounding.

> "Pain, disease, and other disturbances in our bodies are often caused by chronic inflammation. Such inflammation is, in turn caused by positively charged molecules called free radicals. When you make direct contact with the Earth, either by being barefoot outside or via a conductive sheet or mat indoors, the negatively charged electrons from the Earth are absorbed into your body and reduce free radicals and inflammation. This benefit of Earthing is very important because medical research has found that many of the chronic and debilitating diseases of our time have the same cause: chronic inflammation." (Earthing Institute)

In a time in our human history where were are inundated with wifi and constant communication it can be challenging to turn off and get connected to nature. In fact in many outdoor spaces wifi access is readily available which makes it even more challenging to disconnect and connect to the healing qualities of being outside. Think about a time when you had no access to wifi connections or back further to a time prior to internet access, think early 90's or before. Now think about the quality and quantity of outdoor time you had in those situations. You probably had a lot more outdoor time and a lot more balance in your day.

Spending time outside allows the build-up that we collect from the day to get transmuted and cleared. Perhaps you have noticed how a day at the beach or in the mountains helps you to feel lighter and more like yourself again. Since we collect this etheric stuff throughout the day and are spending less time outside, you can imagine how this can take a toll on our quality of life, happiness, and health over long periods of time.

Spending time in nature also allows for the spiritual connections that we have to become cleared out and opened up. Just like your cell phone service has varying bars of connectivity in different places, this is also true for your personal connection to spirit. When you spend time outside your connection becomes cleared and you are able to get a "better signal" to your departed loved ones, guides, angels, higher self, and to God. The more consistent you are with this outdoor time the more easily you will be able to exercise and strengthen your spiritual gifts and increase your connectivity. In fact those who regularly nurture their spiritual gifts tend to make time in nature one of their top ways to increase their connectivity. If you feel guided to increase and nurture your natural spiritual gifts, time in nature will be a great support for you.

It is imperative to consciously carve out time to get outside. It is something that is equally important as the other things on your to do list. In fact, when you move into a balanced place within your life that includes outdoor time regularly, you will actually be able to produce more. Why? Because being outside allows you to decompress from the tension, stress, heaviness, thoughts, to do lists, and noise that is experienced throughout your day.

The challenge for most people is not so much in understanding that importance of getting outside, but in actually implementing it. I have heard pretty much every excuse you can imagine; some of them more valid than others. Trust me, I understand how busy, full, and impacted the modern schedule has become. However, I also know that it is possible to make this connection to nature a priority.

Breathe Through It:

This topic can bring up a lot of stress for some people as they can immediately go into spinning thoughts about how and where they can create more time. They may be running mental lists in their minds documenting every minute and not finding space that would allow for outside time. If you are finding this to be true for you right now, stop; and take a long slow deep breath in through your nose and out through your mouth. This thought process can sometimes lead to feelings of not being able to do "enough" or feeling like balance is an elusive concept which you will not be able to attain. Try to give yourself permission to set those feelings and thoughts on a shelf if they are showing up for you right now.

For others this topic can bring up a great deal of sadness. There are many people who find themselves in situations where they are no longer able to spend as much time outside as they used to and it brings about a lot of emotional feelings. These people tend to be highly sensitive and can feel they are called to spend time outside but aren't sure how to make that happen due to a variety of reasons. These folks tend to feel like a part of themselves is missing when they are separated from nature on a regular basis. If you resonate with this experience, take some deep breaths and allow yourself to release any sadness or other emotions that may be showing up for you right now.

Yet another group may feel that spending time in nature is not something that resonates for them. This group often reports that they can appreciate nature but don't believe it has any real draw for them. This group can sometimes have a take it or leave kind of feeling about being outside. If this resonates for you and you feel that you have turned to this chapter by mistake; hang in there, I promise you that you are here for a reason. So, take a breath and keep reading. You will find that taking small segments of time outside will do a world of good for you. And then you can go back inside.

Activity:

Take an honest inventory of the way you are spending your time. This includes all those little pockets where it feels like there's not enough time to do something so it becomes filled with surfing online or something similar. You may need to refer to Chapter 1 to help you get clear about your schedule.

Once you find some pockets, these can include 5-10 minutes, schedule that time to go outside and place your feet onto soil, sod, or sand. While you are outside, avoid getting onto your devices and instead take some long, deep breaths in through your nose and out through your mouth so you can clean out your lungs. Deep breathing outdoors will also allow you get fresh oxygen while you begin to clear away the build up from being inside. Taking the small pocket of time to decompress while also consciously connecting to Mother Nature will allow you move into a higher frequency. You will find that your stress response begins to slow down and you will unwind from the activities prior to going outside. Your senses will also be activated and as you pay attention to the things that you see, hear, feel and think while you are outside. Many people find that when they slow down and decompress they receive insight, answers, and ideas that will help them in their life. This is a similar experience to having a problem that you can't figure out and then either dreaming about the solution while you are asleep or knowing how to fix the problem when you wake up. Spending time outdoors offers support to us on all levels, physically, mentally, emotionally, and spiritually.

Below you will find some ways to double dip your outside time with other activities. By adding some of these methods into your day you can bank outdoor time and its benefits without losing chunks of your day or feeling overwhelmed by creating large schedule changes.

- ❖ You can eat your lunch outside since you have to eat anyway. Plus, eating outside will allow you to bank your full spectrum sunlight (even if it's cloudy) which will allow you to create serotonin; a brain chemical that allows you to experience a positive mood, more energy, and to sleep better.
- ❖ Go for a walk, run, bike ride or swim outside instead of going to the gym for your workout. Some gyms are now placing cardio equipment outside due to the overall health benefits of being outdoors and the demand from patrons who want to be outside.
- ❖ Go to a park or green belt in your area and take a book, small project, and a blanket with you to enjoy some quiet down time.

- ❖ Push yourself out of your comfort zone and try a new outdoor sport activity. Sign up for Paddle Boarding, Kayaking, SUP Yoga, Hiking, or another outdoor activity that peaks your interest. There are often group classes where you can try the activity to see if you enjoy it before investing in the gear. You may meet some new friends in the process as well.
- ❖ Take your dog to a doggie park and enjoy being outside with your canine companion.
- ❖ Invite your friends or family over for a garden party or potluck and enjoy your back yard or outdoor space.
- ❖ Bring back porch parties in your neighborhood if you live somewhere with a porch. Or, simply enjoy sitting on your porch and watch the world go by.

The truth is that there are infinite ways to include outside time into your daily life. It doesn't have to be taxing, stressful, or one more thing to squeeze into your already bulging schedule. The healing and calming benefits from being outside are well worth the investment of your time. Start with 7 days of increased pockets of time and notice the subtle yet palpable shifts you feel for yourself and your life. I have a feeling you will want to continue with this healthy practice.

21.
Get Grounded

These two words can bring up two different thought processes. Some may think about getting into trouble for missing curfew. Others will think about the need to focus, increase clarity, and connect more with their physical body. For this chapter, we will be focusing on the latter of the two.

You may have heard people refer to someone as being, "very grounded and down to Earth." This is a great way of understanding what this phrase means. Being grounded refers to being centered, focused, calm, and connected to yourself and the things that are going on around you. So, when you feel like your most centered self, you may also refer to that as being grounded. On the other hand, if you are feeling spacey, clumsy, disoriented, or find yourself having trouble focusing; this would be referred to as being ungrounded.

Many people use the analogy of a tree when thinking about being grounded. When you feel grounded, you feel stable, connected, and strong. Similar to a tree with roots running deeply into the ground keeping it rooted, grounded, and strong. We too can make a conscious effort to tap into that grounded energy by learning ways to increase our own grounding, and to notice when we have become out of balance or ungrounded.

Here are some signs of being ungrounded:

- ❖ Easily Distracted
- ❖ Clumsiness
- ❖ Brain Fog

- ❖ Forgetting Things Consistently
- ❖ Feeling Irritable
- ❖ Experiencing Frustration Easily
- ❖ Feeling Spacey
- ❖ Feeling Like You Can't Quite Get It Together
- ❖ Rushing
- ❖ Doing Things Half Way
- ❖ Not Hearing What People Are Saying To You

Being ungrounded can include a sliding scale of the experiences listed above. The experience is similar to how it feels to be sleep deprived but without missing the sleep. Many people don't even realize that they're ungrounded because they've gotten used to the living this way. Instead, they just find ways to adjust to the challenges they are experiencing throughout the day. Unfortunately, this can lead to compounding effects because so much more energy needs to be used to do "regular" tasks when someone is ungrounded. This can lead to burn out, frustrations, and irritability.

There are a several common ways that people become ungrounded. I've included the most common ways that I have seen show up for people over the years. Many people find that they resonate with more than one area. Finding the ways that you tend to get ungrounded can support you in better understanding how to recognize the situation when it happens to you and provide you with ways to shift back to a centered place.

Lack of Balance:

This is a big one for people and one of the most common ways I find that people become ungrounded. People who tend to have a lot going on in their daily schedule resonate with this area. People who tend to be out of balance run a lot of lists throughout their day.

These Lists Can Be:

- ❖ Physical Lists that have been written down
- ❖ Lists that are held in the mind
- ❖ Lists that have been text messaged, emailed, or show up on reminders on various devices.

People in this group often have a lot of people reminding them about the things that need to get done within each day, and they tend to find themselves rushing from one task or activity to the next. People in this group find that they feel exhausted at the end of the day and that there is never enough time to get every item checked off their lists; so they feel perpetually behind schedule.

Staying Indoors Too Long:

This is another common reason people become ungrounded. When too much time is spent indoors, whether that is due to a demanding work schedule or cold weather issues, we can get cut off from our natural rhythm.

Being outside in nature allows us to synch up with our natural body rhythms and allows us to clear from any tension or stress that has built up inside of us. So, when we have several consecutive days or even weeks of inside time banked it can take a toll on the way we feel, leaving us ungrounded, lethargic, and even irritable.

Too Much Technology:

Since technology is such an integrated part of our lives, we often have devices, wifi, and other electromagnetic frequencies (EMF's) near us and running through us on a daily basis. These energies can disrupt cell function, damage DNA, and can lead to other physical health challenges. Some research shows that lethargia, nightmares, and trouble focusing can also be linked to EMF exposure.

Because we are so heavily inundated with technology at this time in our lives, this exposure is also a top contributor to becoming ungrounded. Many people find that they can feel a "fog" lift from them when they go into no wifi zones for breaks to get off the grid.

Lack of Physical Movement:

I find that people who spend a great deal of time being sedentary throughout the day are more likely to be ungrounded than those who move throughout the day. Physically moving the body allows the build up of stress, tension, and other challenging energies to be moved out of the body. Regular movement allows the body and the mind to stay clear, focused, and razor sharp.

Sitting or standing in front of computer screens for long hours every day leads to a sedentary lifestyle. Many people in this situation have a hard time finding ways to incorporate movement throughout their day or they report that they don't realize how much time has passed while working at their computers. This compounding effect from a day in and day out sedentary lifestyle leads to being ungrounded.

Poor Stress Management:

I find that people who have high stress in their lives but don't have healthy ways of managing their stress tend to lean into behaviors which increase being ungrounded.

There are a variety of reasons or factors for this situation; I have included the areas that have shown up the most for my clients over the years. This is not an exhaustive list.

- ❖ Lack of Information about Healthy Stress Management
- ❖ Failure To Commit To Healthy Change
- ❖ Addictions, Including Being a Workaholic
- ❖ Denial
- ❖ Excuses
- ❖ Family History/Family Modeling

As stress increases, our bodies begin to secrete "emergency" support systems and chemicals; this is called the fight, flight, freeze, and fawn experience. These stress responses place our bodies into a fear response rather than our natural response which is rest and repair. We aren't meant to have our fear responses turned on for long periods of time. This kind of stress experience is very taxing on the body and leads to a long list of physical challenges for the mind and body, including being ungrounded.

Breathe Through It:

This chapter can really shine a bright light on an issue that many people aren't aware is impacting them. If you feel a bit overwhelmed by reading this; it's okay. If you feel yourself holding your breath or if you found yourself tuning in and out as you were reading this information, take a nice long deep breath in through your nose and out through your mouth. Good.

Many people find that they resonate with one or more areas and it helps to put some pieces together for them. Often, people tell me that they felt they were the only one's having this experience and they often judged themselves for it. Once they realize that there are many factors that contribute to this experience and that it can be managed they feel a lot better. Being aware of the areas that resonate for you will allow you to make changes and shift your experience quickly. You will find that as you work with the support systems below that you will be able to stay grounded more easily throughout the day. You may also create some support systems of your own which will be a completely personalized match for you and your needs.

Activity:

There are a lot of easy ways to Get Grounded; try some of the ways listed below to see which ways work the best for you. Then, include these techniques in your daily life. You may find that you like to combine different methods at different times of the year depending on your own needs and sensitivity levels.

Eat Grounding Foods:

Eating grounding foods can support your body in getting grounded naturally. Grounding foods include foods which are grown underground, also known as Root Fruits and Vegetables.

- ❖ Onions
- ❖ Garlic
- ❖ Carrots
- ❖ Potatoes
- ❖ Beets
- ❖ Turnips
- ❖ Radishes

Connecting with the Ground:

Physically place your bare feet on soil, sod, or sand to help you connect with the earth. This allows you to get outside while your feet are connecting to the ground which allows you to clear your energy while grounding. This method helps to ground really quickly.

Foot Friction:

This is an easy way to get grounded if you're not able to get outside because you are at your desk or because it's too cold to get outside to place your feet on the ground without socks and shoes. Take off your socks and shoes and rub your feet on carpeting or a throw rug to create friction on the bottoms of your feet. This will help to "wake up" your feet and get you grounded again quickly.

Foot Rub:

This allows you to get grounded easily as your feet get activated through the massage. This can be achieved by asking a loved one to rub your feet, through reflexology, massage, or a pedicure.

Getting Back Into Your Body:

For those who feel spacey a lot of the time, they tend to hold their energy up in their heads and can feel disconnected from their bodies. By gently squeezing your arms, trunk of your body, and legs you help to redistribute your energy throughout your body so you feel grounded again.

Gentle Exercise:

Participating in regular gentle exercise allows the body to clear away distractors that contribute to being ungrounded while simultaneously bringing the body into balance. The key here is to participate in low impact, gentle, restorative movements. Avoid high impact, jarring, or stressful exercises as this can increase the stress responses in the body which can lead to being ungrounded.

Gentle Exercises Can Include:
- ❖ Gentle Yoga
- ❖ Walking
- ❖ Swimming
- ❖ Thai Chi
- ❖ Gentle Bike Riding (such as riding a beach cruiser)
- ❖ Gentle stretching

Balancing Indoor and Outdoor Time:

Getting outside is a quick way to get grounded again. If you feel that you spend more of your time inside than outside, you may want to work through chapter 1 to find ways to shift and maximize your schedule.

Reduce Tech Time:

Most people don't realize how much they interact with their devices throughout the day. People tend to underestimate their time connected to technology. Taking technology breaks can allow for grounding to happen. There is no one way to take technology breaks, but rather the ways that are right for you. You may find that different scenarios call for different levels of tech breaks. Here are a few of the ways you can incorporate tech breaks into your life.

Scheduling 15 minute breaks from technology throughout the day. This will require you to physically get up and remove yourself from your technology. Going outside during these breaks allow you to bank some outside time while also decompressing from your tech. (win win)

Place your devices, including cell phones, tablets, and lap tops in another room when you go to sleep.

Turn off wifi while you sleep.

Leave your cell phone at home while you run small, quick errands.

Leave your cell phone at home while you go for a walk, bike ride, or participate in other outdoor activities.

Go on "off the grid" vacations where you go into a no wifi zone. Some of these vacation destinations also ask that you turn over your devices as you check into their venue. These venues have already removed all technology from the premises for you, many times this also includes clocks. These vacations allow you to detox from technology while you get back onto your natural body clock. These vacations allow you to get grounded quickly.

Any ways that you find to get back into synch and balance will be a great support system for you. You may find that on different days you use different techniques to help you get grounded. This is in no way an exhaustive list of grounding techniques.

As you become more aware of the areas which tend to get you out of balance, you will find that you catch yourself slipping into a spacey or ungrounded state and you can shift back quickly by using any of the methods that resonate for you. By maintaining balance and staying grounded, you will find that you can get more out of your day while feeling more like yourself.

22.

Nap

Here is a topic that tends to bring with it very strong thoughts, feelings, and emotions as soon as it's mentioned. You may have had a strong reaction to the word Nap as soon as you turned to this chapter. Some people feel excited, grateful, and very receptive to napping. While others find napping to be boring, a waste of time, and not very beneficial. Tune into your own reaction right now. Are you thinking that you're glad that you turned to this chapter because you are going to log some nap time later today? Are you wondering if you turned to this chapter by mistake? Perhaps you are thinking about how napping just isn't your cup of tea and you're glad that as an adult no one can make you take a nap anymore. Wherever you are within the nap sliding scale, naps really have a positive impact on our mind and body.

Most people find that they either identify as a Napper or a Non Napper. Within the Napping group, there is another category which includes Cat Napper or Long Napper. Again, people tend to identify with one group over the other. Of course this is not a hard and fast rule, some cat nappers may find that occasionally they are guided to take a long nap and vice versa but for the most part, those within the napping community know which group they are a part of.

Breathe Through It:

If you are feeling frustrated about the idea of napping, please hang in there with me. Take a breath, gently scan your body, especially your stomach and your shoulders. Release any tension or tightness that may be holding space within you. Good. No one is going to force you to take naps, however turning to this chapter means that there is something for you here. You may feel guided to increase small segments of naps into your life occasionally after you finish reading this chapter.

If you enjoy napping and have felt any guilt, trepidation, or have been teased for your napping habits, take a nice, long deep breath. You are not alone in your need for naps and you will find that there's a lot of support and positive effects that come from napping.

So, you may be wondering why napping would receive its own chapter. Sleep, including napping is very beneficial for overall health and wellness. Many people aren't receiving enough sleep throughout the day due to high stress lives and excessive demands on their time. Napping is a useful tool in supporting the mind and body in refreshing itself so that we can have more focus, clarity, and energy to return to our work or other demands upon waking. The body heals and restores itself during sleep time, so taking time to sleep allows the body to go to work on the areas that need support. When the body needs more sleep it provides very clear signs to let us know that it wants to rest.

Some of These Signs Include:

- ❖ Feeling Sleepy
- ❖ Yawning
- ❖ Feeling Heavy or Weighed Down
- ❖ Feeling Lethargic
- ❖ Trouble Focusing and Thinking Clearly
- ❖ Trouble Finding Your Words
- ❖ Making A Lot of Simple Mistakes

Even when these signs show up, many people disregard them or turn to caffeine to try and override the signals to engage in sleep. However, if instead of overriding the natural call for sleep you choose to participate in a nap; the benefits are a win win. A nap allows you to get back into balance as your body goes to work to support your brain and other organs so they can work at a more optimal level upon waking. It's almost analogous to a control alt delete for the body, almost.

In addition to the physical support that comes from napping, many people experience information, ideas, inventions, and solutions to problems while they sleep. Idea people and inventors often report that their information came to them during their dreams. Sleeping with a notepad and a pen on your bedside table can help you to remember the guidance that you receive during dream time by writing everything down as soon as you wake up before you begin your routine. Many people have had the experience of trying to solve a problem all day to no avail and then go to sleep and have the answer to their problem when they wake up in the morning. These are common experiences and benefits from sleeping, including napping.

Some people actually need more sleep than others; and over the years I have found that highly sensitive people often fall into this group. Sleeping can allow highly sensitive people to clear from intense or harsh energy they were exposed to throughout their day. Sleeping can also help people in this group to recharge. Many highly sensitive people find that they need a lot of down time, quiet time, and alone time to maintain the balance that resonates for them. Sleep can be a big part of this balancing recipe.

I've found that highly sensitive people tend to have had this need for down time throughout their entire lives and the sooner they can accept and invest in this need, the better. It's when this group tries to fight their need for more sleep and down time that they can feel off balance. Some clients have told me that they feel guilty for taking naps, or that people within their families or friend circle shame them or make them feel uncomfortable about this type of self care. Others have told me that they feel they could be using the time for another task or activity which seems more "productive" in some way. Sometimes these feelings are self generated and other times they are inflicted upon them by people within their lives. By understanding the health and wellness benefits of napping in addition to their own personal need for balance; I've found that highly sensitive people can learn to embrace this aspect of their personal balance recipe without guilt.

Napping can also be a way for people to connect to their spiritual support team and departed loved ones. Maybe you have had the experience of all of a sudden feeling so tired that you could barely keep your eyes open. You may have thought, I need to lie down, I have to sleep right now. Almost immediately after lying down, you fall into a deep sleep and experience a dream visit with a loved one who has passed, an angel, or a spirit guide. This kind of sleep experience is one of the most common ways the spirit world gives us messages, support, and information. Upon waking, there is a very palpable feeling that lingers longer than a "regular" dream experience. There is also a knowing that you were visited and that you received important messages of support. There is also a longer period of adjusting to being awake again as the sleepy state can linger after a dream visit. The details about the dream and the feeling that it was a real visit remain long after the dream is over.

Activity:

When you notice that you're experiencing the signs of needing a nap, give yourself permission to acknowledge what your body is telling you. Notice what your first reactions are to this information. If you find yourself trying to push the messages down, try to stop and breathe. If your schedule will allow you to take a small nap, great try to give yourself permission to do that. If you can't, try to find a pocket of time later where you will be able to allow your body time to rest and restore. Even 10-15 minute "power naps" or "cat naps" can be very beneficial and supportive.

If you are someone who understands your need for napping but tend to feel guilty about participating in your napping schedule, try to stop and breathe when these feelings show up. Re-read this chapter about the benefits of napping or do some research online so you can gain even more support for your need to nap. Try to release your feelings of guilt around napping and gently share your findings about the importance of sleep with the people in your world if your guilt or shame is being exacerbated by others.

Try different ways to nap, perhaps you could test out the idea, invention, or problem solving methods. Maybe you have been longing to have a spiritual connection during your dream time. You can set up these experiences by intending them prior to sleeping. With time, you can increase your ability to program your dream time so you can experience rest and restore while participating in other support systems at the same time.

With so many ways that napping offers support, comfort, increased wellness, and connection, I hope that you will give yourself permission to embrace napping in any ways that feel right for you.

Part Two

Mental and Emotional Support

23.

Balance

Ahh, yes, the B word, Balance. This concept is incredibly important and if we can find ways to understand and apply it to our own lives we can open doors to the life that we want to live while also enjoying said life simultaneously. However, for most people I find the word balance to be a buzz word; a catch all phrase similar to the word stress. It's easy to place a lot of life issues under buzz word umbrellas because as a culture we hear those words, understand what they mean, and accept them as justifications for why something is the way it is. For example, balance is a topic that many of us talk about regularly and it's something that's talked about in wellness books, circles, magazines etc. however; I find that most people feel they're constantly chasing this idea of balance without really understanding how to implement it within their own lives. So, you may hear someone including yourself saying things like:

- ❖ "I just can't find time to make my needs a priority because I have so much on my plate, I'm in need of balance."
- ❖ "Balance, yeah well, when I have a personal assistant then I can focus on balance, until then this is the way it's going to be, running from one thing to the next, every day."
- ❖ "Balance, that would be great, but I don't have time for that right now, maybe when I go on vacation."
- ❖ Balance, ha ha, what's that?

These are examples of how we use the concept of balance in our daily lives without implementing its support systems.

So, I find that one of two scenarios show up for people most often.

The first is when someone knows a lot about the concept of creating balance, can rattle off examples, sometimes including empirical data about the importance of balance, and encourages loved ones to create more balance in their lives yet doesn't do this for themselves. People in this group feel they are the exception to the rule when it comes to balance. These people believe that since they understand the importance of the concept they are ahead of the game and rationalize that as soon as they have more time, then they'll begin implementing balance into their daily lives. The challenge here is that the "one day" scenario never comes because there is always a special circumstance keeping them from incorporating balance into their life.

The second scenario is with someone who is so bogged down with a laundry list of demands on their time that they genuinely don't believe balance is possible. They may even believe that the idea of balance is another marketing ploy being used to make them feel bad about themselves. People in this group tend to accept defeat before even trying to create balance in their lives because they don't believe it's possible for them to achieve it. This experience fosters the need for more balance which creates a vicious cycle of feeling in need of balance but not being able to experience it because they don't believe it exists.

Sometimes there is a third scenario where people have fallen off the balance wagon due to some extenuating life issue. In these cases, the people in this group know how important it is to get their lives back into balance because it was a regular priority for them prior to their life curve ball. So for these people there is often a small to moderate amount of readjustment time and maybe a redistribution of work or responsibilities so that balance can be a priority again. People in this group often explain how challenging it is for them to be in a place where their needs and down time have been shelved and make a strong commitment to shift their life back into balance even if it means making significant life changes and adjustments.

Breathe Through It:

Because balance brings up so many raw emotions for people, you may notice that there are some places within your body which feel tight right now. Take a moment to gently scan your body for any of those places right now. You may also notice that you're unconsciously holding your breath. Take a breath and as you scan your body, release any tension, tightness, or stress that you find. Telling your body to release is often enough to open up those tight places. If you notice that some of the tension remains, do some gentle stretching while you continue to breathe. Put your arms up over your head and gently lean from one side to the other. The key here is to keep breathing, your breath helps your body to open and release naturally.

You may have identified with one or more of the scenarios above and it may have caused an emotional reaction for you. If you find yourself thinking, "Yes, but…" take another breath. No matter what your personal situation may be, the need for balance is still an underlying issue for you. As you can allow yourself to embrace this truth it will be easier to begin making room for balance within your life. Creating room for balance, even seemingly small amounts of room will lead to big change over time.

Activity:

If you identify most with Scenario 1 then it's time to read chapter 1 again and contact a time management specialist to support you in creating space in your calendar. You may immediately think to yourself, I don't need to do this, this isn't about my schedule, it's about these certain life situations (insert your situation/s here_____) that are demanding more of my time than usual. Okay, if this is your initial reaction I want to emphasize to you that yes, it's time to reach out for professional support with your schedule.

The issue for people who identify with this situation is that there will always be a new scenario that shows up as soon as you've finished dealing with the last issue. Every day, you are shelving your needs until some elusive time, which never shows up. This creates an immediate impact on you as well as a compounding effect. Overtime the impact of neglecting your own personal needs show up and can create big challenges physical, mentally, emotionally, and spiritually.

Let the people in your inner circle know that you need support in contacting a professional so that they can encourage you. Then, ask for referrals, do some research and schedule an appointment with someone you feel aligned with. There are a lot of professionals who specialize in this kind of work and who can teach you how to implement necessary changes which will benefit you in all areas of your life. The big issue here is to take action now, don't put this off. The sooner you reach out or support the better you will feel and the more joy you will be able to experience within your life.

If you identify most with Scenario 2 you may need to make some changes in the way you see your role within your life. People who feel most aligned with this situation tend to be natural self-starters, go getters, and can often lean into perfectionism. Many times people within this group believe that if they want something done right, they need to do it themselves. This creates a challenge because pretty soon they find themselves doing everything nearly all the time. This leads to a lot of pressure, stress, tension, and a belief that balance isn't possible. People in this group believe it's not possible because there's physically no way they could add anything else to their plate.

People who connect with this scenario tend to be very skilled at mastering their schedules, they tend to have very little if any "wasted time" because every moment is accounted for with activities that allow them to be productive and moving toward a specific outcome. It's really important for people in this group to learn how to ask for help and then to receive that help once it's offered to them. People in this group tend to have a genuine fear that if they accept help the task won't meet their expectations and they'll wish they'd just done it themselves. Some of this goes back to control issues while some it's also about healthy communication skills.

If you identify with this group and these feelings, you may benefit from working with someone who understands perfectionism, challenges with receiving, and fears around asking for help. There are coaches and therapists who can provide support and techniques which will allow you to feel comfortable releasing some of your responsibilities to others. Once you can begin to redistribute the responsibilities within your life, you'll find that you can back in touch with who you really are again and you'll realize that you don't have to do everything all by yourself. You'll also find that not only is balance possible it's something that you can enjoy and embrace.

If you identify most with Scenario 3 you would probably identify as someone who for the most part makes balance a priority in your life. You may have made choices in your life that to some may have seemed out of the ordinary but you know they honored your need for balance or an internal guidance system. However, you may now find yourself in the middle of an unexpected life situation which has turned the stress way up in your life. In fact you may feel like a pot that is bubbling over on the stovetop.

Often this can feel even more challenging because you have spent so much time focusing on living your life in a balanced state. In these situations, it's really important to ask for help and to let the people within your life know what you need. Many people in your inner circle may see you as the one they come to for support so it may seem uncomfortable at first to ask for help, but it's important that you do. You may also want to reach out for support from a prayer circle or other spiritual support system.

The truth is that because you are so focused and committed to living your life in alignment with who you are, this is going to be an adjustment for you for a while. However, you will find a way to get things back into balance as you have many times before. Life curves bring trauma with them even if you don't realize that you're experiencing it at the time. Reaching out for support from a therapist who specializes in trauma can also be a huge support system for you. Also, any practices or self-soothing techniques you enjoy can offer another layer of support for you as you move through the initial level of intensity. Because you are so committed to living in balance you may find that you will need to make some changes or shifts to the way you have been doing things to acclimate to your current situation. However, as you continue to honor and nurture your wellbeing to move toward balance you'll find your footing again as you have many times before. The big key here for you is to reach out to your support systems and allow yourself to receive support.

No matter where you find yourself within the realm of balance, I hope you will give yourself permission to take an honest inventory of the way you spend your time. Making time for balance is an investment that yields huge dividends and you are definitely worth the investment. It's okay to be moving toward balance, this isn't about perfection but rather progress. Reaching out for support from professionals can help you to maximize your time and your quality of life by understanding and implementing regular balance within your life.

24.

Burn Out

This has shown up for a lot of clients and in many ways has become common for people. So common, that many of my clients haven't realized that the experiences they've had are connected to burn out at all. I've seen so many people, men and women who have experienced burn out and have compartmentalized it into something else. Some of the most common things I've heard it described as include: aging, frustration, lack of energy, not enough time, and lack of support from others. While these things can be contributing factors to making burn out feel more magnified, they are not in fact to blame for the experience.

With schedules becoming busier, work hours becoming longer, and a lack of genuine down time; people are experiencing burn out more frequently. One of the most challenging things that I've found for people is that in addition to not knowing how to deal with their burn out, they also don't want to identify or accept that they are experiencing it so they try to push through it. Pushing through it is exactly how they got to the place that they're in so this becomes a compounding and vicious cycle. As this cycle is fostered it becomes more and more challenging to deal with as time passes.

So, if you notice that the majority of your time is spent working (in the home or out of the home), managing issues or crises, multitasking with a lot of technology, and barely finding time to manage "regular" day to day tasks, you are on a road that can lead you to burn out. Many people report feeling like there aren't enough hours in the day for them to make their own personal health needs a priority not to mention investing in personal passions or projects. Over time, this kind of lifestyle literally causes people to burn the candle at both ends until they literally burn out completely. The truth is that we aren't made to live like machines because we aren't machines. We need quality downtime away from stimulation like computers, televisions, and smart phones every day. (Yes, every day.) We also need time outside to decompress which tends to get pushed onto the back burner for a lot of people due to their schedules.

In addition to the physical burn out that happens for people with a lifestyle that feels like it has you on a leash, there's an emotional burn out that happens too. Many times people will come in to work with me and they tell me that they feel completely empty inside. When I look, I literally see an image of a well and I can see varying levels of water within that well which tells me a lot about the way they've been living. I've seen some people with no water at all and a cracked well due to making themselves a low priority within their own lives for far too long.

Emotional burn out is as equally challenging as physical burn out and they go hand in hand. While the physical self care gets shelved for other so called responsibilities, so too do the things that make people feel connected to who they are on a core level. The passions, spark, and qualities that make someone feel alive and allow them to contribute to their life purpose and personal joy begins to dim until it feels like it's completely gone forever. The good news is that your personal passions are hard wired inside of you, so the spark no matter how dim can never fully go out. However, neglecting yourself for long periods of time can lead to feelings of being disconnected, depressed, exhausted, and unsure of who you are and why you are here. The joyful or magical parts of life can also feel like they've disappeared completely and life can begin to feel automatic or like every day is the same as the one before. Over time these experiences can lead to serious issues including varying degrees of health challenges for people.

Because physical and emotional burn out work together like best friends, both are experienced together. As things continue to be shelved within your life, both your physical and emotional selves begin to get out of balance until it gets to the point where you can't ignore it anymore. For some people this crisis may show up as a physical health issue, while for others their relationships may experience a great deal of strain or they may completely dissolve. Some experience a deep sense of emptiness or a feeling that they are a visitor within their own life. However it shows up, know that it's a red flag and a "check engine light" letting you know that something needs to change because what you're doing isn't working. These are serious signals and shouldn't be waived off as no big deal or something that everyone experiences. This is a serious issue, one that warrants a genuine investment of your time and energy.

Breathe Through It:

This chapter tends to bring up a lot of emotions, feelings, and thoughts for people across the board. While you may or may not be experiencing this for yourself, it's safe to say that you do know someone within your life who is experiencing this or has experienced this in the past. Take a breath, and if you feel any emotions coming to the surface for you, let them come up and out.

If you find yourself reading through this chapter and identifying with some of the experiences and thinking to yourself that you are somehow exempt or in a special situation, please take a breath. With the deepest respect and gentility, please hear me when I say that no matter what your personal situation may be, when you shelve your needs no matter how seemingly small, you will over time experience burn out. It's important to acknowledge and take ownership of any of the ways that you've been putting your own needs onto a shelf until a better time. The truth is that there is no better time to take care of yourself than now. You are definitely worth it.

If you feel worried because you resonate with some of the feelings, thoughts, or experiences connected to burn out, it's okay; you don't need to panic. The great news is that it's absolutely possible to make some shifts and changes which will allow you to navigate your path back to a place of balance. Just like when you're driving on the freeway, if you take the wrong exit, you can get back on and get yourself going in the right direction again.

Activity:

This activity calls for a couple of things to support you in getting yourself back into a place of balance. You will need a notebook, something to write with, or a blank document on your computer or tablet to get started.

Part One:

Below you will find a writing exercise, this is designed to help you dump your thoughts onto your page. It's important not to over think the things that come through for you or to try and "come up" with an answer. The first thing that comes up no matter what the sentence structure, grammar, or feelings it evokes is the exact right thing. No one will see this except for you, so you don't have to sensor yourself at all. All you have to do is write down the first things that show up for you as you read through the following questions.

- How would I describe my life in 3 words?
- If I had unlimited resources, time, money, and opportunities, what would I change in my life, today?
- If someone offered to finance my dream job and I could be guaranteed that I would be successful, what would I do?
- What beliefs are important to me at a core level?
- How do I support and live my core values each day?
- What issues are important to me?
- How do I support or contribute to the issues that are important to me each day?
- What dreams do I have for my life?
- What dreams did I have for my life when I was younger?
- How have these dreams changed? Why?
- What dreams have I set down along the path of my life? Why?
- Are there dreams that I've set down that I would like to move toward again? If so, what are they?
- How do I feel about my relationships right now?
- What would I like to change about my relationships right now?
- How do I feel about my personal health and wellness right now?
- How much exercise am I getting each week?
- How much sleep am I getting each night?
- Is my life joyful?

- How much time and I investing in creative outlets?
- When was the last time I made time for creativity?
- Do I feel like I am just going through the motions of my own life but somehow feel disconnected from it?
- How much down time away from technology do I get each day?
- How much time do I spend outdoors each day?
- What would I change if I could change anything right now?
- Why haven't I changed that one thing yet? What's holding me back?
- If I could add one thing to my life what would it be?
- How do I wish I could feel throughout the day?
- How do I feel throughout the day?
- What, if anything needs to change in my life? Why?

Part Two:

Take an honest inventory of the things that came through for you. Notice any themes or areas that are showing up for you over and over again. Take a minute to notice how it made you feel to answer these questions. If you are experiencing emotions, let them come up and out and take as much time as you need to feel them.

Re-read chapter one about time management and see where you can make some adjustments to the ways you are spending your time.

Part Three:

Tell a trusted friend or loved one in your inner circle who is supportive of you what you've realized as you've worked through this chapter. Ask them for their honest feedback about what you've found and ask them for support as you make some much needed changes. It's important to choose someone who will lovingly be there for you to remind you take good care of yourself and to support you in changing things about your current life and schedule.

- ❖ Please don't choose someone who could go into competition with you or make you feel bad for wanting to make changes to your current lifestyle.

You may also want to reach out to a professional with whom you feel aligned to gain further support and who can help you map out ways to implement changes. There are many coaches, therapists, intuitive counselors, and advisors who can be instrumental in offering support, insights, and techniques to help you remain committed to yourself and your new way of living.

Sometimes, big life changes come into play depending on what guidance you received about what's no longer working for you within your life. In these situations it can be particularly helpful to work with someone you trust to move through these changes together.

No matter where you are within this experience of burn out, at the beginning, someplace in the middle, or completely burned out; you can make a change. It's never too late to get your life back and to make your needs, calling, and joy a number one priority again. By honoring yourself, you won't neglect your responsibilities or relationships in your life; instead you will be able to give more to them. The people in your life who really love you will support and encourage you as you make these changes. As you refill your own well, you will have more to offer others and you will feel excited, uplifted, inspired, and reconnected to the truth of who you are again. You are absolutely worth the investment. You can do it.

25.

Decompress and Detox From Machines

Technology is a beautiful thing, it allows us to be connected with people and information with the stroke of a key or the swipe of a screen. However, all good things in moderation or so the saying goes. I believe that technology in moderation is an important way to find balance in a world that is inundated with screens and tech time.

Because machines are such a regular part of everyday life, it can become easy to allow technology to dominate our waking hours. It's natural to have more than one screen within arms' reach throughout the day and it's easy to underestimate the amount of time that is spent interacting with technology.

Too many hours logged with tech can reduce the amount of time spent getting outdoors, experiencing 3 dimensional face time, and a much needed break from the electromagnetic frequencies that are emitted from tech products.

Extended time with technology can even lead to:

- ❖ Feeling Lethargic
- ❖ Feeling Heavy
- ❖ Trouble Focusing
- ❖ Insomnia
- ❖ Reduced Attention Span
- ❖ Low Grade Anxiety
- ❖ Challenging Interpersonal Relationships
- ❖ Vitamin D3 Deficiency (Not getting full spectrum sun without filters.)

Taking time to decompress from technology and machines is not only a great way to maintain balance but it's also important for overall health and wellbeing. There are more and more places popping up with a business model to help people detox from their technology. There are unplugged vacations that you can participate in where you experience your entire vacation without access to any wifi at all. Many of these places are in restorative type settings so you can reconnect to nature, yourself, and the people you're traveling with if any at all. Some of these places ask you to surrender or check in your devices when you check into their establishment. Like any detox, there tends to be a window of adjustment for everyone with a sliding scale depending on how heavily you interact with technology throughout your regular day. During the detox, most people report feeling lighter, more clear, and more like themselves again. Many people also report that they were surprised how often they were on a device during the day until it was taken away from them.

While I'm not suggesting removing yourself from the grid entirely forever, I do find that regular unplugging and regulation go a long way when it comes to technology. I've watched clients experience an increase in stress, tension, low grade anxiety, and communication issues over the last 5 years as computers have become smaller and fit into the palm of our hands. Taking time to find detox methods that will support you and your family will yield huge dividends.

Breathe Through It:

Technology can be a challenging issue to look at for some people because they feel this issue doesn't apply to them for _____ reason. Some believe that they absolutely must be on their devices at all times and others underestimate their usage, while some feel that it has no negative impact upon their life. No matter what your usage may be, the truth is that technology does have a challenging impact in addition to all of the positive contributions that it provides.

If you find yourself getting irritated, nervous, or defensive as you've read through this chapter so far, stop and take a deep breath in through your nose and out through your mouth. If you are feeling upset, allow this to be a gentle nudge to you that this is an issue for you to look at a bit deeper. Taking an honest inventory of your daily device usage will allow you to get a clearer picture of how you can move toward balance. Finding your personal recipe for success will allow you to embrace your technology without getting you out of balance in other areas of your life.

Activity:

First, you will want to spend a few days monitoring your technology usage. This is one of those things that's similar to asking someone how long their television has been on throughout the day; it's almost always under reported. So, you will need to print out or create a document with a time table for the entire day in 30 minute blocks of time. Depending on how comfortable you are with self reporting, you may want to enlist a family member and a colleague to support you in documenting every block of time throughout the day for at least 3 full days. This will give you a pretty good idea of what your daily average of use is on any given "regular" day. Technology usage includes any and all screen time throughout the day. This includes televisions, phones, tablets, laptops, and any kind of device including Kindles or other reading devices.

Once you have established your average amount of usage; you will probably notice hot spots of time where you tend to be on a device or several devices more than others. This will help you have a better understanding of the places and the spaces where you can whittle down or completely separate from technology and devices.

There is no one way or right way to detox from devices and machines there are just the ways that are right for you. Below you will find some ideas that you can implement or use as a jumping off place to create your own detox regimen.

No Tech Zones:

These are areas in your home where you declare no tech zones. No matter what the circumstance may be, that rule is respected. Often, dining areas are allocated as tech free zones. Some people make that official dining spaces while others make it across the board, no matter where food is being served whether at a breakfast bar, outside bbq, or at the dining room table.

Bedrooms are another common place where people tend to have a no tech zone. This can support healthy sleeping habits and intimacy.

Out of Sight Out of Mind:

This is a powerful way to reduce and disconnect from technology. The same adage that applies to a place for everything and everything in its place works here too. By creating hidden charging and docking stations, it reduces usage. Some people have drawers or small areas in cupboards that hide unsightly cords while holding all of the tech necessities that are within reach if needed.

All About Timing:

Similar to parents who limited television to a certain amount of minutes per day, having a set amount of tech time per day can limit usage quickly. This also allows people, especially young people in the house to decide how they want to use their minutes.

Setting a shut down time or an hours of usage time for technology is another way to hold a healthy boundary with devices.

Scheduling time in the morning to be tech free can make a huge difference in the way the entire tone of your day will unfold. Even 30 minute to an hour of tech free time can allow you to reconnect to your own natural rhythm before being inundated with infinite communication and to do lists. The same holds true for bedtime; find an amount of time where you can shut down and decompress without devices. This will allow for a more restful sleep.

Go Offline:

This is for those of you who truly want to detox whether that is for 72 hours or an entire "vacation." You don't need to go to a fancy place to participate in a tech detox but it can be much easier to disconnect if you have no way to get connected. You can either ask someone to hold your devices for you or you can unplug your router and go off the grid. This will most likely mean that you can't go to any hot spots or places with access to wifi because then you will get hooked back in really easily.

You may want to investigate some of the places that offer wifi free getaways. You can find a sliding scale of price points from camping all the way to spa like retreats.

No matter what you do to make some healthy shifts and changes to your technology lifestyle, you will experience benefits. While we use machines to help support and enrich our lives, we aren't machines and shouldn't be connected to them at all hours of the day. Find some ways to slow down and get back to that quiet space within while balancing your screen time. I promise you that you can do it and it will be worth it.

26.

Create Time for Fun

Investing in fun is a powerful and important component of life. Fun has the ability to reduce stress, tension, and heaviness from our moods relatively quickly. Fun also works like a time machine and can transport us back to an experience of being children again. Joy, laughter, giddiness, and freedom are some of the emotions and feelings that are stoked during some good old fashioned play time. Play can also support us in experiencing solutions, light bulb moments, and a reconnection to our own selves.

Over the years I have worked with countless grown ups who have felt lost, disconnected, angry, and even numb in their lives. Many reported feeling like every day was the same as the day before and felt disenfranchised with their life. Some also expressed an emptiness and a feeling that there had to be more to life than what they had been experiencing. Many told me that they felt the magic or wonder of life had completely disappeared for them. As we started working together, often we would find that for a long period of time, play and fun had been omitted from their lives. In fact for most people, play didn't even cross their minds as something that was missing, it didn't even register as something that was important or even necessary. For some people, they realized that they couldn't remember the last time that had played.

In addition to not creating time for play; there was another large group of clients who didn't know how to play anymore and they didn't know what they liked anymore. There was a quality of deep sadness for them around this issue because they felt like it underscored the level of disconnect that had been evident in their lives for so long. When I asked them what their favorite pass time was and if they could do anything they wanted what it would be; they couldn't think of anything. For many of these people, this would often lead to a lot of emotions and tears.

Working to find ways to reconnect to the natural inclination to play allowed a deep healing to happen for people. For many people there was a reawakening in a sense, a reconnection to the heart of who they are and a letting go of the heaviness they had been carrying around with them. Once these folks realized that what was missing from their lives was genuine fun and play; it was finding ways to reintegrate it that made the difference in increasing happiness in their lives. In doing this clients felt like their lives went from being in black and white to Technicolor. Many also reported that they were able to reconnect to the magical quality of life they experienced when they were younger.

Bringing fun back into life is not a one recipe kind of thing. It really depends of the individual person and their situation. For some people reintegrating things that they once loved and made time for while they were younger allowed them to bridge the gap. While for others there was an investigation time to really understand what they liked and how to bring those things into their daily life.

Just like with any shift, when things change there are people, situations, and ways of living that begin to shake out of life through the natural process of the law of attraction. So, many people found that once they began investing in fun on a regular basis, they simultaneously said no to people, things, and situations that they had previously been saying yes to out of obligation, guilt, or habit. This combination of saying yes to fun and to honoring themselves while saying no to things that weren't supportive of them led to big changes over time.

Breathe Through It:

If you find yourself resonating with this experience; take a moment to breathe deeply in through your nose and out through your mouth. Pay attention to any tension or tightness that could be holding space within your heart or stomach and give yourself permission to release that tension now. Many people who resonate with this experience lean into a sense of self blame and feel that they should've been able to manage their time or life better and take this as a reflection of some kind of failure on their part. Please don't let yourself go into self blame in this situation. For most people, this is something that happens slowly over time until it begins to add up to a challenging situation. The great news is that once you are aware of the situation, you can begin to make active positive changes. The shifts and changes can be seemingly small or big changes; but no matter what you choose to do to increase fun and play within your world, it will all add up to big positive change. Yes, you can do it.

For those of you who may feel this doesn't really apply to you, please take a moment and breathe. I promise that if you have turned to this chapter these is something here for you. You may already know what it is that brings you childlike joy, happiness, and glee but you've been shelving it for _____ reason/s. This is the right time for you to begin to reintegrate those things back into your life on a regular basis so you can continue to experience a full and happy life.

Activity:

<u>I Know What I Love To Do For Fun and Play</u>

If you find yourselves in this group, great! A big portion of the work is already done for you. The piece that you will want to work on is getting a deeper understanding of why you chose to shelve your personal passions and acknowledge how much time has passed since making that choice. It's really important to avoid the yes, but_____ thought process while taking a look at this situation. No matter what the reason, you still chose to put your fun factor on the back burner. Remember, this isn't a judgement but rather an opportunity to get a deeper understanding of how this happened and to make a conscious choice and effort to reintegrate the things that you enjoy doing back into your life.

For some people it will take making some changes to their schedules to create time to do the things that bring them joy. This is a positive investment of your time, one that will yield big dividends. If you find that you have a hard time executing the shift in your schedule, you may want to work with a Coach or a Time Management Specialist to support you in creating windows of time. This will often mean holding boundaries with yourself and others so that you don't continue to shelve the things that bring you joy.

I Don't Know What I Like To Do For Fun

If you find yourself in this group, great! This means that you get to try new things and see what resonates for you. This is really exciting and allows for brand new doors to be opened for you. One place to start it to think about anything that you wanted to try or learn when you were younger but for whatever reason never had the opportunity. This is an opportunity for you to try those things now. It's also a time to try things that you never even thought you would be interested in. This is similar to being a freshman in college where you can try lots of different things to see what clicks for you. Give yourself permission to step out of your box during this process and to enjoy all kinds of new things while you meet new people. You may feel guided to try some classes, workshops, or events with a supportive friend or family member. That's great, you can invite people to join you on your journey and you can fly solo too; just give yourself permission to try the things that resonate for you or make you think, hmm, that sounds interesting.

There are often community events, and other local organizations where you can try new things without it breaking the bank. Connect with your local community to see what's happening where you live.

Additional Support Systems:

One of the biggest issues I've found when working with people is the belief that they have to schedule out a huge chunk of time to invest in fun. This is absolutely not true, even 20 minutes can make a huge difference in the way that you'll feel. Of course if you want to invest more time, that's great but it's not necessary.

I've found that clients who tend to lean into perfectionism often restricted themselves from fun because they felt it had to be really structured. So, rather than just organically moving with their schedule they wouldn't allow themselves the time to play because they believed they didn't have "enough" time. If this hits home for you, it's important to understand that seemingly small windows of time still lead to joy and fulfillment. In fact multiple windows of time allow you to incorporate more play and fun throughout your schedule, allowing you to reconnect to that joyful place within more frequently. Clients who resonated with this felt a huge sense of relief in knowing that they would still benefit from play time even if it didn't fit into a long time block.

The other big issue is the old out of sight out of mind situation. This really goes hand in hand with creating windows of time for play. Sometimes, simply pulling your stuff out and keeping it in a place where you can see it and get to it easily allows for more regular use. Whether that includes:

- ❖ Musical Instruments
- ❖ Sewing Machines
- ❖ Sports Equipment
- ❖ Books
- ❖ Art Supplies
- ❖ Gardening Tools
- ❖ Or other items

Simply having access to your belongings can increase the amount of time that you use them. Many people feel that they don't take the time to invest in their play time or fun because it feels like a chore to get the stuff out so they can enjoy it. You may want to work with someone to help you arrange your belongings in a way that allows you to have easy access without them taking up prime real estate in your living room. Working with a

- ❖ Professional Organizer
- ❖ Friend or
- ❖ Family Member

who can support you in making space for you to access your stuff can make a world of difference. It doesn't have to cost you a lot of money to make simple yet effective shifts when it comes to placement for your goodies.

The big thing during this process of investigation is to try new things and to allow yourself to reconnect with what you like. You may be surprised how many things you enjoy while meeting some really incredible people along the way.

I hope you will enjoy reconnecting with fun and play. I hope that you will give yourself permission to laugh, play, and enjoy your life with the same level of glee as you did when you were a child. There is often a lot of talk about connecting with and nurturing our inner child. This work is really important because it allows us to bring together all the parts of us on a regular basis. But I've found that sometimes people get confused as to how to achieve this experience. I've found that by increasing fun, playtime, and joy in our day to day lives it not only increases overall happiness but also connects us to our inner child at the same time. We don't need to overthink making time for fun; and I hope that you will reap the benefits of reconnecting to your inner child by investing in your personal joy as an adult today, and every day.

27.

Clean Up Your Friend and Family Circle

This is a big one and one that shows up for people at least one time in their life if not more than one time. This life area can also create a lot of stress for people because it's a really emotional area to look at, so sometimes people try to avoid it altogether. However, avoiding this issue doesn't make it go away, instead it makes it fester and bubble up until it's finally dealt with. The process from acknowledging there's some clean up to do and taking action on it depends on the person. Whether you are a person who takes action immediately in this situation or someone who tries to walk delicately around it until you just can't take it anymore, or somewhere in between, it's an important issue that must be tended to.

Relationship changes and shifts happen organically as we shift and change too. There are some people who will share the majority of our lives with us but many others won't be with us through the long haul, and that's okay. There's a difference between acquaintances or colleagues that shift out of our lives due to life changes, moving, promotions, etc. and the folks who we know aren't a fit for our lives anymore. This chapter is about the latter of these two groups. The people that this clean up refers to are people who for whatever reason are not a healthy or positive contribution to your life.

I find this can be a really challenging issue for people, especially sensitive people. Often times I work with a client who has a hurtful friend, partner, or family member in their life who has been taking advantage of them for a significant amount of time and when my client has finally had enough, they come in to work on the issue.

Here are some of the reasons that I hear when I ask why they haven't left the relationship yet:

- ❖ I don't want to hurt them.
- ❖ If I leave them, they won't have anyone else.
- ❖ I would want someone to give me another chance.
- ❖ They have a nice/good side of them too, most people just don't get a chance to see it.
- ❖ I can see the best in them and want to help them step into that place within themselves.
- ❖ I've invested a lot of time in this relationship.
- ❖ I'm afraid of the fall out if I leave.
- ❖ I have children with this person.
- ❖ I don't know how to leave, I feel bullied by this person.
- ❖ I don't have any other people in my life because I've given so much of my time to them.
- ❖ In my family, we pretend that this person's behavior isn't really happening.
- ❖ My family accepts the bad behavior and there is an unspoken rule that I should too.
- ❖ If I hold a boundary with this family member, I'm afraid everyone else will be mad at me.
- ❖ If I stop communicating with this family member I won't be able to see or talk with the family members that I enjoy.
- ❖ I thought forgiveness meant that I should continue to have this person in my life.

These are just some of the common responses that I've heard, this is in no way an exhaustive list. However, no matter what the reason, if you know that you are in a toxic relationship with someone no matter what the scale, it's important for you to know that leaving and holding healthy boundaries are your right. You don't need to have a reason to say no or acknowledge that something doesn't feel good to you anymore. You don't have to wait until things get so bad that you experience trauma to let you know that you can end the relationship.

Holding onto relationships that have run their course doesn't do anybody any good. Stunted relationships actually keep us from moving forward, from being who we really are, and can make us feel trapped or stifled. Over time these relationships can also create glass ceilings for us because we can start to believe that "this is it" that there's nothing past this group or situation, which isn't true. But these glass ceilings can lead to making choices that limit potential and personal growth. So, it's important to honor your inner wisdom, sinking feeling in your stomach, or moment when you say, "enough is enough" and end the relationship.

Choosing to hold a healthy boundary and dissolving an unhealthy relationship is a loving and respectful thing to do for yourself; body, mind, and spirit. In the big picture, it's also a loving thing to do for the other person involved as well, even if they can't see it right away. It may be hard for you to see that it's a loving thing to do too, but in time it's often easier to see things more clearly. At the end of the day, the most important thing is to honor your own needs and to love yourself enough to say no to the people who are no longer meant to be in your life. You can do it. I promise.

Breathe Through It:

This topic can often bring up a lot of deep emotions and heart hurt. Sometimes this topic can bring up a full bandwidth of emotions including anger, so if you're feeling angry, it's okay. Take a deep breath in through your nose and out through your mouth. Quickly check in with your body and loosen up any clenched muscles while you continue breathing…good. Give yourself permission to feel the emotions that are coming up for you and try not to hold back any tears if you feel them welling up in your eyes. Allowing your emotions to move through you (in a healthy way) allows you to release anything that you've been holding in or pushing down.

Activity:

You will need a something to write with, some paper, or a new document open on your computer or tablet.

You will need to be in a quiet place where you won't be interrupted for 10-15 minutes.

Turn off your phone and any other notifications that could distract you.

Then:

- ❖ Take 3 long deep breaths, in through your nose and out through your mouth.
- ❖ Gently move your shoulders and neck to let go of any tension or tightness that could be hiding there.
- ❖ Answer the following questions without putting too much thought into them, just let whatever is inside of you pour out through your writing or typing.
- ❖ No one will see this but you, so please don't worry about grammar or sentence structure.

Questions:

- Who is no longer a fit in my life?
- How long have they not been a fit for me?
- What are some of the ways that they have hurt and/or violated me?
- How does this person's life style, beliefs, or actions feel out of alignment with mine?
- How do I feel when I am around this person?
- How do I feel when I talk to this person?
- Do I try to avoid or dodge their calls, texts, or messages?
- How does my body feel when I interact with them?
- Do I feel drained or upset after interacting with them?
- Do I find myself going over and over our conversations in my mind after the interaction is over?
- Do I experience hurt feelings or anger when I think about previous interactions with this person?
- Do I feel any physical reactions such as an upset stomach or headache after interacting with this person?

After answering the questions above, pay attention to the way that you feel.

- Do you feel lighter after getting a lot of stored energy out through this writing exercise?
- Do you feel any emotions coming to the surface?
- Do you have more clarity about this relationship and how it's impacting your life?

- ❖ Do you feel tired, drained, or sleepy after this writing exercise?
    - o This exercise can bring up a lot of stored emotions, memories, and hurt. You may want to drink some water and take some down time for yourself before going on to the next activity in your day. You may also find that you feel a bit sleepy or even exhausted after this exercise, if you can take a nap or rest, please give yourself permission to do that. If not, then try to get to bed a little bit earlier if possible so you can give your body a little more rest.

Now that you have a better understanding of this relationship and the need for a healthy boundary; the next step is taking action. There is no one way or right way to hold a boundary or to close the door to a relationship. There are only the ways that are the right fit for you. You may find that including more than one technique is the right fit for you, or you may create your own technique. Below you will find some examples of ways to hold healthy boundaries. This is not an exhaustive list, so please feel free to add your own ideas, resources, and techniques to the one's listed.

Communication:

Depending on the dynamic of the person and your relationship, talking about the situation could be an option. It is very important to be conscientious about using gentle language and avoiding blaming statements or attacking language in any way. Using statements that begin with I feel can help to create an open door for positive communication.

However, if the person you want to talk to is abusive, addicted, or uses manipulation, this method may create more challenges for you.

Therapy:

This option can support you in gaining more confidence, clarity, and support in working through any trauma or negative patterns you've experienced during this relationship. A therapist can also support you in feeling confident in holding healthy boundaries and support you in moving through any grief you may experience by ending a relationship.

If the other person is open to therapy, you could work together with a therapist to create healthy communication and learn some techniques to support a healthy relationship.

Your therapist can also direct you to other services, organizations, and resources that can continue to support you as you make positive change.

Cutting Ties:

If you feel that communication isn't an option, cutting ties and breaking all communication can be a way to hold a firm boundary and allow you to move forward. There is often a grief period that comes with this method, but also a feeling of a heavy weight being lifted from your shoulders at the same time. You may need to change your phone number and other personal details in some situations.

Divorce:

This is very clear way of cutting ties and dissolving a relationship. There is often a grief period included in this method, but also a feeling of a heavy weight being lifted from your shoulders at the same time. You may want to work with a therapist or coach to support you in moving through the divorce process.

Saying No:

In unbalanced relationships whether they be with "friends" or family members the challenging person often uses bullying, manipulation or guilt to try to get the result they're looking for. Learning to say No without guilt or explanation can help to shift these relationships. The pushy or challenging person may try to continue to convince or push you into doing what they want several more times but the more you say No they may stop trying to get what they want from you. Unfortunately, this doesn't work with everyone but it can work.

Sometimes the pushy person will stop asking you for things because they realize you are no longer available to meet their needs; so they move on to someone else. Other times, they may try to implement some other way to get you to meet their needs, such as trying to get a family member or a friend to ask you to do it for them. In these situations it's important to continue to hold your boundary.

When these situations are part of a family dynamic it may mean saying no to activities where the abusive person will be there. This can create a forced choice situation where you have to choose to be put into an abusive situation or miss out on the activity. You can either bring a "safety" person with you to the event, choose to stay a short time or choose not to attend at all.

12 Step Programs:

There are 12 step programs for many life areas, and these support communities are free and available online as well as in person. There are groups for people who find themselves in co-dependent relationships. This is a great support system for people who have experienced one sided, manipulative, and or abusive relationships. Al-Anon is also a great support system for adults who have parents, partners, or friends who abuse alcohol or drugs. You can find these groups in your local area simply by doing a google search.

At the end of the day, no matter what your personal situation is whether it be with family, friends, or both, the most important thing is to honor you feelings and inner guide. You know who is no longer a fit for your life and you know why. You don't have to explain, make excuses, or justifications for your needs and boundaries. You get to choose who is allowed to share your life with you and you never have to accept abuse to appease others.

In moving through this situation, it's a good idea to reach out for support from a trusted professional. Whether you feel guided to work with a therapist, assertiveness coach, a 12 step community, or support group; reaching out for help will be a step in the right direction.

28.

Create Time for the People in Your World

Carving out time for your loved ones is an important and fulfilling experience in more ways than one. Sometimes, however, with the impacted schedules of modern life, it can feel challenging to get those moments in on a regular basis. I've worked with a lot of clients who tell me that it hurts their heart to feel disconnected from their loved ones due to demands on time. Many of these clients tell me that they feel like they only see the people they care about in extreme situations like a wedding celebration or a celebration of life. This can lead to a feeling of sadness and a sense of waiting for "one day" when there will be more time. While there are life changes and moves that can bring loved ones closer, often it's a shift in priorities that creates a bridge to more time with our friends and family.

We're at a place as humans where we're the busiest we've ever been. With the extra demands on what can seem like every minute of the day, there is also a sense of less life satisfaction that comes along with this pressure on our time. I find this to be especially challenging for people who live far away from their loved ones which creates an additional factor in connecting.

For some people the distance or lack of regular connection can become too much to bear and a life change is made to physically close the gap. For others this may not be possible for whatever reason and so there is an element of grief, small but significant changes, and acceptance that come into play. Overall, even with all of the wonderful advances in technology that we enjoy, there is a need to connect with people we love in real life. There is a hard wired need we have for connectivity and the experience of connecting with our loved ones is very important.

Loved ones can be anyone that's part of your inner circle and someone that you feel genuinely connected to. Sometimes people tell me that they feel guilty wanting to choose to spend time with a particular loved one instead of another. At the end of the day, the people you feel connected with and desire a connection with are the ones that you're being guided to spend time with. It's about feeding and nurturing your relationships and yourself by investing in one on one connection and quality time. Any investment that you make in this area will yield big dividends.

The truth is that there will most likely never come a day when there is more time. It's important to make the most of the time that you have right now. Even seemingly small shifts can lead to huge positive change. Creating healthy boundaries for yourself so you're investing in the people and experiences that resonate with you will allow you to experience a more full and rich life. Relationships are a very important part of a full life and your desire to invest in more time with your loved ones is divinely guided. There are ways to reconnect with loved ones on a more regular basis and you are deserving of the changes which will allow that to come to fruition in your life.

Breathe Through It:

This chapter can bring a lot of emotions, memories, and pent up feelings to the surface. For many this topic can bring up images of holidays, celebrations, and other moments in time where they feel they missed out, or wished their loved ones were with them to mark that special day. It's natural to have these feelings and if you find that some emotions are coming to the surface for you right now; give yourself permission to move through them.

Activity:

There is no one way or right way to increase the time spent with loved ones. There are only the ways that are a right fit for you, right now. As your life shifts and changes, so too may the ways that you connect with the people in your world. I've included some of the ways that former clients and I have come up with to increase connectivity. This is by no means an end all be all list but rather an opportunity for you to get some ideas that may work for you and hopefully spark some ideas of your own.

Set The Date:

Getting an event into the calendar is often half the battle. When something is scheduled and treated the same as any other appointment or work commitment it's so much easier to actually move forward with the event. Often what happens, is there's a lot of talk of getting together or pre-planning but there is no date set. This can lead to a lot of time passing without seeing the people you are trying to get together with. Get it into the schedule and treat it like any other commitment.

Ask For Help:

Due to the demands on time, schedules are pretty tight. There's usually someone who wants to get everyone together but it's a lot of work for one person to be in charge of all of the organizing, food, etc. The thought of putting something together alone can make someone say, No way, I don't have the time to take that on right now." So, by asking everyone to pitch in and be responsible for bringing and or doing something it takes the pressure off of everyone and allows for a pleasant and relaxed get together. This easy and gentle hosting style often allows other people in the group to feel comfortable stepping up as a host the next time. This can lead to more regular visits and quality time.

Small But Significant:

Sometimes clients tell me that they want to spend time with their loved ones by doing big splashy kinds of things. While this is great and a lot of fun, I find that people can overlook the fun that can come from seemingly small yet significant time together. If your loved ones live close by, getting a cup of tea, lunch, or simply hanging out while one of you is prepping food or doing "regular" things is still precious time together. These small but significant moments together can make wonderful moments and memories. It's important to acknowledge the smaller windows of time for connections because they are equally valuable as big or fancy celebrations.

Meet In The Middle:

When there is a significant distance between you and your loved ones it can be challenging to make the trip as often as you may like. There can be a lot of pressure to make the visit "perfect" because you don't see one another very often. Because there is no such thing as perfect, this can lead to a lot of stress and pressure. Meeting in the middle can be a great way to take the pressure off of one person doing all the traveling and one person doing all the hosting.

Relocation:

For people who feel a deep ache and calling to be closer to their loved ones, it may be time to consider relocation. Living a great physical distance from loved ones can take a toll over time. For some, they are able to manage the distance and work with the small but precious time that they have with their loved ones. However, for others it can be too much to bear. I find this especially true for people who want their children to be near their extended family. For many people, advanced education and professional careers can lead to location changes away from the family unit. Depending on how far away and how many years it's been there can be a call to make a physical move to be closer to loved ones. It's important to consider all the aspects of life that will be altered by a significant change like this. However, for those who know they're being guided back to their family, it will feel like a welcome change.

Screen Time:

While this chapter is about making time for physical visits and connections, there is something to be said for screen time. This is especially true for those people who live far away from their loved ones or who may be separated from them due to life circumstances. The blessing of modern technology is that we can actually see and connect with our loved ones through our cell phones, tablets, and laptops now. There is something to be said about being able to actually see the people we love while talking to them. There is another level of heart opening that happens when connecting through screen time which can make the miles separating you feel obsolete. Scheduling screen time in just like any other date helps to keep the visit locked into your plans. Screen time dates are a wonderful way to help to take some of the sadness out of the distance you feel while being separated from your loved ones.

Any way that you feel guided to reach out and connect with the people in your world will be worth it. We're not here for an unlimited amount of time and the way we spend our days is the way we spend our lives. Giving yourself permission to spend time, even seemingly small amounts of time with the people you love will increase your happiness, joy, and life satisfaction. I promise, you are worth it!

29.

Clean Up Your Inner Junk Drawer

Just like cleaning out junk drawers and closets in your home, it's important to clean out the inner junk drawer as well. Inner junk drawers can hold lots of stuff including but not limited to, gossip, negativity, sarcasm, limiting beliefs, complaining, and negative self talk. These kinds of things can create challenges and glass ceilings in moving forward and in living a life that feels full, happy, and joyful.

Similar to physical spaces, inner junk drawer "clutter" can creep in little by little almost without being noticed for a while. Then all of a sudden you realize that you've got a whole lot of stuff around you that you don't need or want anymore. Sometimes you may not realize that you're carrying around clutter until someone mentions that you could be more positive, or should look on the bright side, or that they haven't called you because it's hard to be around you etc. Those moments can be a really big wake up call. Other times it can be more subtle, you may find that you are exposing yourself to drama filled situations, media, or people who begin to make you feel off balance and less like yourself. No matter how your inner junk drawer gets full, it's important to give it a good clearing on a regular basis.

Even the most positive and forward focused folks can still benefit from a regular cleaning or clearing. Just like professional organizers continually clear, purge, and organize their homes, so too does this technique benefit everyone. If you feel unsure about your ability to make positive changes in this area of your life, allow me to reassure you that you can do it. Sometimes, it can feel overwhelming if you've been living a certain way for a long period of time, but that doesn't mean you can't make positive changes, you can. Just like a client who doesn't know how to organize their homes, they can reach out for support to learn how to make changes while they work with a professional.

Breathe Through It:

This chapter can bring up a couple of things for people. Some people may feel that this doesn't apply to them because of _____. However, there is a difference between working through healthy emotions due to a challenging situation and negativity, sarcasm, and consistent complaining. This isn't about adopting a Pollyanna kind of attitude where you choose not to acknowledge challenging life situations. This is about getting connected to the places and spaces within your own life where you could be slipping into behaviors that aren't suiting you or the life that you would like to live.

This chapter isn't about placing blame, shame, or guilt, but rather offering you support in finding the patterns and behaviors that could be creating glass ceilings for you. This chapter is an opportunity for you to get clear on what is ready to leave your inner junk drawer and help you create space for new people, situations, and opportunities.

The other big issue that can show up for people around this topic includes social situations. Some people feel a connection between friends, family, and colleagues by participating in these behaviors together. It can feel like an insiders club for people who like to use these kinds of things as buffers or conversation starters. Shifting away from these behaviors can lead to shifts in relationships, but you will benefit in the process.

Activity:

Making changes in this area can look a lot of different ways depending on your personal situation. There is no one way or "right" way to clean out your inner junk drawer, there are only the ways that are right for you. As you work on different areas of your drawer, your changes may look differently.

Below you will find a list of some ideas that I've collected over the years, this is by no means an end all be all list but rather a jumping off place for you. Hopefully this list will spark some ideas for you so you can create some changes that work for you and your situation.

Pinky Promise:

Choose a very trusted friend or loved one for this technique. Please choose someone who will support you without teasing or downplaying the work that you're doing. Once you find this person, ask them to gently but consistently tell you when you are slipping into the behavior that you're choosing to clean out of your life. For example if you want to let go of complaining, ask your accountability partner to kindly let you know when you're complaining. Then, thank them, and try to find a way to either reframe what you were saying or don't say it at all.

As you may imagine in the beginning this could be a bit of a shift for you, but as you continue to receive support and feedback from your friend, you will find that you shift that old pattern quickly. This is a powerful way to clear out a behavior that creates a lot of clutter.

Gossip:

This area can have a large umbrella of things which fall under it. First, acknowledge which things are under your gossip umbrella. Then, once you know what they are you can begin eliminating them.

One of the easiest ways to get gossip out of your life is by no longer paying for it. If you tend to purchase gossip rags or watch gossip television (including reality style television) stop. Physically removing these things from your home will make a huge impact on your life. You will also notice that you have a lot of "free time" on your hands after letting these things go.

Feed Scrolling can be another way that you're absorbing gossip which can also be a huge time waster. If there are people in your social media communities who are drama filled or Debbie Downers, clean up your list.

Be conscientious of the things that you say to others. Are you a gossip? Do you find that the way you make conversation with others is by disparaging someone else? If so, ask a trusted person in your life to support you in ending this bad habit. Being a gossip can lead to having a group of people in your world who aren't of the highest integrity and can push integrity filled people and opportunities out of your life quickly.

Media Meltdown:

If you're highly sensitive, you may find that negative headlines or conversations can take a huge toll on you. This can lead to depression, anxiety, and even trauma. This can also lead to feeling and believing that there aren't reasons to be happy because you feel consumed by warning type messages. This belief or experience can then roll out into the way that you move through your world which can have a negative impact on your relationships with others and yourself.

If this is something that rings true for you, it's important to acknowledge this experience and then adjust accordingly. It doesn't mean you should bury your head in the sand and choose to ignore situations; but it does mean that limiting exposure to negativity is important for you. Reducing the amount of time you invest in headlines, videos, or news outlets can support you in finding a balance between awareness and personal peace.

Negative Self Talk:

This pattern of saying hurtful, belittling, or judgmental things to yourself negatively impacts all area of your life. This habit can lead to creating limiting beliefs, glass ceilings, and a fear of making changes. Like any clean out process, acknowledging the issue is the first step. You can work with an accountability partner for this issue if you feel guided. However, it's often a good idea to work with a therapist, trauma specialist, or professionally trained coach who can give you tools which can help you to uncoil from these harsh thought patterns. It is possible to stop negative self talk and it's a worthwhile investment of your time to reach out for help if this is a part of your life right now.

Saying No to Say Yes:

Anytime you make changes in your life no matter what area that may be, sometimes you need to adjust your boundaries. So, as you dedicate yourself to clearing out you inner junk drawer, you may find that there are people and situations which no longer resonate for you. This is a natural and organic part of change. This isn't a negative reflection of you nor is it a reason to discontinue your healthy clean out. Give yourself permission to create new healthy boundaries that resonate for you as you move forward and allow people who honor those boundaries to come along with you and release the ones who don't. Many times, participating in simple shifts will allow people to organically shake out of your life on their own. Be gentle with yourself as you move through this process because grief and sadness are a natural part of change, and remember to go at your own pace.

As you move through this important work, you will notice that you feel better and more like your true self. Sometimes people also find that they physically feel different, even lighter and younger. This is an important investment in your wellbeing and life satisfaction; and something that will upgrade every area of your life. As you focus on creating a positive, happy, and healthy life, you will experience it alongside people who want the same for you and for themselves.

If you find that this is challenging for you or you aren't sure where to begin, reaching out for support is a powerful way to begin to make these worthwhile changes. You are worth it. You do deserve to be happy and to have positive people in your world. You can do it. It's never too late to make a change in the right direction.

30.

Financial Literacy

Finances are a part of all of our lives, but I've found that some people have a more comfortable or confident relationship with it than others. Financial literacy doesn't focus only on how much money you have saved in your bank account or how much debt you have incurred. Financial literacy is an umbrella area which asks you to look at how well you work with your money, your understanding of investing, the way you handle your money, how you feel about money, who may be connected to your money, and how other people interact and treat your money.

Sometimes this subject can make people feel nervous, anxious, or downright confused. For some people, they take the attitude that they don't want to know what's happening with their money and don't want to look at it for fear of _____. Other people can tell you down to the cent how much money they have in their accounts, how much money they budget for every area of their life, and updates about all of their investments. Some people find themselves somewhere in between these two examples. However, no matter where you find yourself, there's always an opportunity to get more comfortable and informed about your finances.

In addition to learning about how you can manage, invest, or increase your financial status, there is an emotional component to this area as well. Some people can feel the emotional connection that they have to money and others may not realize that it's there. Some people have intense memories of the way their parents managed money and may find that they have similar money patterns now as adults. Whether you realize it or not, you're in a relationship with your money which means that there is an emotional connection tied to it. So, what does that mean? It means that in addition to understanding how to work with your money responsibly it's also important to understand your emotional connection or emotional relationship to it as well.

Breathe Through It:

Take a moment and notice how your neck, shoulders, and stomach feel right now. Now, tune into your chest area, are you holding your breath? Do you feel any tension or tightness in your body? If you do, that's okay. Take 2 deep breaths in through your nose and out through your mouth. Good. Now roll your shoulders and release any additional tension that you may be holding onto including any tension in your face. Noticing how your body reacts to thoughts about finances is a powerful tool for you. This information can support you in understanding your relationship and emotions connected to your finances. You can move toward a place where you feel more confident, literate, and comfortable with your finances. Yes, you can and it doesn't matter what your situation is now or how it may have been in the past.

Activity:

You will need a something to write with, some paper, a journal, or a new document open on your laptop or tablet. You can also speak into a voice recorder if you would like to listen back to your answers at another time.

You will want to carve out about 15 to 20 minutes for this activity where you won't be interrupted. Turning off your phone, email, or anything else that could ding or ring when you are doing this will be very helpful for you.

Take a couple of deep breaths and relax your body. Then, when you feel ready, I want you to answer the following questions with the first thing that pops into your head. Don't worry, no one will see anything that your write down, this is just for you. Please don't try to come up with the "right" answer or a socially acceptable answer. The more honest you can be, the more you will get from this activity.

- ❖ Do I feel confident in my current financial situation? Why?
- ❖ How do I deal with my financial responsibilities?
- ❖ Do I find myself getting nervous or uncomfortable when I check the mail?
- ❖ Do I know how much money I owe to each business I have accounts with?
- ❖ On average, how much money do I have left over at the end of each month after all of my bills are paid?
- ❖ Do I balance my checkbook after each transaction?
- ❖ On average, how much money do I put into my savings account each month?
- ❖ Do I have a budget for this year? If so when was the last time I updated my financial planning?
- ❖ Do other people have access to my money? If so, who? Why?
- ❖ How do I feel about other people having access to my money?
- ❖ Would I ever allow someone else to have access to my money? If so, who? Why?
- ❖ What investments do I have?

- How did I choose to make the investments that I've made?
- Do I know how much money or value I've accrued since investing my money?
- How did my parents deal with money?
- How did my parents work well with their money?
- What challenges did my parents have with their money?
- What issues came up for parents around money?
- What kind of relationship did my parents have with money?
- What habits did my parents have with their money?
- How did my parent's habits impact my life?
- What money habits have I implemented in my own life that my parents modeled to me?
- What money habits or patterns would I like to change?
- Do I feel comfortable with my financial literacy?
- In what ways would I like to improve my financial literacy?
- How do I feel when I think about money?
- How do I feel when someone talks about money?
- Do I have enough money? Why?
- Do I feel comfortable knowing that I can easily get more money?
- Do I know how to increase my income?
- Is it easy for me to receive?
- Do I believe I am worthy of having financial freedom? Why?
- What money beliefs have I been told throughout my life? Who told me these beliefs?
- Which money beliefs do I believe, today? Why?
- How do I feel about money?

Okay, now that you've finished answering these questions, take a look over your answers. You may notice a theme showing up for you which can help you better understand the area/s you're being guided to shift or change. Now if looking over your list brings up some emotions for you, that's okay. Breathe, and let any memories, thoughts, feelings, or experiences come to the surface for you.

Now, it's important to increase your overall financial understanding and make some changes where you've been guided. There are many ways to do this and there's not just "one way" or a "right way." There are only the ways that are right for you.

Here are a list of some people who can support you:

- Financial Planner
- Financial Advisor
- Financial Aid Counselor
- Mortgage Consultant
- Personal Accountant
- CPA
- Book keeper
- Personal Banker
- Therapist

You can also go to your local bookstore and go to the finance and business section. You will find a lot of different authors who specialize in a variety of areas within the financial literacy umbrella. You can also go to your local library and see what they have to so you can borrow the books rather than purchasing them if you would prefer.

It's really important to choose professionals to work with that you:

- Like
- Feel Comfortable With
- Feel Respected By
- Feel Talk to You as An Equal
- Believe to Understand Your Needs
- Feel Confident With
- Trust
- Would Want Connecting With Your Money
- Want to Work With

These are all really important factors to take into consideration when hiring someone to support you. Sometimes really sensitive people become timid about asking questions because they don't want to seem like they don't understand something and they don't want to waste someone's time. While these are understandable feelings, it's really important to push through those experiences because you want to make sure that you are choosing people who you feel are the best fit for you. It's also important to remember that just because someone you like or respect works with a particular person, it doesn't mean that person will be the right fit for you. Please trust your gut reactions to the people that you interview and choose the professionals who are the right fit for you.

You can also create a support group with trusted friends or colleagues and brush up on your financial literacy together. Some clients tell me that they have a meeting once a month to discuss a different topic with their group and often bring in a professional to teach them about their topic of the month. This can create a community which will allow you to feel comfortable learning new things while also knowing that you aren't the only person working on their financial relationship. This can also create a safe place to ask questions and to get support from the people within your group.

No matter how you approach making healthy changes to your financial relationship, you will yield positive dividends. Remember that it's okay to go at your own pace and to start where you're standing. Try not to focus on all the things that you don't know but rather approach this topic as an opportunity to learn more and to increase your financial situation in the process. It doesn't matter how old you are or how much experience you have with money. You do have the ability to make positive changes in this area, and you can start today.

31.

Framily

Framily is a made up word which is a hybrid of friend and family. This word refers to the friend family that you create for yourself; sometimes this is also referred to as your tribe. This is a powerful group of people that you have in your inner circle who you love and support and who do the same for you. This group doesn't usually have biological family members within it; it can but usually this group is made up of non-biological (or adoptive) family members. A framily tends to be filled with people who you feel deeply connected to and they become the family you create for yourself.

I work with a lot of highly sensitive people and one of the most common themes that I find among them is feeling disconnected or very different from their biological (or adopted) families. Many clients report feeling like the odd one out within their family. Some feel that everyone in their family speaks the same language while they feel like complete strangers who were never provided with the information on how to be a member of that particular family. Others report feeling and knowing that they were placed into their families to be helpers and support people but always knew they weren't really a part of the family. Rather, they always knew they were providing some kind of service and found themselves on the edges or fringe of the family dynamic.

The experience of feeling like an outsider within the family can be very lonely and challenging. Some people try a variety of ways to try and bridge the experience of being the different one within their family. Often times it can lead to more heart hurt, sadness, and even in some cases isolation. If this hits home for you it's really important for you to know that you are not the only one and this isn't because you aren't trying hard enough to fit in with your family.

In addition to feeling disconnected from primary family relationships, I find highly sensitive people can also experience challenges within friendship relationships. In the same way that families can single out the helper within the family, acquaintances and colleagues often do the same. So, the sensitive person can then experience a repeating pattern in their life where people only connect with them for support, help, or to gain something. (Many people aren't doing this use the sensitive person, some are, but many don't realize they're doing it.) This can feel overwhelming and can lead to a compounding effect where the sensitive person feels like an outsider yet again.

I find that there are two main pathways that people take who find themselves in this situation.

First: They continue to interact in social situations and within their relationships on a somewhat surface level. Because the sensitive person feels that people don't want to take the time or care to get to know who they really are, they feel like they live two lives. The life when they're around others which feels like a caricature of who they really are and then their true life which they experience for the most part when they're alone.

Second: They pull away almost completely from any kind of social situation to the best of their ability because it's too draining, hurtful, and lonely.

Overtime, both of these pathways can lead to sadness, loneliness, and the belief that they don't belong anywhere.

Breathe Through It:

If you're reading this and you feel a tug at your heart and a lump in your stomach because you relate to this situation, breathe. It's okay. You're not alone and nothing is wrong with you. This topic brings up so much for highly sensitive people and they can often recall many experiences in their lives, even as children where they felt isolated, different, and outside of the cultural family and or friend norm.

Take a few moments to pay attention to any thoughts, memories, or feelings that are coming up for you right now. Then, gently scan your body for any places or spaces where you could be holding any tension. (Especially in your neck, shoulders, chest, and stomach.) Take a deep breath, in through your nose and out through your mouth as you simultaneously release the tension in your physical body. Good. Do this 3 more times or until you feel your body release and relax.

You may even feel guided to journal about any memories that came up for you that still evoke a lot of emotions. Healing is a process, and even if something happened _____ time ago, it doesn't mean that it's no longer impacting you. The more you can feel and move through your emotions as they come to the surface the more you will be able to clear away another layer.

Activity:

Building a Framily

Creating a Framily is a powerful way to not only create and foster real and lasting relationships, it also allows you to create a community which matches who you are. Framilies allow you to be yourself while experiencing the same level of love, support, honesty, and dedication that you so easily give to others.

Building your Framily is something that will happen organically, you can't rush the process but you have to invest the time and energy along the way. So, that means that you as a highly sensitive person have to let people see and meet the real you. I know, that can feel really frightening especially if you've had challenging experiences with family and "friends" in the past.

However, the only way you will be able to find your people is by letting yourself be seen. There's no one way or right way to do this. There's just the ways that are right for you; and these things may vary based on how you're feeling on any particular day.

Here are some suggestions on how to begin building your family:

- ❖ Go to places that you like and meet like minded people
  - o Bookstore
  - o Café
  - o Art Supply
  - o Music Venue and or Music Store
  - o Animal Sanctuary
  - o Volunteer Organizations

- - Theatre or Play House
- ❖ Join an organization that resonates with you and your beliefs and passions
- ❖ Take a class
- ❖ Join a community, including online communities

Once you find some places that feel like a fit for you; be yourself. This may feel a little bit awkward at first because you may feel some old anxieties or fears come up for you. It's important to give yourself permission to be the real you so that the people who match you will find you. In fact the more that you can let down and be the 100% real you, the easier it will be to find members of your framily.

Give yourself permission to say yes to invitations and activities with these new people who match you and who take the time to get to know the real you. Overtime you'll find that you have incredibly loving people in your world, in fact you may even call them your very own framily.

I've worked with people who thought they could never have equality based and loving relationships in their life and wanted to give up all together. However, having even one or two framily members became a huge game changer for them in so many ways.

Love yourself enough to let yourself be seen, the whole you, quirks and all. Love yourself enough to bring your framily members into your life. You'll find that there are so many loving, supportive, and kind people who would be overjoyed to call you framily. I promise you, you're absolutely worth it.

32.

10 Minute Quickies

We are living in a time where humans are over stressed, working nearly around the clock, and in almost constant communication due to technological advances. While there are a lot of positives that come with technology there's also a down side that people may not talk about but can definitely feel on a daily basis. We no longer have a time of the day where the calls stop and the time belongs solely to us. There's no more allocated down time or off the clock time. At a time in our history where you can reach someone no matter where they live on the planet with the click of a button, we're learning how to create and experience balance within our day to day modern lives.

While there's a lot of talk about the importance of carving out down time on a regular basis, the rubber meets the road when it comes to implementing this down time. There has been a lot of empirical research investigating the sliding scale of health issues, relationship breakdowns, and other negative side effects of our current communication issues. You can find information about the importance of slowing down, unplugging, and mastering your own schedule in nearly every periodical available; scientific and mainstream.

The real issue becomes why it's so challenging for people to implement change in this area. Nearly every client I work with has some aspect of this situation as an area to work on within their lives. Of course there's a sliding scale depending upon the person's life and work demands but across the board it's an issue that everyone seems to want to reign in on some level.

I've found that the issue isn't so much about failing to acknowledge that it's a problem and has become an invasive part of their life but rather how to carve out the time to help them feel more like themselves again. The slippery slope comes in when people already feel overscheduled with to do lists and don't want to add anything else to those lists. The things that tend to get dropped off the lists become things like:

- Self Care
- Downtime
- Rest
- Creativity
- Exercise
- Sleep
- Getting Outside Into Nature
- Eating Good Food
- Connecting With Loved Ones In Person

In fact, many times clients will tell me that they have trouble breathing and feel tightness in their chests throughout a lot of the day. Some have told me that they don't remember the last time they spent a portion of the day doing something for themselves. Many people also report that they feel guilty taking any downtime for themselves because they feel they should be doing something more productive and tackling more items on their to do lists.

One of the most common beliefs I find in this situation is that the person has every intention to make time to rest, go outside, get to yoga, read a physical book, or do something else for themselves. In fact, for many people it's on the list of things to get done that particular day. They believe that as items get cleared off the list, the list will organically move up and they will finally be able to do something for themselves once their name reaches the top. However, as items get checked off the list, new tasks auto fill into the same spaces, so their name never moves to the top. In some cases this can go on for weeks, months, and even longer. This leads to burn out. This also leads to a compounding effect where the person feels like they're failing and that something is inherently wrong with them. This is not true.

Breathe Through It:

If this topic resonates with you and feel overwhelmed, anxious, or stressed while reading this, please take a moment to breathe in through your nose and out your mouth. This isn't meant to create even more overwhelm for you but rather to identify the multifaceted layers of this issue and to reassure you that this is an issue that nearly everyone is working through in varying degrees. Even if you feel like you're at an extreme end of the spectrum, that's okay. In fact it means that there's lots of room for you to swing the pendulum back; even if that means moving it little by little in increments that feel doable for you.

Some of the physical red flags the body begins to wave when it's time to make some changes in scheduling include but are not limited to:

- ❖ Increased Stress and Stress Symptoms
- ❖ Weight Change, Weight Gain or Weight Loss Rather Quickly
- ❖ Sleep Disturbances Including Insomnia
- ❖ Bloating and or Weight Gain in the Lower Abdomen, Hips, and Thighs
- ❖ Exhaustion
- ❖ Fatigue

- ❖ Lethargy
- ❖ Intense Mood Swings

It's important to talk with your health care professional if you're experiencing any symptoms that are unusual for you. But these will give you an idea of some of the common experiences that can show up when your body is out of balance.

Activity:

I've found that similar to investing small amounts of money into a savings account (or even into a piggy bank) yields big dividends over time; so too does investing in your down time. Because people are so overscheduled it can be challenging to find ways to maximize time especially in the beginning of making changes to your schedule.

So, I've found this method to work really well without creating additional stress, or worry about making big changes to your schedule. I call it the 10 minute quickie. (I know, feel free to call it anything else that feels right for you.)

Four times a day you are going to participate in a 10 minute quickie. It's really imperative that you don't write these 10 minute sessions into your book or schedule. For those of you who still use a physical calendar like I do, I understand how much you love connecting with your day planner, but this technique works best another way.

In your cell phone or in your electronic calendar that you can connect to your phone, you're going to schedule in 4 ten minute blocks of time. If you prefer to set an alarm right into your cell phone, you would set it up just like a wake up call. Choose 4 times throughout the day and schedule your phone alarm to go off. I recommend choosing a tone that's different from your actual wake up alarm tone.

If you know which times of day are particularly challenging for you, set an alarm for those times. Then, when your alarm chimes, treat it with the same respect as you would any other important and VIP task in your schedule. When your alarm chimes, physically push away from your work and "stop, drop, and breathe."

You can do this at your desk, but if you can also get up and walk around or go the rest room to get away from your work that would be great. Then for 10 minutes, focus on your breathing without doing anything else. Don't check your email, social media, text messages, news updates, etc.

Many people don't breathe properly which can lead to the heaviness or tightness in the chest which comes from mouth breathing. (Mouth breathing is a stress response not our natural breathing state.) So, after you strop, drop, and breathe you'll want to take a deep breath in through your nose, hold your breath at the top of the breath for a count of two, exhale out your mouth, hold the breathe again for a count of two and repeat. You'll notice that your entire body begins to release, relax, and move into a state of quiet release. Pushing away from your work and solely focusing on your breathing will help to calm and clear your mind and support you in coming back into a state of balance and respite. It's possible to do this breathing technique anywhere since you're always breathing; the important thing here is to actually do it.

If you can walk around or even get outside during these 10 minute quickies, that's even better but it's not necessary.

I like to write in a positive message for each of the 4 alarms as another layer of support. So, if you tend to have mantras or affirmations that really help you, program them into your alarms so when it shows why your alarm is going off you'll read one of your favorite mantras before you stop, drop, and breathe.

This is an effective and easy way to begin to bring down time and balance back into your schedule. This doesn't take a lot of time and you don't need to go anywhere or spend any money to benefit from this exercise. Ten minutes makes a huge impact in the way that you'll feel as you begin to implement this technique in your day to day life. I've found that by adding this simple shift into the day, people feel more grounded, more focused, and less stressed. People have also told me that by using this method, they were able to make even more scheduling changes because they felt better, worked more effectively throughout the day and had more time to invest in themselves.

33.

Affirmations and Mantras

People have been using affirmations and mantras for hundreds of years to support them in a variety of life areas. In our western culture, the work of Louise L. Hay has been prominent in supporting people in understanding the benefits and positive change that comes from using affirmations and mantras in our daily lives. We now have research that supports the positive changes and shifts that come from adopting and including affirmations and mantras into our lives.

Affirmations and mantras can be one word, a small phrase, or a longer sentiment to support a specific area of your life. I find that many people gain a great deal of support from including mantras into their world. I also find that affirmations and mantras support people in releasing or breaking glass ceilings that they previously held for themselves for one reason or another. I find that sometimes people hold onto limiting beliefs that a person of position set for them whether that was a teacher, parent, work supervisor, or partner. Many times people are unaware that they're still holding onto these glass ceilings but areas of their life reflect that they are in fact holding themselves within a boundary that doesn't need to be a part of their life. Changing the way you speak about yourself allows your brain and body to change the way that you do things which allows you to make changes in the way you move through your world. Limiting beliefs become self fulfilling prophecies which can compound the belief that we aren't _____ enough. However, by shifting something as seemingly small as the language you use, you can shatter those glass ceilings. A new self fulfilling prophecy can then begin; one in which you're able to experience forward motion in an area where you may have felt it wasn't possible in the past.

Are actions a part of this process toward positive change? Absolutely! One of the largest stumbling blocks that I've found in working with clients within this area relates directly to this piece about action. Affirmations and mantras open the space for change to begin to take place and for that change to continue. However, actions steps must be taken to create the positive changes that you're trying to enact. Sometimes clients tell me that they're spending a significant amount of time investing in their mantras but they don't feel like anything is changing for them. When we talk about the ideas, nudges, or feelings they've received about taking action they nearly always tell me they've been feeling like they should do _____. This is the next piece in working with affirmations and mantras; it's walking through the open door that presents itself by changing the way you've been thinking about yourself up to this point. Taking action is what leads to the next piece of your life shifting, moving forward, and new opportunities coming together. As you continue to take action you will be presented with a new door to walk through and then another one and so on.

Think of the analogy of someone who wants to have their own website but doesn't feel they have what it takes to make that happen. The person could create affirmations and mantras to support them in seeing themselves as someone who can achieve their goal of having their own site. Maybe they need to work through some self esteem and self worth issues. Perhaps there's also some old fear or messages about their technology skill set, and perhaps someone told them in the past that they aren't the kind of person who has what it takes to be a blogger, online shop owner, or to maintain an online presence. While working through these glass ceilings eventually there will come a time when the person needs to either learn to build out a site on their own or hire someone to help them. All the mantras in the world won't create that site, action must be taken to bring the dream or desire into fruition. However, the affirmation and mantra work can help to bolster their self esteem and confidence level so that they feel ready to reach out and take action. Affirmations and mantras work hand in hand with the physical human action steps which allow change to happen.

Everyone can use these powerful tools to bring positive changes into their world. In fact there is no one way to use these tools, there are a variety of ways and the best way is to use the one's which resonate with you. I've seen people change extreme limited beliefs systems by changing the way they talk about themselves and I've watched them let go of painful life experiences in exchange for more peace and happiness. It's possible for you to incorporate these tools into your own life too. It doesn't have to take a lot of time or energy to implement them.

Breathe Through It:

If you're reading this and you're thinking, "Yeah I want to believe that this could work for me and my situation but here's all the reasons that it won't work, _____." Take a deep breath and release the list that you're running through your mind about all the things that could go wrong or how this doesn't really apply to you. The truth is that the list that you're running through your mind and that you carry with you through the day is a mantra. Believing that in some way your situation alone won't allow you to benefit from using affirmations is in and of itself a glass ceiling that you're reinforcing daily. Your list of why this doesn't work is your affirmation.

By no means am I trying to diminish a challenging life situation, challenge, or any grief that you could be experiencing. However, affirmations allow us to first become cognizant of the personal beliefs and limiting thoughts we place upon ourselves which can ultimately keep us in the same place for long periods of time.

Incorporating a mantra doesn't cost anything at all, and the benefits in the way you will think and feel about yourself will pay you back in large dividends. The truth is that how we feel about ourselves drives the direction of the way we move through our world.

Moving in the direction of the life that you want for yourself, even if in small increments is worth it. You're worth it. It is possible for you to move from where you are today, right now in this moment to a place that you want for yourself. It can begin by the way you talk and think about yourself. Rebuilding the foundation of your life begins from within.

Activity:

There are many ways to incorporate affirmations and mantras into your daily life. Below you'll find some ideas to get you started. This is not a be all end all list but rather something to get you started. Please feel free to adjust the ideas below to make them your own and create something especially for you based on what feels like a fit for you.

- ❖ Write positive phrases on post it notes and tape them to your bathroom mirror so you can read them while you're getting ready in the morning.
- ❖ Program your mantras or affirmations to go off as alarms on your phone at specific times of the day.
- ❖ Walk your mantras into your body by repeating your mantras while you walk or go about your day.
- ❖ You can create an MP3 file on freeware like Audacity or Garage Band with your affirmations and mantras and listen to them while you're doing chores, working out, or when you're taking some down time.
- ❖ You can use a physical tactile system like mala beads. You can say your mantras as you move bead by bead through the 108 beads on a mala.
- ❖ Create a wallpaper for your computer with your affirmations or mantras so you see it when you sit down to work.
- ❖ Write your mantras on a piece of paper and place them in a special place in your home or office so you can work with them during quiet moments of your day.

Here are some Affirmations and Mantras that you can use and adapt to your own needs. Again, please adjust these so they work for you.

- ❖ I am loveable
- ❖ I am love
- ❖ I am whole, healthy, and complete
- ❖ I am smart
- ❖ I bring a lot to the table in all areas of my life
- ❖ I am comfortable in my own skin
- ❖ I love myself

- ❖ I allow my true self to be seen by others
- ❖ I let go of hiding my true self
- ❖ I am capable of moving outside my comfort zone
- ❖ I am capable of creating a life that I love
- ❖ I am worthy of living a life of happiness, peace, and joy
- ❖ I am peaceful
- ❖ Kind loving people are a part of my life
- ❖ People respect me
- ❖ People treat me with kindness and love
- ❖ I respect myself
- ❖ I am comfortable saying no
- ❖ I know where my boundaries are and I honor them
- ❖ I honor my boundaries with everyone within my life
- ❖ I know who I am and I love myself
- ❖ I know that I'm perfect just the way I am
- ❖ I am comfortable choosing a life that resonates with me and my dreams
- ❖ I honor the goals that I set for myself
- ❖ I take time to rest, rejuvenate, and relax on a daily basis
- ❖ I let go of any guilt in taking care of myself
- ❖ I know that taking care of myself is an investment in my overall health and wellbeing
- ❖ I choose to honor the natural rhythms of my body
- ❖ I know what my body is telling me and I listen and take action accordingly
- ❖ I sleep peacefully at night
- ❖ I give myself permission to rest
- ❖ I am gentle with myself
- ❖ I am healthy
- ❖ I take care of myself
- ❖ I treat myself with dignity and respect

- I fuel my body with fresh fruit and vegetables
- I honor my body
- Exercise is natural for me
- I enjoy exercise
- Moving my body is good for me body, mind, and spirit
- Moving my body feels natural for me
- I let go of things and people who are weighing me down
- I let go of the past
- I clear the clutter in my life so I can feel light and free
- I live in a clean and organized home
- I am worthy of living in a home which rises up to greet me
- My home is welcoming, comforting, and soothing to me
- I live in a safe home
- I believe in myself
- I invest in myself
- I use positive thoughts, language and imagery to describe myself
- I invest in my creativity
- Creativity is natural for me
- I enjoy creating things for myself and others
- Creativity is a worthwhile investment in all areas of my life
- As I invest in creativity, I feel calm, supported, and nurtured
- My creative expression is an important part of who I am
- I respect my creativity and make time for it regularly

- ❖ I allow myself to receive
- ❖ It is easy for me to receive
- ❖ I am valuable
- ❖ I am worthy of receiving good
- ❖ Receiving feels natural for me
- ❖ I am abundant
- ❖ I open my arms to receive the blessings and abundance available to me now
- ❖ I see myself as abundant
- ❖ I know that this is an abundant planet and there is more than enough for everyone
- ❖ I have healthy and loving friendships in my life
- ❖ My partner is kind, compassionate and respectful of me and my needs
- ❖ The people in my life treat me with respect, understanding, and love
- ❖ I am a great friend
- ❖ I am a loyal and trustworthy person
- ❖ I easily attract kind and honest people into my life
- ❖ I believe in myself
- ❖ I know that I can follow my dreams
- ❖ It's safe for me to make life changes
- ❖ Change feels good to me
- ❖ I commit to my dreams and to myself
- ❖ I keep my promises to myself
- ❖ I know that I am enough
- ❖ I allow myself to feel my feelings
- ❖ My feelings are valuable and trustworthy
- ❖ My sensitivity is a gift
- ❖ I honor and respect my sensitivity
- ❖ I listen to and trust the feelings that I get
- ❖ I know that it is safe to trust my feelings
- ❖ I trust myself

Part Three

Spiritual Support

34.

Prayer

Prayer is a spiritual tool that can support you in opening up to information, ideas, solutions, divine guidance, and divine intervention. Prayer also opens the doorway for a conversation and relationship between you and the divine.

There are many ways to pray, some of them are very formal while others are more natural or organic forms of praying. There is no one way or right way to pray, as all prayer is equally valid and valuable. Finding the ways that feel like a fit for you is what's important. When you find a prayer practice that feels like a fit for your style and your life you will make time to foster and nurture it while also enjoying your time in prayer.

There are two umbrella types of prayer if you will, supplication and affirmative.

Supplication Prayer is a style which focuses on asking for help. Such as, "Please help me with _____."

Affirmative prayer focuses on using statements made in the positive and focusing on gratitude for the help already being given. Such as, "Thank you so much for resolving and healing this _____."

There are lots of feelings about which style is a better fit; however all prayer is heard and answered. The more that you nurture your prayer practice, you'll find the style that works best for you. You may find that on some days or in some situations one style is better for you and that you enjoy using both prayer styles.

Breathe Through It:

Prayer can bring up a lot of emotions, memories, and at times challenging feelings due to any kind of negative experience that may be connected to prayer for you. If you're experiencing any stress, tension, or intense memories right now, take a moment to breathe. You may want to physically move your body to shake out any trapped emotions that could be showing up as tension. If you feel like tears want to come to the surface, give yourself permission to let them come up and out.

Sometimes prayer can be connected to a traumatizing experience with an organized religion, an outcome of a situation where it may feel like your prayers weren't answered, or even feelings of guilt or shame. It's important to allow yourself to move through your feelings without stuffing them down or believing that you should or shouldn't feel a particular way due to the length of time that has passed since the incident.

If you find that you're experiencing a lot of intense emotions surrounding this issue on a consistent basis, you may want to reach out for support from someone you trust. You can reach out to a therapist, grief counselor, trusted friend, family member, or other trusted professional.

Activity:

As you invest time in your prayer practice, you will notice that you can easily move into a place of open dialog and connection with the divine. On your pathway to finding and creating a practice that works for you, you may want to try different kinds of prayer.

Below you will find some suggestions to increase your prayer practice. These are by no means the only ways to pray, but rather a place to get you started in finding the ways that are a fit for you and your practice. Please create and nurture your practice in the ways that are right for you.

Structured Prayer:

This can include attending formal church or temple services, reciting formal prayers either silently or out loud, or participating in any prayer rituals that you enjoy. (Example, praying at a specific time each day.)

Prayer Groups:

There are many ways to participate in prayer groups. Most spiritual communities have a prayer group or groups that people can join. There are virtual prayer communities available at the click of a button if you don't feel comfortable or don't know where to go to join an in person group. You could also start a prayer group with like minded friends and or neighbors.

Prayer Beads:

Prayer beads have been used as a way to mark or count prayers for many years. Some people really enjoy the process of saying a prayer for each bead on the string. There is also a beautiful tactile connection that happens as you hold the beads in your hands. Prayer beads can be found at most spiritual bookstores and sometimes at places like yoga studios and other spiritually minded places.

Mala Beads, Rosary Beads, and Prayer Bracelets are common prayer beads that are easily accessible. They come in a variety of shapes, sizes, colors, and materials. If you enjoy having a physical connection while you pray you may enjoy trying prayer beads.

Personal Prayer/Internal Dialog:

This type of prayer is often an internal dialog and silent prayer (not always). This prayer style is often more individualized and organic and something that you create. Some people describe this style of prayer as a conversation where you feel free to talk in the way that feels right for you. Many times this prayer is silent but not always. If you feel guided to talk out loud that's great too. There is no one way or right way, simply the way that is right for you at the time. I find that because this prayer style is so personal, people find what feels like a fit for them and really enjoy nurturing their personal prayer/internal dialog practice.

Global Scheduled Prayers:

This style of prayer can be done in person or virtually with a group of people who are praying for a common issue or cause at a specific time. Many people will join together to pray for a common reason, such as global peace. Often people will choose a time to pray and then either everyone prays at the same exact time to amplify the prayers or people will create a wave of prayers by praying at the same time in their own time zones. For example, either everyone will pray at 1:00 pm pacific time; or everyone will pray at 1:00 pm no matter where they live.

Bedtime Prayers:

Praying before bed is often a common time that people pray. For some, this is a part of their daily prayer practice and can be the time during the day when they do their prayer. For others this may be one of the times they pray throughout the day. Praying before bed helps to clear from anything that has happened throughout the day and can support a letting down and clearing of the mind. It's also a perfect time to ask for good dreams, protection during dream time, and protection over your home and all who live with you while you sleep.

Some people use a specific prayer for bedtime, especially with children while other people use a more personalized or internal dialog style prayer.

Special Event Prayers:

These are prayers that you may say for special events that happen within your life. For some people these kinds of prayers may be used every day depending on their situation.

Some examples include but are not limited to:

- ❖ Travel
- ❖ Exams
- ❖ Children (Praying for your children or someone else's.)
- ❖ Loved One with High Risk Employment (Such as Police Officer, Social Worker, Fire Fighter, Emergency Room Health Professional or Other First Responder)
- ❖ Any Specific Issue (Job Interview, Moving to a New Home, Giving a Lecture)

Prayer Lists:

Prayer Lists can be formal and informal. Many spiritual communities have prayer lists where people can add their names and prayer requests and people within the community or congregation will pray on their behalf. Many times there is a specific amount of time that the community will pray for everyone on the list and it is often disclosed when you submit your name or the name of a loved one.

You can start a prayer list if you feel guided, and you can add the names of loved ones and or issues you're passionate about and then create a prayer practice for your list. You may feel guided to let people know about your prayer list or you can invite people to be included in your prayer list if you feel so inclined.

Outdoor Prayer:

Some people find that their connection to spirit is most accessible to them when they are outdoors within nature. If you enjoy being outside and find that your mind and body clear when you're outdoors, you may find that you enjoy outdoor prayer. Again, there is no one way to do this, just the ways that feel most comforting and supportive for you.

Some people find that walking while praying helps them to focus and get clear communication time with the divine. Some people describe this prayer as a full body experience because of the tactile component. Movement also increases oxygen which allows for clearer thinking which can support more focus while praying.

If you enjoy doing repetition prayers, you may enjoy walking while repeating your prayers.

Writing Prayers/Prayer Letters:

For people who love to write and who feel their communication is most clearly articulated through writing, this may be a prayer style that feels like a fit.

The writing can be done with a computer, tablet, or a paper and pen. Set aside a little bit of time, and then when you feel guided, you can write your prayer. Some people enjoy writing their prayer in a letter format, but it's not necessary. Use whatever writing style you enjoy, including lists, letter, or freeform.

Once the prayer is finished you can choose to keep it somewhere special or you can release it. If you've typed it and you want to release it you can simply delete it or you can print it out and physically release it.

For hand written and printed prayers, you can release your prayer in any way that feels right for you.
Here are a few suggestions:

- ❖ Outside in a well ventilated area, you can light your prayer allowing it be released as the paper burns away.
- ❖ You can bury your prayer in your garden or flower bed.
- ❖ You can place your prayer into your compost bin.

SOS or Emergency Prayers:

These prayers are exactly what they sound like, they are the "I need help now" prayers. These prayers are powerful and even though they may be short and to the point, they are no less powerful than a long formal prayer practice.

God Box Prayers:

A God box is a box where you can place prayer requests for yourself, your loved ones, any issue that you need help with, or anything at all. A God box can be anything that you want to use to hold your prayer requests. Some people will get a box and decorate it with things that they love and that represents them. Some people will find a box that's already made and designate it as their God Box. You can use a Mason Jar, Coffee Can, Shoebox, or anything you have around your home. Decoupage, glitter, stickers, or anything that you want to use to decorate your God Box will work.

Once you have your box, simply write the prayer requests you have on pieces of paper and stick them into your box. This work especially well if you find yourself having trouble letting go of a particular situation. By placing your requests into the box you're asking God to take your situation from you and to intervene and give you help.

You don't have to worry about how you write your requests or what the paper looks like that you place into your God box. Just breathe, write, and release.

I hope this chapter has inspired you to nurture or begin a prayer practice that matches you. I hope that it's also sparked some ideas of ways that you can personalize your prayer practice. Remember there is no one way or right way to pray; there are only the ways that are right for you and they may change from day to day or depending upon your situation.

35.

Meditation

There are so many benefits gained from investing in a meditation practice on a consistent basis. In the last 10 years there has been an influx of data, research, and information about the physical, mental, emotional, spiritual and overall and well being benefits that are connected to meditation. You can even find articles and information about beginning a meditation practice in mainstream magazines; including the ones about gardening and creating beautiful homes. The benefits of meditation are not new, in fact they have been well known and documented for many, many years. What is new, especially in the western world is the influx of meditation practices and principles being folded into the fabric of our modern world. You no longer have to hunt for a meditation group, instructors or classes, nor feel awkward mentioning your practice in varying social and professional circles.

With all of the information and access to meditation you may think that it would be easy for people to make meditation a part of their everyday life. For some, it is and they nurture and foster their meditation practice consistently. For others, I've found it can be a little bit more challenging. I've had clients tell me that they don't know where to begin because they feel inundated with so much information. Others have told me that they feel like they won't be able to meditate correctly so they don't try. Some have told me that they have such a challenging time focusing that they become frustrated and stop their practice before it really begins.

No matter where you fall within the meditation practice spectrum; the big key is in finding the style or styles of meditation that are a good fit for you. While meditation itself brings positive benefits to everyone, it's not necessarily a one size fits all when finding the meditation style that is right for you. So, if you've gone to your best friend's meditation group, the one she swears you're going to love because she knows you as well as you know yourself and you don't have any desire to return to that group, take heart. Just because one meditation style is a fit for someone, doesn't necessarily mean that it's going to be a fit for you and that's okay. It also doesn't mean that you aren't able to meditate nor does it mean that meditation isn't for you.

Most often when I've worked with clients who feel they've bumped into a wall around this topic, it's because they haven't found the right fit. A lot of times it's also because they don't realize the big umbrella that is meditation. Many times they're already meditating but don't realize it because it looks differently than they expected.

Breathe Through It:

If you feel a bit overwhelmed just reading about meditation, that's okay. If you notice any tension or tightness in your neck, shoulders, and chest; take a moment to breathe and move your body. If you're telling yourself any kind of messages about how you're the one person who can't meditate, or that it's too hard, or _____. Stop the story you've been telling yourself about your ability to meditate and be open to the possibility that you just haven't found the right style for you yet.

If you're reading this and you feel a knot in your stomach and you find yourself thinking, gosh I really need to get back to my practice, take a breath. Remember that if you've taken a break from your practice, it's okay; you can begin again at any time. Give yourself permission to reconnect with your personal practice and give yourself permission to release any feelings of guilt around taking a break. It's okay to take a break.

Activity:

Giving yourself permission to try new and different ways to meditate will allow you to find the styles that are right for you. You may find that one particular style really speaks to you and feels like coming home. Or you may find that a few styles really feel like a fit for you depending on your particular situation or disposition on any particular day.

Below you will find some suggestions to begin or increase your meditation practice. These are by no means the only ways to meditate, but rather a place to get you started in finding the ways that are a fit for you and your practice. Please create and nurture your practice in the ways that are right for you.

Guided Meditation

This kind of meditation is great because you don't have to do anything or try to make anything happen. If you find that meditation has been challenging for you in the past or you are worried that you won't be able to quiet your mind, this may be a style that works well for you. All you have to do when participating in Guided Meditation is relax and listen, similar to listening to someone read you a story. If you enjoyed people reading to you as a child (or an adult) you may find that you really resonate with this style of meditation.

In honor of supporting you in trying different styles of meditation; here is a link to a Free Meditation MP3 that I created. http://eepurl.com/b93pc1 Just type this link into your browser and download your free meditation. I created this to support you in releasing stress and tension and increase rest, relaxation, and rejuvenation. I sell this in my store but I want you to have the opportunity to experience the benefits of guided meditation as my gift to you.

Group Meditation

This style of meditation can cover a large group of meditation styles as a whole. So, you may find that there's an opportunity to participate in a Group Guided Meditation session or a Group Chanting Meditation Session. It simply refers to participating in a meditation experience with a group of other people.

Savasana

This style of meditation happens at the end of a yoga class and is a very relaxing and restful meditation. Depending on the instructor, this meditation can vary from class to class.

Lotus Position Meditation

This tends to be the image many people imagine when someone talks about meditation. You may have had that experience yourself. This style of meditation is often pictured in movies and even silk screened onto t-shirts. It's called Lotus position because it refers to the yoga pose called Lotus Pose or Padmasana. With feet crossed over the knees, the person rests the backs of their hands on their knees, palms facing up as they meditate.

This is a wonderful yoga pose and posture for meditation if this resonates for you. Please don't try to force yourself into Lotus Pose if you aren't currently practicing yoga. If you would like to bring yoga into your life, please work with a trained professional yoga instructor. Yoga is a wonderful way to meditate while learning about the principles and applications of meditation.

Visualization Meditation

This style of meditation can be solitary or experienced in a group setting. During guided meditations, many times you will be lead through a visualization experience. You can experience visualization meditation on your own by getting quiet, closing your eyes, slowing your breath, and visualizing things, places, or people that feel comforting for you. Often times this style of meditation is referred to as "going to your happy place" which is often depicted in movies with a character in their therapist's office. There is no one right place to go during this style of meditation, just what is right for you.

Chanting/Toning/Sound Therapy

If you enjoy sound and sound therapy, this may be a great fit for you. There are numerous musicians who have MP3 files and CD's you can purchase and use during your meditation. You can learn to chant and tone as well as play sound therapy instruments. There are also many group meditation circles you can attend where the musician/sound therapist plays incredible instruments while you rest, lie down, and listen.

Conscious Breath Work

There are many different kinds of breath work that you can learn. Each will allow you to have a better understanding of the importance of breath, how to deepen your breathing, and ways that the breath contributes to overall health, wellbeing, and your meditation practice.

Moving Meditation

This is one of the most common forms of meditation and often times isn't recognized as meditation. When you participate in a Moving Meditation you are physically moving your body in a way that you enjoy; and as you relax into the activity, you begin to move into a meditative state.

Here are a few examples of a Moving Meditation:

- ❖ Walking
- ❖ Running
- ❖ Dancing
- ❖ Yoga
- ❖ Riding a Bike
- ❖ Swimming
- ❖ Hiking
- ❖ Fly Fishing
- ❖ Washing Your Car (If you enjoy washing your car)
- ❖ Gardening
- ❖ Creating (Makers, Writers, Artists, Designers, Inventors)

Any activity that you enjoy which allows you to get above your racing thoughts and decompress while moving, places you into a state of Moving Meditation. This is one of the reasons people feel so good when doing activities they enjoy and why they feel less stressed after participating.

Music

This could easily be placed into the Moving Meditation section above. However, it's important to know that music allows people to move into a meditative state even if you aren't playing an instrument. Listening to music, creating music, and singing or humming along to music allows you to move into a meditative state.

Communing with Nature

Nature has a natural calming effect and by taking time to get outside in nature, your body will begin to organically rest and let down. You may notice that after being outside for only a few minutes you begin to breathe more slowly and feel tension and stress begin to fall away. If you enjoy being outdoors, this may be a great meditation style for you. Because there are so many things to do outside, you can combine being outdoors with other moving meditations that you enjoy if you feel guided.

You can also make a conscious effort to increase your connection to your senses while outside by:

- ❖ Getting quiet and listening to the sounds you hear
- ❖ Noticing the fragrance of the plants and air
- ❖ Noticing the colors around you
- ❖ Feeling the different textures around you

By doing this you will find yourself physically slowing down and simultaneously moving into a gentle and meditative state.

36.

Spiritual Connection

Many people have told me both professionally and personally that they would like to deepen their connection to their spirituality. Many of these people would then rattle off their own personal list of why they felt disconnected or in some way blocked from this relationship. Some of the most common reasons included fear, not knowing how to connect, belief they couldn't connect, past family/personal trauma, and pain from previous spiritual experiences.

What I know for sure is that everyone, yes, everyone can increase their spiritual connection. Like everything, small steps and actions lead up to big change over time. Sometimes people would tell me that they didn't want to invest the time in fostering a closer relationship with spirit but instead wanted it to just appear out of thin air. A few people have told me that they wanted to go to bed one night and wake up with their connection strong and crystal clear the next morning. While I believe that may be possible for some people, I've found that like all relationships, investing in them regularly leads to healthy, strong relationships over time.

If you find yourself in the camp that wants your connection to deepen really quickly and feel a bit discouraged at the thought of years of nurturing, take heart. The truth is that you can yield the outcome that you want and contribute to its growth based on the rate that you nurture and invest in the relationship. Depending on how much time you give to your spiritual connection, you can adjust the time frame allowing you to move toward your goal more quickly.

Your connection to spirit is like any other relationship that you have in your life. The more that you put in, the more you get out in equal measure. This doesn't have to feel hard, frustrating, or like chores. In fact, it really shouldn't feel that way; it should feel gentle, supportive, and comforting.

There's no one way of fostering this personal connection, there are only the ways that are right for you. They make change from day to day or based on what your needs are at any particular time. As you pay attention to what feels right to you, you will find the right way to invest in this very special and valuable relationship.

I've found that as people invest in this connection, their lives can change in profound ways. There's almost a deep shift or clearing that begins to happen from the inside out. Calm, simplicity, and their core values become evident to them and a deep priority. Things, people, and old ways of living often get released from their lives during this process. I've seen people become genuinely happy, make huge life changes, and embrace health and healthy living more than once. I've also found that people feel lighter, look younger, and have a renewed excitement for their life. I've also found that people stop making themselves last on their list and choose to live the life that is right for them, even if it takes a great deal of courage.

Breathe Through It:

This topic can bring up a lot of issues for people and if you're feeling a lot of emotions coming to the surface or sitting in your chest, it's okay. You may want to take a moment to sit down and move your shoulders and relax your stomach muscles. Do a quick body scan, beginning at the top of your head. Release any tight or tense muscles that you find. Good. Now take a couple of long slow deep breaths, in through your nose and out through your mouth.

If you're noticing any challenging thoughts, memories, or fears coming up for you around this topic, you may want to journal about it or talk to a trusted friend, loved one, coach, or therapist.

Activity:

One of the most supportive ways I found to connect to spirituality is by getting quiet. At this time in our human experience we are inundated with noise, interruptions, and constant contact all day long. It can be challenging to get peace and quiet which can make it even more challenging to foster a relationship with spirit. So, clearing away the chatter and white noise is a powerful way to begin this journey.

Just like any other relationship you have, creating time that's scheduled into your day and week will allow you to stop and invest in the relationship. Even if you're really busy, it's important to honor the time that you've created for this relationship.

In the beginning, taking small segments of time, 15 or 20 minutes is a great place to start. Then, create a space that will allow you to nurture your connection.

Turn Off Your:

- ❖ Phone
- ❖ Computer
- ❖ Tablet
- ❖ Radio
- ❖ Any other noise making device

It's not enough to turn these devices onto silent or to face away from them. Knowing they're on and possibly seeing lights flashing breaks your connection with what you're doing and divides your attention. If you feel anxious thinking about disconnecting from your devices for 15 or 20 minutes, then it's even more important that you spend time powered down and disconnected from them on a regular basis.

Once you've created a calm quiet space to connect, you can choose to use any form or modality of connection that feels right for you. I've listed some ways you can connect below; please know this is not a be all end all list but rather a jumping off place for you to create your own style of connection.

Journaling:

Writing about your feelings and desires for your personal connection to spirit can help you to get a clear understanding of the kind of relationship that you want. This can also open up any issues or fears that could've in the past created some challenges for you in this area.

Meditation:

This is a wonderful way to calm and quiet your mind while exercising your spiritual muscles. Meditation is the bread and butter if you will of spiritual connection. Just like if you wanted to increase your physical muscles, you may begin to work out or hire a personal trainer. Meditation strengthens the spiritual muscles which allows you to have clear communication and insight. There are many ways to meditate. If you're newer to meditation you may want to review the chapter in this book about meditation and try some methods that stand out to you. If you've taken a break from your meditation practice, you may want to pick it back up again.

Prayer:

Prayer allows you to calm and quiet your mind while also connecting to your spiritual support system. There are many ways to pray, and honoring the style that is right for you will be the right fit. You can also ask for support in increasing your spiritual connection during your prayer practice. If you are new to prayer you may want to read the chapter on Prayer in this book. If you have gotten away from your prayer practice and feel guided to get back to it, this may be a good time to reconnect.

Classes and Workshops:

There are a variety of courses and workshops available in person and online covering a large cross section of spirituality. If you feel guided to work with an instructor, you may want to do some research about the courses that are available to you. Like any course work, it's very important to find an instructor that matches you and who has a high integrity and the skill set to teach. Not all courses and instructors are created equally. If it's possible to meet with or connect with (even through websites or social media pages) to get a feel for the person, it would be a good idea. Choosing happy, healthy, and high functioning instructors who walk their walk are a good choice.

Spiritual Tools:

There's a wide range of spiritual tools to help you cultivate your connection to spirit. Whether you feel guided to

- ❖ Read passages or channeled messages from a favorite spiritual book
- ❖ Enjoy using oracle cards to receive a message
- ❖ Feel guided to attend spiritual retreats or prayer groups
- ❖ Travel to and visit spiritual power places on the planet

spiritual tools are a wonderful way to open the door to your connection to spirit.

Solitude:

Taking time away from others just to be with yourself and connect to the things, beliefs, and desires that are important to you is a powerful way to connect to your higher self. You don't have to go away or spend a lot of money to do this. You can do this in the comfort of your own home by carving out quiet time where you won't be interrupted or disturbed by others. If you feel your home is too busy with people coming and going, you can go to a local park, the beach, or other quiet place where you can be alone with your thoughts. It's incredible how quickly we can tap into our higher self and to our spiritual connection when we're away from distractions. It's almost analogous to a heavy velvet curtain being lifted from us so that we can hear, think, see, and feel what we're being guided to do.

Exercise:

Moving and strengthening your physical body allows you to be a clear channel for communication and connection. Your body is the instrument that you've been given to live in while you're here. So the more that you can keep it clean and strong, the better it will allow you to nurture your spiritual relationships.

Personal Passions:

When you invest in the activities that bring you joy, you open up to your higher self. Anytime that you can move into that place where you're connecting with your higher self, it makes it easier to connect with spirit.

Whether you enjoy,

- ❖ playing music
- ❖ writing
- ❖ cooking
- ❖ designing
- ❖ stitching
- ❖ exercising
- ❖ inventing

or any other passion that brings you joy, it is a worthwhile investment.

The more often you connect, in any way that feels right for you the stronger and more clear your connection will be. Go at your own pace and try to be gentle with yourself. This process should be a positive and rewarding experience not one that feels heavy or depleting. You may notice that at the beginning it can be a little bit uncomfortable or awkward but like anything new, there's a little learning curve involved. There could also be some residual nervousness or anxiety from being disconnected from your devices too. Breathe, and go at your own pace.

This is your relationship and you get to choose how to nurture and invest in it based on what you know is right for you.

37.

Energy Work

Energy work is an umbrella term that includes a large group of energy treatment modalities. Energy treatments, which are sometimes referred to as energy healings have been around forever. However, energy work has made its way into more traditional healing environments in the last couple of decades. There are hospitals that have energy work professionals on staff to support patients during their recovery.

There have also been more mainstream people and publications mentioning energy work in the last several years. For example, Dr. Oz has talked about Reiki on his television show and about the efficacy of energy work. There are spas that offer energy treatments on their service menu and it seems that energy treatments and energy professionals are available in more and more places.

Some of the common questions that people ask me about energy work include:

- ❖ What does it feel like?
- ❖ What does it do?
- ❖ Why would someone schedule a treatment?

These are all great questions. The truth is that each energy treatment or modality has its own unique or individual feeling. If you think about the different kinds of massage treatments that are available at a spa, you can get a better understanding of how energy treatments feel different yet move toward a similar goal. Massage helps to move blocks, tension, or tightness from the physical body while bringing the body into a rested state. However, the different kinds of massages achieve that goal in their own individual ways. Depending on the needs or sensitivity of the client, people are drawn to a particular kind of massage over another. This is very similar to the different energy treatments that are available on the treatment menu.

Energy treatments also work to release tension, tightness, blocks, or unease from the physical body, emotional body, and the energy body simultaneously. These treatments often feel relaxing, restorative, gentle, and calming leaving the client feeling lighter and more like themselves when they leave.

There are many reasons people feel guided to schedule an energy treatment.

- ❖ For some, they want to receive support in shifting out anything that feels off, heavy, or stressful within their body.
- ❖ Some people feel guided to maintain a consistent schedule of honoring their self-care and energy treatments are part of their wellness system.
- ❖ Others enjoy the feeling they receive during and after the treatment and enjoy the process.
- ❖ Some combine energy treatments with other physical support systems to move toward their overall health and wellness goals.
- ❖ Some people use energy treatments as a way to help them rest, relax, and restore.

The body, similar to a building is a container and can pick up and hold onto stress and tension. Over time those energies can get trapped inside the body which can lead to physical and even emotional heaviness. If you've ever walked into an attic space or a basement that hasn't been aired out in a while you've experienced the feeling of trapped energy. It can feel heavy, dense, and sometimes has a strange smell. An energy treatment is similar to opening a window, decluttering, and clearing out the attic or a basement. Once it's done it feels like a whole different space, one that's been returned to its former glory. Energy treatments can help to move out those heavy energies that feel stuck inside the body, so that the person feels more like themselves again.

Breathe Through It:

If this seems overwhelming or odd to you, that's okay. There's a lot of information about a large variety of energy treatments available and you can use this as a jumping off place to learn more about them if you feel so inclined. No one is going to force you to have an energy treatment if it doesn't feel like a fit for you.

If you feel excited or interested in learning more about this but aren't sure which treatment is right for you, that's okay. Take your own time to learn more about the different modalities that are available and pay attention to the way you feel when you learn about each one. Your body will tell you what you feel attracted to. Often times, you can find practitioners who offer mini group sessions so you can go with a friend or family member to test the waters and see if it's a fit for you.

Activity:

There are so many different kinds of energy treatments that it's important to research and find the one or ones that are a fit for you. After finding one that really stands out to you, it's really important to find a practitioner who feels like a fit for you. Just like you would look for a dentist, therapist, or massage therapist that you felt comfortable with and felt was a fit for you, so too is it important in finding an energy treatment professional.

You can research people by:

- Visiting their websites
- Sending a message through their contact form
- Calling to ask them questions about their work
- Connecting with them in a group setting prior to scheduling an appointment.
- Asking a trusted friend or family member for a referral

If at any time during your research process there is something that tells you that a particular person doesn't feel right to you, heed that wisdom.

Below you will find some common Energy Treatment Modalities that you may want to learn more about. This is not a be all end all list but merely a jumping off place to spark your interest. Please look into and research any modality that seems interesting to you.

- Reiki
- Chakra Balancing
- Crystal Therapy
- Pranic Healing
- Polarity Balancing
- Angel Therapy®

Once you find a modality that resonates for you and you've found a practitioner that you trust and who feels like a fit for you, schedule your session. You may want to start with a group style session so you can attend with a friend.

I recommend bringing a notebook and something to write with to your session. Many times, practitioners will include a portion at the end of the session where they provide you with information about what shifted, released, and any messages that came through during the session. There may also be follow up instructions and things to expect after the session. It's nice to be able to write these things down so you can reflect on them at a later date.

I tell my clients that similar to a dream state, we think we're going to remember everything that happened and was discussed for days and weeks after the session. However, like a dream sometimes we don't remember everything they way we thought we would. So, writing things down can be a great support to you. It's also nice to have a catalog of any feelings, thoughts, or insights that come to you during or after your session.

Enjoy your energy treatments and exploration into the energy work world. There are so many wonderful things happening and available to support you as continue to move forward on your personal path of peace.

38.

Aromatherapy/Essential Oils

Aromatherapy and Essential Oils have been used for overall wellness and balance throughout human existence. There are writings about the use of plants from many groups throughout history, including but not limited to indigenous tribes and ancient Egypt alike.

Today, we still use plants and oils to support our overall health and well being, and can find or access these support systems in easily accessible places. For example, in most health food stores there's an entire section devoted to essential oils, tinctures, body oils, and other plant based products. There are books about how to use oils for a variety of different issues in mainstream bookstores and I've seen diffusers being used and sold in traditional health care professional offices. It seems that the ancient knowledge and connection with the plant kingdom is being integrated into our modern life and becoming even more available to us.

The benefits from using Aromatherapy and Essential Oils is vast and you can easily find volumes on the subject if you feel guided to learn more about this topic. But, you don't need to be an expert in the subject to benefit from their use and can find ways to incorporate the benefits into your regular day to day life.

I'm a big fan of using Essential Oils and have found that they can make a big positive impact without taking a great deal of time out of your day to enjoy them. There are so many ways to incorporate them into your life, and depending on your lifestyle, personal style, and overall goals, I believe there's a way for everyone to enjoy the use of oils in their own life.

I use oils in my private practice to help create a space that feels welcoming, comforting, and uplifting for clients. I also use oils in my home depending on what I feel will be a good fit for a particular season or feeling that I want to foster, or to help with a particular issue, like a sleep disturbance or stress.

You probably already do this within your home too. Perhaps during the Autumn season you have a desire to smell spices, apple cider, or pumpkin, and light a candle with those combinations. This creates a scent and overall feeling in your home that feels comforting and in alignment with the season. Some candle companies, not all, but some have toxins inside their candles so when you light their candle, the chemicals are being infused into your home and you and your loved ones breathe those chemicals in and they go into the body. Using pure grade essential oils will allow you to get all the benefits of the comforting scents without any of the harmful chemicals.

Essential Oils in addition to smelling wonderful can also aid in soothing physical symptoms within the body. There are many oils that are naturally anti-bacterial and anti-microbial too; so infusing them into your home can naturally clear and purify the air. Using essential oils can help create balance for you physically, emotionally, mentally, and spiritually.

There are so many ways to use and enjoy oils. If you're being guided to learn more about them or incorporate them into your life, give yourself permission to enjoy the process.

Breathe Through It:

If you're noticing that there's any tightness in your body or you notice that you're starting to hold your breath. That's okay, take a deep breathe in through your nose and out through your mouth. Sometimes, people can feel a bit overwhelmed thinking about all of the information that's available on this topic. Even if you're brand new to learning about Essential Oils or Aromatherapy and they're not something that you've ever used before, that's okay. I promise that you don't need a graduate degree in plant science to receive the benefits of using oils. In fact, the great thing about learning something new is enjoying the process and going at your own pace.

There are a lot of great books available that cover the most commonly used oils including their benefits and ways to use them. In fact some of my favorite books are written in a "hand book" style so you can flip to the oil or issue that you're wondering about and you can find the information easily. You can find these books at your local bookstore or by researching from the comfort of your own home online.

If you're intrigued, interested, or feel guided to use oils, then take this as an opportunity to learn what kinds of oils you enjoy and try different ways to include them in your daily life. Relax, enjoy, and have fun with the process.

Activity:

Because there are so many ways to use oils I've included some of my favorite ways below. This is by no means a complete or be all end all list. This is simply a starting place for you to get some ideas of how you can bring oils into your life. I hope you'll be inspired to create some ways of your own and share those ideas with the people in your world.

- ❖ Diffuser:
    These are available in a sliding scale of price ranges and sizes. There's something for everyone, there are even some that can play music. Try to avoid oil "burners" these usually require a tea light to heat the oil. These burners are often made of metal and sit close to the tea light creating a lot of heat on the oil. Heat can break down the chemical component of the oils which means that you don't receive their full benefits. (Sometimes the metal begins to burn too creating a not so nice smell.)

    What I love about using an oil diffuser is that you receive all the benefits of the oils and you don't really have to do anything. Once you add the oils to the water and turn it on, it does all the work and you can relax and enjoy the atmosphere and the aromas while you do whatever you want to do. Just remember to turn it off when you leave the room.

- ❖ Bath Treatment:
    If you're a bath person, you may really love this oil treatment. In addition to whatever you like to add to your bath whether it's sea or epsom salt, or bubbles; essential oils can make your bath an even more relaxing experience. Simply add a few drops of the oils of your choice and feel your body unwind at an even deeper level during your bath time.
    - o Lavender helps with relaxation and gentle sleep
    - o Chamomile helps with relaxation

- o Eucalyptus helps to increase deep breathing and can open the sinuses
- o Bergamot helps to reduce stress, tension, and low grade anxiety
- o Lemon is invigorating, brightening, and can help to increase joy and energy.

❖ Stove Top Simmer Pot:
These are great especially during the cold season when you may be using the heat or a wood burning stove a lot. Using any kind of heat for long periods of time can dry out the air in your home. Dry air can lead to itchy skin, dry or stuffy sinuses, and dry scalp. Dry air, especially if you use a wood burning stove can lead to damage in your wood furnishings.

Place a large stock pot onto your stove filled with water and add several drops of essential oils in any combinations you enjoy and turn your stove onto medium heat. Allow the pot to simmer and steam so your entire home is infused with oils and moisture. This will make your home smell great while also helping to moisturize dry skin, scalps, sinuses, and your wood furnishings all at the same time.

Never leave your home with the stove on and keep your pot on the back burner away from small hands. It's important that you keep an eye and ear out while you use this method so that you can turn off your stove as the water runs low or refill it with more water.

You can also add live herbs from your garden, and spices from your pantry to your simmer pot. The options here are endless.

- ❖ Linens:
  You can freshen up your linens by adding a few drops of your favorite oils to a small bottle of water and spritzing your linens lightly. (You don't want them to be wet but just have a light spritz.) You can do this after you get your linens out of the dryer so that they are ready to go onto your bed. Or, you can spray your pillow slips before you go to sleep. Lavender is a popular choice for linens because it helps to increase relaxation and helps with sleep. But any oil that is comforting and relaxing to you will be a great choice.

  If you or a loved one has trouble sleeping you may want add several drops of lavender oil onto a couple of the flat cotton make up removers and place them inside the pillow slip for even more support. This way you don't have to moisten the linens too much but you'll breathe in more of the oils.

- ❖ Room Sprays:
  These are so fun and easy to make. You just need a spray bottle, water, and your favorite essential oil or oils. Simply combine, shake, and spray. This helps to give your room a pick me up if you feel like it could use a refresh. If you include Eucalyptus or Tea Tree oil then you will also purify the air because these are both naturally anti-bacterial and anti-microbial. Instead of spraying a harsh toxic

spray that smells like a lavender field, or a rosemary garden, you can infuse your room with the pure essential oil of the real thing. (win, win)

- ❖ Aura Sprays:
  Not only do these smell great but they revitalize you and help you to feel refreshed. These are a great way to give yourself a pick me up especially in the afternoon if you feel your energy start to drop. These are easy to make and all you need is a small spray bottle, water, and the essential oil or oils of your choice. Simply combine, shake, and spray.

These sprays are often sold in natural food stores and boutiques. Some of the common one's that are sold include rose water, lavender water, and tea tree water. You can make these combinations or something entirely unique just for you. It's important to hold the water bottle away from you and avoid spraying your clothing. Essentials oils like all oils can stain clothing. (Also, avoid spraying your technology as water damages electronics.)

- ❖ Yoga Mat Refresh:
  Yoga mats go through a lot and you can make your own mat refresher that is free from toxins. Any essential oil combination that you enjoy is great. I also like to include a few drops of Eucalyptus and Tea tree oil because of their anti-bacterial and anti-microbial properties. Add your oils to a spray bottle filled about three quarters full of water. I also like to add a little bit of witch hazel, and a couple of drops of an organic liquid pure castile soap. Shake all of

your ingredients, if you add the castile soap you'll see some bubbles inside the bottle. Spray directly onto your mat and wipe clean. This works really well and it will leave your mat smelling really good. The next time you get your downward dog on, you'll breathe in all those essential oils….ahhh.

- ❖ Body Application:
  You can apply essential oils to your body to receive their benefits. It's important to use a carrier oil when applying your oils to your body. If you don't use a carrier oil, you could experience a stinging effect, irritation, or tightness if you have sensitive skin. You can use coconut, almond, sesame, or another carrier oil to apply your essential oils.

  Some of the common places people like to apply oils include, but aren't limited to:
  - Bottoms of Feet
  - Back of the Knees
  - Wrists
  - Ear Lobes
  - Chest
  - Spine

  It's important to talk to your health care professional before applying essential oils directly to your body. It's also important to avoid any oils you may be allergic to and if you aren't sure about your personal allergies, you may want to work with an allergist prior to applying oils to your body.

I hope this chapter has inspired you to find some ways to incorporate essential oils into your daily life. I also hope that it has shown you how easy it is to enjoy essential oils and that you can start using them today. If you feel guided to learn more about this topic, great, but you don't have to spend a lot of time researching before enjoying all of the benefits of oils and aromatherapy.

39.

Guided Action Clears Tension

This topic can bring up a lot of feelings for people, especially if you're a highly sensitive person. (Since you're reading this book, I would venture a guess that you are indeed a highly sensitive person.) Over the years I've found that there are some things that tend to be really big challenges for people. They are the things that get connected to many other life areas and can create tension, stress, and a feeling of being stuck. This is one of them. Whether I was working with professional students, clients of a large cross section, or talking with a friend, this issue came up time and time again.

The issue is understanding why it's important to take guided action and then giving yourself permission to begin taking that action in the present. Here's an example of a very common experience I've found over the years. Someone will tell me that they feel lost, disconnected from themselves, and that the joy or magic of their life has somehow become dim or feels completely gone. They tell me that each day feels the same as the one before and that their life feels almost like it's on automatic. They also tell me that when they're away from their life, they feel more like themselves but when they are back home again and in their normal day to day life, they feel disconnected again.

Often these people will also tell me that they don't feel fulfilled by the work that they're doing, the relationships they're in, or the location where they live. Many will describe a physical discomfort within and around their body as well. Sometimes it shows up as a low to medium grade anxiety, restlessness, trouble sleeping, a pressure within their chest, or a pressure that feels like something outside of them is weighing them down. They will also tell me that they know or feel that they're supposed to be doing something else and that it feels like they are under pressure to do it now.

When I ask them what they feel they are supposed to be doing, they more often than not can tell me almost immediately.

- ❖ Move
- ❖ Change careers
- ❖ Go back to school
- ❖ Leave my unhealthy relationship
- ❖ Get into counseling
- ❖ Completely change my food and health priorities
- ❖ Write
- ❖ Start a business
- ❖ Quit drinking or using drugs
- ❖ Reconnect with my family
- ❖ Create healthy boundaries with my family
- ❖ Let go of unhealthy "friends"
- ❖ Start saying no

These are a few of the common answers that show up for people over and over again but this is by no means a complete list.

When I ask them why they haven't begun taking action on the guided action steps they've been receiving, I would often hear a version of:

- ❖ Well, you see I can't really do that just yet, because_____.

Or

- ❖ Well, once, I do _____ then I'll have more time and resources to do what I know I'm being guided to do.

Or

- ❖ I'm so used to living this way and I know what to expect with this version of my life. I don't like it at all, but I'm scared that making changes could be harder so I would rather just keep doing this since I know how to do it.

Or

- ❖ I'll just wait until I retire, or my kids move out of the house or until I have more free time.

Or

- ❖ I'm too old to change what I'm doing now. A career change and university life are for people much younger than me.

Or

- ❖ This is the way everyone feels, no one feels satisfied with their life. People are just pretending to be happy, why fight it, this is just the way it is.

These are very common responses that I've heard many times over the years. When I ask them about what they're doing to try to quell that physical feeling that shows up inside the body or the pressure they're feeling outside of their body these are the things that I hear:

- ❖ Alcohol, Cigarettes, or Drugs
- ❖ Shopping
- ❖ Social Media/Internet

- Television/Movies/Gaming
- Food
- Drama
- Helping Others Rather than Themselves
- Diversion Tactics/ Delay Tactics
- Obsessive Cleaning
- Waiting for Perfect Timing
- Pretending it's Not Important/Pipe Dream
- Creating "Business"
- Negative Self Talk
- Spend Time with People Who Aren't Following Their Guidance or Taking Action

The problem is that none of these things will help to move anyone closer to what they're being guided to do. So, a paradox can occur for people. They aren't happy or fulfilled but aren't taking any action to move toward the answer to their prayers which is to do _____. So, the person chooses to delay or put off the divine guidance they're receiving which begins the cycle of unhappiness and angst again. Over time this can feel very compounding and increasingly challenging.

> The truth is that nothing will take that physical and emotional strain away except Taking Guided Action. The answer is to Do what you're being guided to do.
>
> The action quells the anxiety, worry, angst, pressure, and tension.

Only taking guided action can accomplish this. After the temporary numbing agent begins to wear off whether it's alcohol, food, shopping, or something else, those old feelings show up again. The reason it feels like alarm bells are going off, is because they are. The urgency that is felt inside the body is a genuine message that you're receiving about the importance of making divinely guided changes now.

None of us have an infinite time to do the work or live the life we are called to live. The truth is that we all have a finite time line here. The pressure you feel to move toward the life you're waiting for and that you are truly aligned with is there as your personal support system. That pressure you feel is leading you to your happy life.

The challenge is to acknowledge that you are being divinely guided when you are given repeated messages to change_____. Then, to actually begin taking action on those life areas, now. Even if it seems like this isn't the perfect timing. The truth is that there will never be a perfect time to make a change or move toward the life that you're wanting to live. The only time that is available is right now.

Because of the complexities of modern life, most people won't have the opportunity to take a month off to focus on the changes that they want to make. The great news is that these changes can be made in small but significant ways throughout the day. Just like a savings account, seemingly small investments add up to big change over time. The same is true here and this is the way to move toward the life that you know and feel is right for you while simultaneously clearing out the tension, anxiety, and pressure that you're experiencing.

What you'll find is that by taking any action, even if it feels tiny to you will lift that pressure, anxiety, and tension that you're experiencing. Plus, you will be moving toward what it is that you've been guided to move toward for a significant amount of time.

Once someone understands this and then chooses to take action, two things usually show up.

The first is a feeling of not knowing how to get support which can lead to old habits of pushing divine guidance to the back burner. If you notice this happening for you, breathe and ask for help. It's important to reach out for support from people in the realm in which you are moving.

So, if you are being guided to go back to school, reach out to a guidance counselor.

You will need to have people in your circle who can support you and give you guidance as you make these important life changes. These people will help you to stay inspired, motivated, and informed of which steps to take and will most likely give you additional resources and put you into contact with additional support people as you take these steps.

The second issue that can often show up is overwhelm. Sometimes once the decision is made to make changes, a whirlwind of all the things that need to be done begins to show up in your thinking space. This can feel daunting, heavy, confusing, and can lead to paralysis. While it's important to have a good understanding of the working parts and the bigger picture of the changes that you're making; it's critical to take things one step at a time. By taking things one step at a time you can keep overwhelm at bay while continuing to move forward. When overwhelm creeps in it can create a freeze up and discourage you from moving forward. This can happen to anyone and it's not a judgement about your ability to move forward. Just breathe, take a break and reach out to your support system so you can get going again.

I've watched people completely change their lives by deciding to start listening to their divine guidance and begin taking action. I've seen people who've been pushing against their guidance for more than half of their lives finally stop resisting and move into more joy than they ever thought was possible. It doesn't matter how old you are or how long you've been resisting. Giving yourself permission to begin now is the biggest gift you could ever give to yourself. Asking for support and doing the work, even seemingly small steps is the lock in the key that leads to the life you know you're being called to live.

Breathe Through It:

If you're finding that this is bringing up a lot of emotions for you and maybe even releasing some tension from your body, take a breath. Sometimes even acknowledging this experience can help to shift some of the pain and heaviness that you've been carrying around with you.

Many people tell me that they think they're the only ones who feel this way, so there's a component of feeling isolated or embarrassed about this experience. If you've thought that you're the only one feeling this way, I promise you that you aren't. In fact, you're in good company and part of a large community of people who understand how you feel.

You may want to take a moment to move through your emotions; a lot of times this topic can bring up feelings of grief. If you enjoy journaling, this may be a great opportunity to write down the things you're thinking or feeling. Treating yourself with tender loving care and gentility is a good idea. This is a big topic and it's okay for you to feel your feelings.

Activity:

Below you will find a list of some ways to help you get started in taking guided action toward the calling of your heart. This is by no means a complete or be all end all list. Please allow yourself to be inspired to create the action steps that are right for you. These are not in a specific order of importance, please follow your guidance as to which steps to take first. It doesn't matter so much what your actions steps look like as long as you take action.

- ❖ Tell Someone You Trust
  Find someone in your world that you can confide in about what you're being guided to do. Please choose someone who will genuinely support you, cheer you on, and believe in you.

  Please avoid choosing someone who may feel jealous or competitive with you. People who may feel threatened by you making life changes isn't a good choice for a support person. It doesn't mean that you're judging them but you need to choose someone who will be 100% in your corner.

  If you don't have a physical person you can tell, you may want to connect with an online support community or connect with a support group in your area. It's very important to have a support person in your world as you begin to make important life changes.

- ❖ Contact a Professional in Your Field
  Connecting with a professional in your field can give you a lot of information and insight into how they got to where they are within their field. It will also give you an opportunity to ask questions about what it's like to do what they do and any of the things that you've been wanting to ask someone.

  You may want to contact several people so you can get a large breadth of information and stories from different people. You will most likely find some people who feel like a good fit for you and can foster a relationship with them. These people can give you referrals and information that can lead to more support for you and help you in moving forward.

  If you feel shy about reaching out to someone, that's okay, it's natural to feel shy when you're first moving out of your comfort zone. You can send an email or a message through their contact form to initially make contact. After you make that initial contact, you'll find that it gets easier and easier for you to make contact with people in your field.

- ❖ Work with a Counselor
  Sometimes making changes can bring up a lot of emotions, past experiences, or challenges that you may want support in working through. Reaching out to a counselor, therapist, or life coach can be a great support system for you. It's important to find someone who is a genuine fit for you. It's okay to

interview more than one person until you find the person you feel comfortable working with.

If you're going back to school, you'll want to work with an academic advisor or an academic counselor. These professionals are a wealth of knowledge in all things academia, how to go back to school, referrals, support systems and support people who will be able to help you with your specific situation. These people are often extremely kind, compassionate, and are helping oriented. They often have extensive psychology backgrounds and are great people to talk to because they are genuinely connected to supporting people in moving toward the direction of their dreams and goals.

- ❖ Create a Timetable
Set a timeline for your overall goal as well as for the tasks and activities that you will need to accomplish to move toward your overall goal. This is a game changer in making real and lasting change. If you get something down in physical writing with deadlines and goals, it's easier to commit to taking action. Being able to see the actionable steps and the time frame in which they need to be finished allows you to focus on one thing at a time. This method also allows you to experience the reward of finishing things which helps with momentum, excitement, and a feelings of accomplishment.

- ❖ Get Enrolled or Onto Any Time Sensitive Lists
  Find out about any enrollment deadlines or important time sensitive issues that apply to your situation. Get onto any lists that will notify you of when you need to apply or take action on something. Knowing when time sensitive issues are happening allows you to move forward in a timely matter and allows you to meet your deadlines.

- ❖ Research Information Pertinent To Your Situation
  Spend time researching about the changes you're being guided to make. With the presence of the internet, you can easily do some research from the comfort of your own home. This will not only give you information, inspiration, and momentum but it can also lead you to important people, timelines, and opportunities which can move you closer to your desired outcome.

- ❖ Hold Firm Boundaries
  Anytime you decide to make changes, no matter how big or seemingly small, your day to day life will need to change too. It will be very important to make sure that you honor your personal deadlines, goals, and commitments to yourself during this process. You will have to get comfortable holding boundaries with people and situations that drain your time or energy. As you commit to making positive changes for you and your life, some things will organically begin to shift out. This is a natural part of life and it will be very important to hold firm to the vision that you have for yourself.

You may have to practice saying no to people who are used to you saying yes. You may have to let a few things go by the wayside as you adjust to your new schedule and allocation of time. These are natural experiences that come from making change. This is why it's really important to have a support person in your circle. When things feel tough or you feel like you could use a reminder about why you're making these important life changes, you can reach out to your support person.

The more that you hold healthy and firm boundaries around this new life that you're building, the easier it will become. As if by magic, as you hold those boundaries, people within your world will begin to respect you and your boundaries more than ever before. Will some people shift out of your life? Yes, most likely someone or a few people will shift out, and that's okay. It means that you're making space for people and situations which honor and match this new phase of your life. That is worth holding boundaries for, I promise.

- ❖ Invest Time Every Day
  Consistency is the biggest support system in making and sustaining change. You've probably heard that old adage, "Inspiration gets you started, dedication keeps you going." It's really true, when you take time to invest in your changes every single day. (Yes, every single day) even if you can only get 5 to 7 minutes, you'll find that you keep going. When you wait for a day in the week where you have a

large chunk of time, it's easy to get distracted and let your goals get put back onto a shelf.

Commit to your goals and to yourself in the same way that you commit to brushing your teeth and combing your hair every day. It doesn't matter so much what you do each day in the direction of your dreams, but it does matter that you do something. Every action you take is an investment in the changes that you are making.

- ❖ Have an Accountability Partner
  This is a powerful way to keep committed to your schedule and overall goals that you have for yourself. This can be a trusted friend, counselor, therapist, coach, mentor or person from a support group. It's important to choose someone who will hold you to your weekly check in's and call you on the places or spaces where you may be sliding into old patterns. It's also important to choose someone who will cheer you on, inspire you, and bask in as much joy as you do when you have successes.

  This may be the same person you chose as your support person or it may be someone else. Having an accountability partner helps you to maintain your commitment to yourself because you know you have a weekly check in to discuss the action steps you committed to for that particular week. You could also choose to be an accountability partner for someone else and work as a team to support one another each week as you both move toward the life that you're being guided to live.

The divine guidance that you've been receiving is exactly that, it's an answer to the feeling that you have inside, the feeling that something is off; the feeling that something isn't right. Your divine guidance is a map leading you to the life that you know is right for you. Please give yourself permission to honor your divine guidance. Please give yourself permission to begin today, right now, right where you're standing; please give yourself permission to honor yourself. This is your life, right here, right now, and you deserve to honor the guidance that you are receiving about making important and lasting life changes.

40.

Choose You

So often working with highly sensitive people, I find that they tend to place themselves last within their world. I find that some people unconsciously do this perhaps because of an expectation starting when they were very young from older family members. While others consciously place themselves last in their world, becoming bystanders within their own lives in some respects.

I find that along the way, there is often cross over between these two examples. Many highly sensitive people are naturally very aware of their own feelings and the feelings of those around them. Many highly sensitive people are highly empathic which allows them to feel the feelings of everyone around them and the environment in which they live.

Many times, the highly sensitive person within the family takes on a lot of responsibility and adult roles at a very young age. Because of the acute sensitivity and awareness, the child begins to be cut off from their own needs, desires, or even playtime. They become seen as a mini adult and begin to be treated as such by parents, teachers, and other authority figures. As a highly sensitive person, helping, supporting, and trying to stabilize others feelings is natural; however it begins to foster a pattern of placing others needs above their own. It also creates an unhealthy situation where adults encourage and foster this self-denial and self-sacrifice in the highly sensitive child and give them praise, accolades, and other rewards which teaches them that this behavior is positive and deserves rewards.

This scenario often continues for the highly sensitive person in all areas within their lives. Many times these people can attract takers since they are so used to giving. These relationships can show up as unbalanced friendships, unhealthy relationships, challenging family dynamics, and unhealthy working relationships.

Some of the common feelings highly sensitive adults report feeling include:

- Disconnected from themselves
- Compartmentalized
- Lonely
- Burned Out
- Taken Advantage Of
- Underappreciated
- Lost
- Misunderstood, Even by "Close Friends, Family, and Partners"
- Empty
- Waiting for Their Turn to Arrive
- Devoid of Joy or Happiness
- Guilt
- Confusion

Some of the common experiences that people within this group report include:

- Waiting for Perfect Timing to Move Forward with their Needs
- Once Everyone Else is Taken Care of Then They'll Give Themselves Permission to Focus on Their Life
- Waiting For Someone to Give them Permission to Follow Their Dreams

- This is usually unconscious, due to so many years following rules and waiting for someone to tell or ask them to do something.

This can be a very challenging life shift to make for highly sensitive people because they tend to be hard wired to help others. So a push pull situation can show up for them around this issue. They want to take care of themselves but feel obligated to help everyone when they see someone they love in need of help or if they are asked for help.

However, it's imperative that the highly sensitive person receive support in setting healthy boundaries with everyone within their world. Yes, everyone. This is usually a process that can take some time because the sensitive person has to practice changing the way they've been moving through their entire life up to this point. It's absolutely possible to continue to be a highly sensitive, empathic, caring person while also taking care of themselves and supporting the people within their world.

Reaching out for support from a professional counselor, therapist, or coach who specializes in working with highly sensitive people can be a huge support system. There's a deep need for boundary setting, but also in releasing guilt that can show up when saying no, and learning that they're needs and desires are equally important as those of their loved ones.

One of the other areas where this tends to show up for people is when they feel that they reach an age where they feel things should have been "different by now." This is a different time for each person based on their own beliefs about how their life should be progressing. Often because the highly sensitive person puts themselves last for so long, one day they finally realize that they haven't made time for themselves in years, and in some cases decades and it starts to scare them.

This is a breakthrough and can lead to a huge positive shift, allowing the person to understand that they've been living out of balance. This often begins the process of learning to bring their life back into balance. This process of balance also allows the person to truly learn to appreciate themselves, love themselves, and accept themselves outside of the box of what they've done for people. For most highly sensitive people they've learned to equate love, support, and acceptance through acts and service rather than with who they are. This shift allows for a healing in this area and allows the person to truly understand and accept that they are loveable and deserving of love, joy, and happiness just for being who they are and not solely for what they bring to the table.

As the pendulum begins to swing back into balance, the feelings of compartmentalization, being misunderstood, and feeling disconnected begin to lesson and even disappear. As the highly sensitive person begins to choose themselves, often for the very first time, their relationships change for the better. They attract people, situations, and opportunities that are in alignment with who they are in truth.

I've seen people completely change their lives by working through this pattern. I've watched people begin to live their life and honor their own hopes and dreams while feeling fully present in their lives. Someone once told me that she felt like she was finally the main person in her life instead of all of the background people in other's lives.

One of the biggest fears that people have told me they had about bringing their life back into balance was that they didn't want to turn off their ability to feel things so deeply. I want to underscore here that if you have that fear, you can give yourself permission to let that go. Empaths feel deeply and creating a healthy balance within their life won't reduce, dampen, or in some way diminish that beautiful gift. I've found that in setting boundaries, choosing to honor their own needs and desires, empaths actually find they feel things more deeply. This shows up because they stop denying and pushing down their own feelings, needs, and dreams which allows them to tap into even more of that beautiful sensitivity and empathy within.

Breathe Through It:

As a highly sensitive person you may be experiencing a flood of emotions and memories. Take as much time as you need to allow your thoughts and feelings to move through you. You may even find that these thoughts and feelings have been holding space inside of you for a very long time. You may have thought that you were the only one who's thought or felt this way.

You may want to take a moment to just be and take some long, slow, deep breaths in through your nose and out through your mouth. If you feel guided to journal, talk, or cry, give yourself permission to be where you're at and go at your own pace. This is a big topic and it can unearth a lot of past memories, pain, and sadness. Treat yourself with tender loving care and know that allowing yourself to move through your feelings about this issue is the beginning of a big positive shift for you.

Activity:

There is no one way or right way to begin to move toward living a more balanced life, one where your needs are no longer last on the list or less valuable than others' needs. There are only the ways that feel right for you. This could change from day to day depending on how you're feeling or what you're working through.

I've found that working with a professional who understands highly sensitive people can lead to positive lasting change. It's important to choose someone who feels like a genuine fit for you and to know that you can say no to them if you feel they aren't right for you. (Even if other people tell you that they're great.)

Creating a support system is important because as you make this important change, everyone and everything in your life will be impacted. You'll want to have at least one person within your world who you can lean on and receive support from during this transition.

This person can be a:

- ❖ Trusted Friend
- ❖ Counselor
- ❖ Therapist
- ❖ Coach
- ❖ Mentor

It's important to choose someone who will be there to support you and not turn into a situation where you're supporting them.

There are also a lot of support groups available that can offer you comfort and support from people who truly understand what you're experiencing. You can research support groups in your area from the comfort of your own home.

❖ Co-Dependent Anonymous may be a group that could be supportive for you. This group often has highly sensitive empathic people as members.

There are in person and online groups available depending on your needs.

Whether you choose to reach out for

❖ Support from a Professional and Work With Them One on One
❖ Attend support groups
❖ Attend Assertiveness Training
❖ Read and Apply Tools from Personal Growth Books
❖ Incorporate Spiritual Support and Tools Into Your Daily Life
❖ Attend Workshops
❖ All of the above
❖ Or Create and Participate in Support Systems not Included Here

it's important that it feels like a fit for you. It's important that you find what works for you. Please give yourself permission to reach out for a support system that you feel attracted to and know that you are worthy and deserving of living a happy and healthy life.

Give yourself permission to make yourself a priority within your world. Your life is happening right now and it's important that you create the time to move toward the calling of your heart. You are the only person who can do this for you. Yes, helping is in your nature and it's a beautiful thing but you must also help yourself. Your dreams and desires are equally important to those within your world, no matter who they may be. As you honor yourself, everyone in your world benefits.

41.

Life Long Learning

Choosing to be a life long learner adds so much interest, variety, and breadth to life. I often think of life long learning as the bright bold patterns and textures within the fabric of life. Even after traditional schooling and academia is over, there is still so much to learn.

I've found that sometimes when people feel that something is missing from their lives, but they can't quite put their fingers on it, many times it circles back to learning. This is a common experience I've heard many times from a large cross section of clients, it goes something like this:

"I just don't feel inspired in my life. I feel like the days are all running together and I miss feeling like there is something to look forward to. I don't mean a special event but more of something to experience or do that is different from my regular life responsibilities."

When we look deeper into this feeling, what I've found over and over again is a feeling of wanting to learn or try new things. For most people, there is a window of time where professional education is at the forefront and a main focus in life. After school is finished, there's a transition into a professional working life that tends to have minimal if any further formal education or school setting.

As time moves along many people feel that something is missing in their life. When looking at their overall life situation, what shows up is that they haven't taken the time to learn or try anything new in a long time. When the changes, new experiences, and cross section of exposure that comes from school is no longer a part of life, it's easy to get into a routine of things that tend to be the same.

The great news is that there are infinite ways to continue to foster your thirst for learning. For some people this may include going back to school. For others it will mean stepping out of their comfort zone to enroll in courses, workshops, and activities that they've been wanting to do but have been waiting until there's more time or for an optimal time.

If you think back for a moment to a time when you were in school, you probably remember how busy and impacted your day was. In addition to attending classes, there was homework, studying, working, and other responsibilities to maintain all at the same time. Somehow, all of those things got done. The same thing applies here, even though it seems that there may not be enough time, somehow almost as if my magic, once you're enrolled, the time shows up.

This issue usually (not always) has people who fit into one of two groups.

Group One:

The first group are people who feel a deep pull to go back to school. Many people in this group left school prior to graduating. There's a feeling inside for them that feels heavy and can lead to sadness or guilt over time because they didn't finish. The issue isn't so much in why they chose or had to leave school prior to graduation, it's that a part of them still wishes they had finished.

Going back to school and finishing will be the thing that helps people in this group release the heaviness they've been carrying around since leaving school. If someone really feels a deep regret about not finishing, this is the one thing that will quell that feeling for them. This can be connected to self worth and self esteem issues as well. Leaving school could've created a belief that there are glass ceilings in place for them because they didn't finish what they started. These beliefs and feelings can lead to making choices from a place of feeling unworthy or less than others within their world.

Reaching out to an Academic Advisor to get information about how to return to school after a leave of absence can help to get the ball rolling and create excitement about finishing. I really want to underscore here that it's truly never too late to go back to school no matter how long you've been away. As a former university faculty member and academic advisor I can tell you that students are in classes from all ages and if you're being guided to go back to school, please give yourself permission to honor that guidance.

People who feel guided to go back to school for advanced degrees or programs can also find themselves in a space of feeling guided to go back to school but may feel too much time has passed etc. Sometimes, people are worried that they won't have the studying chops that they used to have. Like all things, being a student is a lifestyle, and you can get back into the swing of things more quickly than you may realize. The deep call within you is there for a reason and if you know you're being guided back into a traditional classroom, the please honor that call.

Group Two:

People in this group feel guided to learn something new and to try new things but don't really know where to begin. They usually have a desire to meet new people and to be exposed to new ideas, activities, and experiences.

Many people in this group have an area of interest that they tend to lean into.

For example, perhaps someone is interested in learning how to:

- white water raft
- paddle board
- surf

You can see that this person is interested in learning about outdoor physical activities which also include water.

The big shift for people in this group is to get clear on what they want to learn or experience. Many times when you first ask someone in this group what they want to learn, they'll say, "I don't know, anything I guess." But the more that you talk with them, you see that they have a clear area of interest. Some people will have more than one area which is great.

Once people in this group have a clear understanding and idea of what it is they want to do or learn, it helps them to get inspired to take action. It's almost as if a fog is lifted from them and they feel excited and ready to get out there. You can almost see a spark of joy being relit for people within this group once they realize that it's absolutely possible for them to find a group or course that can help them learn something they've wanted to learn.

Breathe Through It:

While realizing what area or type of life long learning resonates for you is liberating and exciting; it can also lead to feelings of nervousness. For some people, this shift can lead to feelings of uncertainty about taking the next steps.

Sometimes thoughts like:

- ❖ What if I can't do it?
- ❖ Will I make friends?
- ❖ What if it's not for me?

begin to show up which is natural. If you find that you're experiencing these thoughts, take a deep breath and release. Take a moment to release any tension in your neck and shoulders and your stomach.

Trying something new is always an opportunity for growth. Just like everything else in your life, you've done things for the first time and now they're easy for you. If something really isn't a fit for you, you can choose not to continue. No one is pressuring you to do something that doesn't work for you.

Activity:

If you find yourself if Group One:

Contact an Academic Advisor at the University or Community College in your area. You will most likely need to make an appointment to go into the office and discuss your personal situation. You may need to obtain a copy of your transcripts from your previous school. Most if not all of these documents are available online now and you can download them for a nominal fee.

Academic Advisors are a wealth of knowledge and information and are often kind, compassionate, and supportive people. They work with people who are re-entering academic life or who are participating in academic life every single day. You can ask them oodles of questions and if they don't have the answer for you, they can get you in touch with the exact right person for you.

If you feel nervous to reach out to an Academic Advisor, you may want to ask a trusted friend or family member to sit with you when you make the initial call to schedule your appointment and/or to attend the appointment with you. Please make sure you choose someone who you feel is a genuine support person for you and who understands how important this action step is for you.

After you have your appointment you will have a clear idea of the action steps that you need to take to get back into the program that is right for you. You'll also have information about important deadlines and resources that can further support your re-entry into academia.

If You Find Yourself in Group Two:

You will want to spend some time doing research about the activities that are available in your area. You'll also want to spend some time getting clear about what it is that you want to try or learn. You don't have to limit yourself to one area, but getting clarity on what sounds exciting and interesting to you can be a big help.

Below you will find a list of some places to start your search. Please know this is not a complete or be all, end all list. This is simply a jumping off place for you to get started and inspired.

- ❖ University or Community College
  There are often programs where you can pay a reduced fee to take a variety of elective style classes at local universities and community colleges.

- ❖ Specialty Shops:
  Private Groups and Activities are often hosted by owners or employees within these privately owned stores. Sometimes there are classes and workshops offered within large chain stores too.

  Whether your interest is in:
  - Biking
  - Hiking
  - Water Sports
  - Pottery
  - Knitting
  - Sewing
  - Painting
  - Playing a Musical Instrument

You may find that there are a lot of groups and classes available for every skill level.

- ❖ Adult Education Classes:
  Most communities have a version of Adult Education Classes available. You may want to check with your chamber of commerce to find out more about what your community offers. These programs offer classes from Art to Yoga and everything in between.

- ❖ Meet Up
  This is an online community where you can see a lot of activities that are happening within your community and all over the globe. You can search activities and classes by topic or area of interest and see what's happening in your area. You will need to create an account (it's free) to join and participate in the groups.

- ❖ Volunteer and Non Profit Groups
  There are a lot of non profit and service based groups that offer classes, workshops, and activities. Many service groups have a theme that they focus on, so finding a group with a theme that interests you can lead you to like minded people, courses, and workshops.

Life long learning is a gift we give to ourselves. There are so many things to learn and experience in life. When we start to feel ho hum or find that life feels a little monotonous, it may be time to invest in a new activity. Not only will you enrich your life and learn something new, you will most likely meet new people who share common interests with you. Giving yourself permission to continue learning and trying new things will broaden your life experience and add more colors and textures to your personal tapestry of life.

42.
Set Up Your Day

In this busy and modern life, it can be easy to feel like your day is taking you from one activity to the next, rather than you being in control of your day. This is by no means a judgement on you and is definitely not a fun feeling. By the end of the day, you can feel exhausted, like you've been in a whirlwind and surprised that the whole day is already over. If you've experienced this before, trust me you're not alone.

With technology creating longer and longer work days for people, and opening the door to nearly non stop communication and an expectation for all access availability, it can feel like there's never any time to slow down, nor any time just or you.

Over time this can lead to feelings of overwhelm, burn out, and a desire to get away. In some cases it can also lead to health challenges. It can also lead to a belief that you have to push harder, go faster, and accept these encroachments into your private time. You may even feel guilty holding a boundary with clients, family, and friends when all you want to do is take 20 minutes of uninterrupted time to eat your dinner without being inundated with emails, text messages, and messages from your website contact form.

This way of living isn't natural since we are humans and not machines. In the late 1990's when people opened their homes and arms to the internet, we've seen private time and traditional business hours go by the wayside more and more each year. Now that we carry our computers around with us in our pockets and handbags aka smart phones, it's even more challenging to hold a boundary between our down time, recharge time, family time, work, communication, and time with others. The lines have been blurred and we're seeing and experiencing the impact in our daily lives.

This doesn't mean that you have to succumb to this way of living forever nor does it mean that something is wrong with you if you don't enjoy living this way. The shift comes in taking your day back. I know it can feel daunting to think about that and it may even feel challenging to imagine shifting the way you move through your day, but it is possible.

Breathe Through It:

This can bring up a lot of tension, stress, and worry for people. You may be thinking of all the ways that this won't be possible for you because of your personal special situation. If you're noticing any kind of physical resistance to this idea in addition to making mental lists about why this won't work, please stop for a moment and take a long, slow, deep breath.

Okay, good. I'm not suggesting that you avoid or neglect your personal or professional responsibilities in any way. In fact, by embracing some shifts to your current lifestyle you'll be able to get more done while also balancing and investing in your own needs. You'll also experience a richer quality of life rather than feeling like you're being dragged from one activity to the next while feeling like a bystander in your own life, simply going through the motions.

Activity:

One of the most powerful ways to begin to shift your schedule back to what works for you is to set up your day. This may mean getting up 20 minutes earlier than usual and avoiding all technology, communication, and to do lists. (Not even a quick peek just to check one quick thing.)

For This Activity You'll Need:

- A Pen or Pencil
- A Piece of Paper or A Notebook
- Quiet Space In Your Home

You'll need to go into a quiet place within your home with a physical pen and a piece of paper. For 20 minutes without any technology find a comfy place to sit down and start with some nice, slow, deep breaths in through your nose and out through your mouth. Relaxing your neck, shoulders, chest, stomach, and lower back. Good.

Then, imagine yourself right from where you're sitting sending love out to your entire day ahead of you. See, feel, hear, or know that you are sending love ahead to you as you:

- Get ready for your day,
- Load up your vehicle or other transportation method
- Send love to yourself as you are moving through your morning routine
- Eating lunch
- Moving through your afternoon routine
- Late afternoon routine
- You're traveling home

- ❖ When you're home for your evening routine and winding down from your day
- ❖ Getting ready to go to sleep

Then Answer the Following Questions on Your Piece of Paper or In Your Notebook:

- ❖ What do you notice or feel as you do this exercise?
- ❖ How does it feel to send love to yourself prior to your day beginning?
- ❖ What kinds of things did you see, hear, feel, or know as you participated in this exercise?

Now close your eyes again and send love to the people, situations, and activities that you will encounter as you move through your day today. Good.

- ❖ How did that feel?
- ❖ What kinds of things did you see, hear, feel, and know as you participated in this exercise?

Now on your paper, I want you to write the answers to the following questions. Write the very first thought, feeling, vision, or words that you hear.

- ❖ How can I reduce the amount of excess that I have during the day?
  - o The first kind of excess that you think of is the kind of excess that you're working on shifting. (Texting, calls, emails, interruptions, etc.)
- ❖ How can I reallocate some of my activities or responsibilities to people who are capable of taking them on within my world?

- ❖ How can I create more healthy boundaries in my day that will allow me to honor myself, my family, and my clients?
- ❖ What does my soul want right now?
- ❖ How can I honor myself by giving my soul what it needs?
- ❖ What changes am I being guided to make to bring my life more into balance for myself?
- ❖ What is the vision or dream that I have for my life?
- ❖ How can I move toward that vision?
- ❖ Who or what are detractors from that vision?
- ❖ What am I being guided to do to reduce or eliminate these distractors from my life, today?

Take a minute to look over your answers. Pay attention to the way you feel, physically, mentally, emotionally, and spiritually.

When you feel ready, give yourself permission to get up and to begin your day. Try to avoid going onto your tech devices for a little longer so you can gently ease back into your morning routine.

You'll find that when you set up your day and take 20 minutes for yourself prior to jumping into your to do lists and routines, that your day unfolds more gently. You'll also find that all day long you greet that love and support energy that you sent ahead of you during the morning.

Taking 20 minutes for yourself helps you to feel more clear, focused, and in control of your day. This activity also helps you to receive clear guidance about what changes you're being guided to make and why. As you give yourself permission to honor the changes that you're being guided to make, even seemingly small changes, you'll reap big benefits. Your work, clients, family, and friends will also get more from you because you'll be more present. Your life will feel more fulfilling for you because you'll be investing much needed time into yourself while simultaneously creating more balance to your overall lifestyle. Win. Win.

43.

Refilling Your Well

With all the things that you do each day, whether that's work, family stuff, daily to do lists, and everything in between, it's important to refill your well. A lot of times the things that refill the well is the stuff that can get pushed to the back burner or semi-permanently shelved all together.

What I find especially true for highly sensitive people is that a lot of the times, they forget that they've shelved something. In addition to the regular responsibilities of life, and all of the good work that you're doing to create positive change, sometimes along the way your well begins to run a bit dry.

When the well starts to run dry, you may feel or experience:

- Tired
- Brain Fog
- Clumsiness
- Sleep Disturbances
- Food Cravings
- Increased Irritability
- Frustration

The longer that you keep going without slowing down, you may increase these or other experiences which keep you feeling off kilter or not quite like yourself.

Refilling your well is fun, joyful, and creates a sense of you feeling like yourself again. The great news is that there's lots of ways to refill your well. Part of the fun is finding the ways that you enjoy and investing in yourself regularly.

Often, we invest a lot of time in removing things, people, and situations which no longer rise up to greet and honor us. This is really important work and something that always increases your overall quality of life. However, after the removing phase, sometimes we forget to add in some of the fun stuff too. Because highly sensitive people also tend to be self starters, self sufficient, and can lean into perfectionism, sometimes they forget that they've been shelving their fun due to managing all of their other responsibilities.

It's important to continue to hold healthy boundaries, honor your responsibilities, while also filling up your well. This is the fun stuff and it's important to understand that it's equally as important as everything else you invest in or make time for within your world. If you find yourself thinking that something else is more important, or that you'll get to it when you have more time, imagine your well becoming drier and emptier. The goal here is to have your well not only full by running over so that you have more than enough joy and you-ness to spare and share with others in your world without depleting or emptying yourself in the process of moving through your day to day life.

Breathe through It

Okay, so you may be feeling or thinking that this is one more thing to add to your list. Trust me, this is so not another thing to add to your list of to do's every day. Take a breath, and exhale. Good.

This is the stuff that makes you smile, giggle, laugh out loud, and helps you feel more like you. This is the stuff that makes you feel happy to be alive. This is the stuff that helps you to remember that there's magic in life and that you're a part of it. This is the stuff that feels like coming home to you. This is the stuff that nurtures that part of you that makes you who you are. This is the good stuff. Guess what? You deserve the good stuff because you're amazing!

Activity:

Below you will find a list of things that can help to refill your personal well. This is by no means a be all, end all list nor is it in any kind of order of importance. This is simply a list that will hopefully spark your creativity to create some well fillers of your own.

Your job here is to dive into the things that make you feel giddy, joyful, happy, and _____. Give yourself permission to go for it and like moisturizer ads used to say, "For optimal benefit, apply daily."

Apply your joy daily my dear.

- ❖ Read a Book
- ❖ Go to the Beach
- ❖ Have Lunch with a Friend
- ❖ Go For a Walk in Your Favorite Park
- ❖ Pick Up Your Creative Outlet Again
- ❖ Plan a Grown Up Slumber Party
- ❖ Rock Out to Your Favorite Music
- ❖ Sign Up for a Class You've Always Wanted to Take
- ❖ Treat Yourself to a Spa Day
- ❖ Call a Friend and Gab on the Phone Instead of Texting
- ❖ Host a Party or Event
    - o Porch Party, Garden Party, or Good old fashioned Pot Luck Party or Game Night

- ❖ Ride A Bike
- ❖ Roller Skate
- ❖ Eat Your Favorite Meal
- ❖ Host a Costume Party in the Middle Of Summer
- ❖ Indulge in a Movie Marathon (Great snacks and all)
- ❖ Create a Surprise Dinner for Someone You Care About.
- ❖ Listen to Live Music at Your Local Coffee House
- ❖ Say "Yes" to an Invitation from a friend
- ❖ Listen to old records or C.D's
- ❖ Look through old photo albums and take a walk down memory lane
- ❖ Buy a Coloring Book, Crayons, and Markers and Go For It

It doesn't matter so much what you do, as it does that you do something that brings you joy and happiness. As you invest in things that bring you joy, not only will you feel more like yourself, you'll also bring balance back to your world. Your life will feel more enriched and more fun, and you'll have more time to give to the things and people that are important to you. Keep taking good care of yourself and find ways to add sparkle and joy into your day, every day. It doesn't have to take a lot of time, but you're definitely worth it!

44.

Honoring Number 1

You are number one within your own life and it's important to remember that and to take action to honor this truth. Honoring number one is not the same thing as the old adage, "looking out for number one" which has a negative connotation. Looking out for number one implies doing whatever it takes to get ahead even if it means hurting someone else in the process.

This is the exact opposite of the meaning behind honoring number one. Many highly sensitive people confuse these two sentiments and think that they refer to the same principle. Because of the natural gentle qualities of highly sensitive people they would never want to hurt or take advantage of someone else, and can sometimes move away from focusing on themselves too much. Sometimes because of wanting to separate themselves from this negative connotation, sensitive people can forgo honoring themselves more often than they may realize.

While focusing on accomplishments and accolades isn't a top priority for most sensitive people, it's important to acknowledge all of your hard work, contributions, and the ways in which you move through the world. As adults there tends to be less and less people telling us that we're doing a good job, that we're making a difference, and that we're making people proud of us. So, we have to be that person for ourselves. Does it mean that you have to stand in front of the mirror and say glorifying things to yourself as you get ready? No, not all, but please feel free to do so if you feel so inclined. However, it does mean that it's important to take stock of all that you're doing and contributing just by being yourself.

I find that highly sensitive people tend to undervalue the contributions that they make by thinking or saying, "Oh it's no big deal, anyone could've done what I did." However more often than not it is a big deal. In addition to undervaluing themselves, sensitive people can tend to forget all that they're doing because they're so used to moving through the things on their lists each day. They forget to stop and think about how much they're actually doing because they can become preoccupied with getting to the next item on their list.

It's important to take time to reflect upon, to talk to, and to treat yourself in the same ways that you talk to and treat others within your world. If someone you cared about did the same exact things that you do every day, how would you talk to them? How would you recognize them for all that they do? Exactly, you would choose words carefully to highlight all of the components of their contributions and you wouldn't tell them that their insight, efforts, and contributions were no big deal. So too, must you treat yourself in this same way.

While it may feel awkward or uncomfortable at first; like anything, the more that you do it, the easier it will become. Taking time to treat yourself with kindness, compassion, and love is a healthy habit to nurture and foster. If you find yourself slipping into a space where you're being hard on yourself, using negative self talk, or pushing yourself to do more, to go faster etc. stop and take a breath. This isn't a time to get down on yourself for pushing yourself too hard. This is a time to acknowledge yourself for getting into a pattern that isn't serving you. Once you notice it, you can stop, reframe and then go on with your day.

In these times, it can help to talk to yourself in the same way you would talk to a small child around age 8. You may even want to imagine talking to yourself at the same age. What kinds of things would you say to your 8 year old self? What kinds of language would you use? Would you give the 8 year old you a break or an opportunity to shift the way you were doing something?

This reframe can make a powerful difference in the way you treat yourself and the way you move through your world. As you shift the way you treat yourself, others will automatically respond and align themselves with this new level of respect and care as well.

Breathe Through It:

If you feel uncomfortable with the thought of creating ways to honor yourself, that's okay. You may not have had a lot of experience doing this in the past. You may not have had anyone teach you how to do this or to emulate this to you growing up. Even if this is one of the first times that you will begin this nurturing practice, you can do it. Small changes over time lead to big change. As you begin to honor yourself, you simultaneously give others within your world permission to do the same thing.

Activity:

Below you will find some ways that you can use to begin to honor yourself and make yourself number one within your world. This is simply a list to help get you started so you can create some ways that are tailor made for your needs and life. This list is in no particular order of importance.

- Take 15-20 minutes for yourself each day doing something just for you
    - This doesn't include chores, running people across town, or answering emails
- Find ways to show yourself that you appreciate yourself.
    - Treat yourself to flowers, a tea, or something that you've been wanting
- Tell yourself, I love you
- Let go of the things that you can't control
- Slow Down
- Breathe
- Do something just for you, just for fun
- At the end of the day reflect on the things that you did and say 3 positive and supportive messages to yourself
    - You may want to journal about these things each night for 30 days
- Leave positive affirmations and notes in places that you frequent reminding you to make yourself number one within your world.
- Send yourself alarm text messages with positive messages about yourself.
  Things like:
    - I'm a great friend
    - I love myself
    - I bring a lot to the world simply by being myself
    - I am worthy of love
    - I deserve joy
    - I make time for myself
- Remind yourself that as you make yourself the number one priority in your life, everyone benefits.

When you take care of yourself, everyone in your world gets the best version of you.

No matter how you move toward making yourself number one within your world, give yourself permission to enjoy the process. Remind yourself that the things that you're doing are acts of self love. Give yourself permission to go at your own pace, treat yourself with tender loving care, and talk to yourself the way you talk to all of the people within your world; with kindness and compassion.

Just in case someone hasn't told you lately.

You're doing a great job! Keep up the great work.
It's okay to take time alone when you need it. It will help you feel more inspired and excited about your life. You make this world a better place simply by being you.
You are loved.

Epilogue

You may realize that each of these areas whether they were placed into the physical, mental/emotional, or spiritual parts of this book impact all areas of your life and experience. In truth everything that we choose to do or not do impacts us not only in every area of our lives but also on every level of our existence. As multidimensional beings we are always creating an impact on ourselves, our lives, the lives of others, and the planet. As you continue to honor yourself, your needs, your vision, and your calling; you will simultaneously continue to increase the quality and breadth of your life and the lives of those around you.

The more you can continue to focus on the core level of your inner personal happiness, truth, and self-love, you will continue to move in the direction of your true north. Your internal compass is always guiding you from its home which can be found within your heart.

My wish for you is that you will continue to tune in and connect with your heart direction every day. May all of your days be filled with people, life experiences, and opportunities that rise up to greet you; creating more depth and beauty within the fabric of your life.

With deepest love and gratitude,

Kristy~

Acknowledgements

I want to thank all of the lovely people who've allowed me to work with them over the years. Connecting with each of you has been a true gift in my life.

A big thank you to Rudy for encouraging me to follow my own true north every day. I appreciate you and I love you.

Thank you to Sophie for spending many hours laying on top of my feet or next to my feet purring on the days that I wrote from my home office. The company and purring was much appreciated.

To Team KMA, thank you so much for the constant support, guidance, and nudging when I needed it, especially on the days that I didn't feel like writing.

References

1. Doreen Virtue, Constant Craving: What Your Food Cravings Mean and How to Overcome Them 2011

2. Dr. Emoto, The Healing Power of Water 2004

3. Wikipedia, Referenced amount of water in the human body

Notes

Notes

www.ingramcontent.com/pod-product-compliance
Lightning Source LLC
Chambersburg PA
CBHW020732160426
43192CB00006B/200